FIREBRANDS

FIREBRANDS

THE
UNTOLD STORY
OF **FOUR WOMEN WHO**
MADE AND **UNMADE**
PROHIBITION

GIOIA DILIBERTO

The University of Chicago Press CHICAGO AND LONDON

The University of Chicago Press, Chicago 60637
The University of Chicago Press, Ltd., London
© 2024 by Gioia Diliberto
Published 2024
Printed in the United States of America

33 32 31 30 29 28 27 26 25 24   1 2 3 4 5

ISBN-13: 978-0-226-81967-9 (cloth)
ISBN-13: 978-0-226-81968-6 (e-book)
DOI: https://doi.org/10.7208/chicago/9780226819686.001.0001

Library of Congress Cataloging-in-Publication Data

Names: Diliberto, Gioia, 1950– author.
Title: Firebrands : the untold story of four women who made and unmade
    prohibition / Gioia Diliberto.
Description: Chicago : The University of Chicago Press, 2024. | Includes
    bibliographical references and index.
Identifiers: LCCN 2024011408 | ISBN 9780226819679 (cloth) |
    ISBN 9780226819686 (ebook)
Subjects: LCSH: Boole, Ella A. (Ella Alexander), 1858–1952. | Guinan, Texas. |
    Willebrandt, Mabel Walker, 1889–1963. | Davis, Dwight, Mrs., 1887–
    1955. | Prohibition—United States—History.
Classification: LCC HV5089 .D555 2024 | DDC 344.7305/4109252—
    dc23/eng/20240412
LC record available at https://lccn.loc.gov/2024011408

♾ This paper meets the requirements of ANSI/NISO Z39.48-1992
(Permanence of Paper).

for DICK
and for JOE

CONTENTS

PROLOGUE

I N 1920 WHEN THE NINETEENTH AMENDMENT to the US
Constitution gave American women the vote, it was seen as a seis-
mic shift that would transform lives and events. Its immediate
impact, however, was shockingly modest. Women did not rise to the
top of either political party or get nominated for high office. They
did not achieve equality with men or unite in a forceful bloc to push
for women's causes. They didn't even vote in large numbers. Though
women had shown remarkable talent and tenacity in the drive for
suffrage, it would be decades before they exercised real political
clout. With one outstanding exception: Prohibition. The fraught
and turbulent years of the Eighteenth Amendment—from 1920 to
1933—placed women, including the subjects of this book, upfront on
the public stage. These women did not think of themselves as revolu-
tionaries, or even feminists, but they forged a path for those who followed to press for more power and influence. Their lives evoke one of
the biggest, most brutal political clashes of the twentieth century, and
yet they missed history's last call. Today they are mostly forgotten.

Ella Boole, the stern and ambitious leader of the Woman's Christian Temperance Union (WCTU), campaigned fiercely to introduce
Prohibition and fought desperately to keep it alive. Mabel Walker

Willebrandt, the most powerful woman in America at the time, served as the top federal prosecutor charged with enforcing Prohibition. Silent film star Texas Guinan ran New York City speakeasies backed by the mob and showed that Prohibition was not only absurd but unenforceable. And Pauline Morton Sabin, a glamorous Manhattan aristocrat who belatedly recognized the cascading evil of Prohibition, mobilized the movement to kill it.

Overshadowed in most accounts of the era by tales of the disruption and violence of Prohibition, Repeal reflected a stunningly rapid shift in public attitudes. In 1933, a more than century-long, high-minded push to alter the behavior of millions of Americans ended. Most remarkably, Repeal represented a tidal turnaround for the nation's women, who'd been the chief zealots in the drive to ban liquor. As one headline of the day proclaimed, "Women Who Doomed Rum, Now Cheer Repeal! Mass Phenomenon Amazes All."

This is the story of how it happened.

REBEL WOMEN WERE PART of the Jazz Age zeitgeist, and the women in these pages stand out as leaders in the new, post-suffrage era of politics. Their activism is the first expression of women's political activity after the passage of the Nineteenth Amendment, and they form a link between the age of "True Womanhood" in the nineteenth century and the 1960s era of so-called women's liberation, when Betty Friedan's *The Feminine Mystique* landed on best seller lists and the National Organization of Women (NOW) began advocating for women's rights.

Firebrands unfolds at a time, like our own, of extreme political divide, toxic prejudice, weak leadership, and charges of fake news that feels startlingly familiar. It was clear by the mid-1920s that Prohibition had failed, but the politicians in power lacked the courage to stand up to Dry America. A fanatical minority dominated electoral politics. The Drys claimed that intoxicating liquors had wrecked the family and the nation, though an undercurrent of the movement played on fear and contempt for city dwellers, wealthy elites, and recent immigrants. The Drys denounced their opponents as liars and held a death grip on Congress by voting in lockstep, while threatening to target candidates who did not back their demands. The parallel with politics today is obvious.

This book is not a scholarly history, nor does it offer fully realized biographies of my characters. Rather, it is the story of how women fought for power at a particular moment in American life when they had little status and faced rampant sexism at every turn.

AFTER WORLD WAR I, America was torn apart by the Eighteenth Amendment, which banned "the manufacture, sale, or transportation of intoxicating liquors" and was ratified by the requisite thirty-six of forty-eight states on January 16, 1919. Later that year, Congress also passed the Volstead Act, which provided for the enforcement of the Eighteenth Amendment. Both measures went into effect the following January.

Prohibition so divided the nation, warned muckraker Ida Tarbell in a widely read 1929 pamphlet, that it could spark another civil war. Women had recently won the vote, the most basic right of democracy, and many had strong feelings for or against Prohibition, but they now faced a perplexing dilemma. Should they work from the traditional American party system or seek change as outsiders in their own separate feminine sphere, shunning the male-dominated backroom politics of often corrupt dealmaking? From their opposite sides of the Prohibition fight, Ella Boole and Pauline Sabin built on the momentum of suffrage and advocated fiercely for women's place in politics. They knew their power to affect change rested in their ability to mobilize their followers, to build coalitions, and to strengthen relationships within their groups.

When most people think of the Woman's Christian Temperance Union today, if they think of it at all, they conjure pigeon-breasted scolds railing against drunken men. Ella Boole was precisely that, but at the same time a formidable leader who declared war on anyone who opposed her and had the ear of presidents from Woodrow

Wilson to Franklin D. Roosevelt. Though the WCTU had the mis-guided mission of keeping America Dry, it was far ahead of its time in fighting for a host of social justice issues, including equal pay for equal work (a slogan it coined), prison reform, and stronger penalties for sex offenders. Ella believed fervently that intoxicating drink was the enemy of her sex. She claimed she was doing God's work in fight-ing to preserve Prohibition, but she acted more like a general than a minister. At meetings, rallies, and membership conventions, and in her myriad writings in the *Union Signal*, the WCTU newspaper, she urged women voters across the nation to develop the skills to work together as a unified Dry Army.

In the 1920s, Ella relied on Mabel Walker Willebrandt as her chief ally, though unbeknownst to Ella, Mabel was not a teetotaler herself. Mabel's passion was the law, not Prohibition. She went after violators of the Volstead Act with a ferocity that amazed the drink-ing men in power, who had been counting on the ineffectuality of this young, inexperienced woman. She pioneered the use of tax laws to lock up America's top bootleggers, but failed to put Texas Guinan, New York's most notorious speakeasy hostess, out of business (only the mob accomplished that). When Mabel left office in 1929, she dropped out of public life for good, embarking on a lucrative private practice representing movie stars and Hollywood moguls, famous aviators, and even a California fruit industry that made ingredients for homemade wine.

Despite Mabel's defection, Ella made the huge error of thinking that American women would continue to support Prohibition. It took Pauline Sabin to prove how spectacularly wrong she was. Char-ismatic, beautiful, prominently connected in the corridors of power, and immensely wealthy, Pauline by background represented the American aristocracy. Still, she knew how to speak to women from all walks of life and ethnicities and gave them a new common goal after suffrage. Until Pauline came along, as scholars of Prohibition have noted, no one had the vision to mobilize American women against the Eighteenth Amendment. Pauline challenged her supporters to act on their commitment to the group she started, the Women's Organization for National Prohibition Reform (WONPR) by taking on leadership roles of their own. She held frequent workshops to train members in the art of speaking, lobbying, and writing pamphlets that expressed an urgency for change. "Have you impressed upon your senators and congressmen that you demand unqualified repeal?" reads one pamphlet. "As citizens, as voters, it is our job."

Her speeches galvanized the crowds of working girls and housewives who flocked to hear her in town halls and village squares. To the scores of immigrants who heard her on the radio and saw her in newsreels at movie theaters, she was the very model of American womanhood. Pauline's enemies, in particular Ella Boole and those bone-dry men of the Anti-Saloon League, distrusted her wealth, her polish, and, perhaps most of all, her beauty—the dreamy golden looks that dazzled three husbands and five presidents from Warren Harding to Harry Truman. The press also adored her. She was an oft-photographed heroine in the Jazz Age of roadsters, diamonds, and gin—the feminist answer to F. Scott Fitzgerald's Daisy Buchanan, who threw lavish parties at her own Gatsby-esque mansion while leading a movement that changed America.

The "Sabines," as the press dubbed Pauline's followers, were an unlikely sisterhood of flappers, housewives, factory workers, students, nurses, writers, teachers, society matrons, and shopgirls who shared a conviction that Prohibition was ruining the nation by creating a culture of violence and corruption. They battled the forces of Dry America across a teeming landscape of bootleggers, gangsters, federal agents, and temperance fanatics. At the same time, they faced down cowardly politicians (many of them secret drunks) who were under the sway of a fervent Dry minority.

THE FOUR WOMEN PROFILED HERE shared an ambition to push the boundaries of society's norms. At a time when women had few opportunities to enter the professions or achieve elected office, they refused to let their gender hold them back. As they strove for self-fulfillment, they found ways to support themselves financially and emotionally, often in the face of heart-wrenching pain: the loneliness of widowhood, the challenges of single motherhood, and the unspeakable tragedy of losing a child. The years 1920 to 1933 were the most important of their lives. They had all been born in the nineteenth century and came of age at a time when a woman's personal autonomy was severely limited. Women couldn't own property in their own names, or even hold on to those names when they married. They couldn't vote or sit on a federal jury, and their professional opportunities were slight.

Of the four, I discovered Mabel Walker Willebrandt first, when I came across her picture on the cover of *Time* magazine from August 26, 1929, while researching another project. It astounded me that I'd never heard of this attractive young lawyer who had once been the highest-ranking woman in the US government. I wondered what other high-achieving women had been lost to history, so I looked through all the *Time* covers from 1920 to 1933. Few women were featured except for an occasional opera diva or tennis star. Then I saw Pauline Sabin on the cover of the issue from July 18, 1932, and it struck me that Prohibition could be explored in a new way—as feminist history; it was women who had driven Prohibition into law, a woman who was in charge of enforcing it, and a woman who led the crusade for Repeal.

The link between suffrage and Prohibition has been well documented. For more than a century, women had been crucial to the fight to impose Prohibition on America—from Susan B. Anthony and Elizabeth Cady Stanton, who tied suffrage to temperance, to the hatchet-wielding saloon buster Carrie Nation and Eliza Trimble Thompson, a judge's wife who led a band of women in 1873 to fall to their knees and pray outside the saloons of Hillsboro, Ohio. These women thought a liquor ban essential to stop men's abusive, irresponsible behavior and set them on the path of righteousness. Temperance was the #MeToo movement of the nineteenth and early twentieth centuries, seen as essential protection for women and children against the evils and degradation of drunken men. But women had no power to affect change without the vote.

Frances Willard, the forceful second president of the WCTU from 1879 until her death in 1898, helped expand the appeal of suffrage beyond radical activists like Anthony and Stanton to reach ordinary American women. A former college president, Willard argued persuasively that women could use their votes to keep their communities Dry and improve their families' lives. But she left her successors, including Ella Boole, a complicated racial legacy. Though Willard's parents had been abolitionists, she courted White southern women at the expense of Black women in her fight for suffrage, a battle she passionately and, as it turned out, correctly believed would lead to Prohibition. At the same time, the WCTU was the first national women's reform organization that welcomed middle-class African American women and offered Black and White women a chance to participate in an interracial organization, albeit in segregated chapters. Though African American women did not have leadership roles in Pauline Sabin's organization, they were recruited as members. Like the WCTU, WONPR offered an opportunity for working-class Black and White women to work together toward a common goal.

After women won the vote, the men in power assumed they would vote as a bloc, a severe misconception that has persisted in the years since, despite much evidence to the contrary. In the 1970s, the Equal Rights Amendment, designed to guarantee equal legal rights to all citizens regardless of sex and first introduced in Congress in 1923, seemed sure to finally pass, until the anti-feminist godmother Phyllis Schlafly mobilized conservative women to stop it. More recently, the 2016 US presidential election disproved the assumption that an overwhelming majority of women wanted a female president, as just 54 percent of the women who voted cast their ballots for Hillary Rodham Clinton, and only 48 percent of women over fifty.

In the early 1920s, however, the idea that women were a unified political force had the unintentionally salutary effect of leading to the passage of two laws that suffragists supported: the Sheppard-Towner

Act of 1921, which provided federal funding for maternity and child care, and the Cable Act of 1922, ensuring that American women who married foreigners would not (as my grandmother did) lose their citizenship and, crucially, their votes. Male legislators worried that female voters would hold it against them if these measures failed to pass. Later, when the Prohibition fight showed that women could be as divided as men politically, the men in power stopped heeding women's demands. President Herbert Hoover cut funding to the Sheppard-Towner Act in the late 1920s and failed to appoint Mabel Willebrandt US attorney general, as she believed he would.

AS I TALKED TO the descendants of Pauline Sabin and Mabel Willebrandt and examined Mabel's papers at the Library of Congress and Pauline's papers at the Schlesinger Library in Cambridge, Massachusetts, and in a private archive in Chevy Chase, Maryland, poring over letters, diaries, and other documents, I began to see intriguing shadows beyond the well-worn stories of Jazz Age gangsters and flappers. It struck me that Repeal was the perfect vehicle to illuminate how women struggled for power in the years immediately *after* suffrage. It's a struggle that reverberates today. The forces of the present, including the ascendency for the first time of a woman to the US vice presidency, has sparked a need to reevaluate how women conceived and used power in the past and how public policy embodies and confronts socially defined visions of womanhood.

The myriad books, articles, essays, and films on Prohibition touch on the lives of the subjects in these pages. My contribution in bringing them together in one narrative is to show, I hope, not only how Prohibition shaped their interconnected lives, but also how it revealed the struggle of women post-suffrage to win influence in American politics. Some readers might take offense that I call Ella Boole, Texas Guinan, Pauline Sabin, and Mabel Walker Willebrandt by their first names throughout this book, as if my use of their given names implies a lack of respect for their stature and importance. But I feel I know these four as intimately as if they were members of my

own family. To address them as Boole, Guinan, Sabin, and Willebrandt would seem awkwardly formal and distancing. After all, my
chief interest in them has been as flesh-and-blood women. I've tried
to bring them as vividly to life on the page as they once were on the
American scene.

ONE

◇

SEND A MOTHER TO THE SENATE

T FIVE O'CLOCK on August 17, 1920, the day before votes for women became law, Ella Boole sat in a hot, cramped office on West Thirty-Ninth Street in Manhattan verifying names on her petitions to run for the US Senate. She needed three thousand registered voters to put her on the ballot for the Republican primary in November, and she had spent long hours peering through rimless spectacles, painstakingly matching signatures to addresses, hoping she had enough. A fan set on a wood filing cabinet did little to dispel the heat, and sweat beaded her forehead and neck. At sixty-two, Ella was tall and raw-boned with wavy gray hair gathered in a knot at the back of her head. She wore a simple dark silk dress with a pin in the shape of a white ribbon above her heart, a badge of purity that she'd sported since her girlhood in Van Wert, Ohio, as a junior member of the Woman's Christian Temperance Union. Now she was vice president of the WCTU and heir apparent to the presidency, reward for her tireless leadership of the cause that defined her life.

Though Prohibition had become law eight months earlier, the fight to banish alcohol was far from won. Illegal liquor flooded America. Weak, haphazard enforcement of the Volstead Act did little to discourage bootleggers and speakeasy operators, and already a bill in Congress threatened to chip away at the Eighteenth Amendment

Ella Boole, the president and "moral Napoleon" of the Woman's
Christian Temperance Union. WCTU Archives, Evanston, IL.

by legalizing beer with a low alcohol content of 2.75 percent. Now
Ella hoped to carry on her battle from the Senate. "The very permanency of Prohibition depended on" her success and that of other
Dry candidates, Ella told a reporter from the Elmira, New York, *Star
Gazette*. She carefully hid her ambition lest she appear selfish and
unwomanly, casting her candidacy in altruistic terms. Running had
not even been her idea, she told anyone who asked. Her candidacy

had been the brainchild of Mary Garrett "Mollie" Hay, the life partner of America's most famous suffragist, Carrie Chapman Catt. The
founder of the League of Women Voters, Catt had just led her army
to triumph in Tennessee, the thirty-sixth and last state required to
ratify the Nineteenth Amendment.

Ella accepted the challenge, not for personal advancement, she
insisted, but for the good she could do by bringing about laws to
protect women, children, and the home. She didn't have a choice but
to join the race, as no suitable man had stepped up to challenge the
Republican incumbent, James W. Wadsworth Jr., the senior senator from New York and a committed anti-Prohibitionist—a so-called
Wet—who'd also fiercely opposed suffrage. The distinguished Elihu
Root, who'd been President Theodore Roosevelt's secretary of state
and served as secretary of war under both Roosevelt and President
William McKinley, had declined to run. So did the president of Cor-
nell University and several upstate congressmen.

Any of these men would almost certainly have a better chance
than Ella in the Republican primary. The social tsunami that had
resulted in the Nineteenth Amendment had barely opened the door
to women who wanted a life in the public sphere. And yet Ella was not
discouraged. She expected the majority of New York's newly enfranchised women to vote for her and also a large swath of the state's
men, though the mere mention of her name evoked sneers from
New York's drinking men, who had contempt for any do-gooding
woman out to ruin their fun. They would swallow their bootleg with
less pleasure, however, as one journalist noted, if they understood
Ella's power, her unfailing strength and grit, her eloquence, persua-
siveness, and executive talents that showed the very "hallmark of
genius." The newspapers favored pictures of Ella looking stern in
frumpy hats and clod-hopping shoes and resembling the cartoon
versions of humorless reformers, who were "stuffy with causes and
sententiousness," as the *New Yorker*, the era's bible of uber sophis-
tication, put it. But the photos belie the intelligence and speaking
gifts that gripped Ella's audiences and made legislators "whimper"

when she testified before Congress, as she often did. To be sure, she was prone to making sweeping claims she didn't back up. "Prohibition has made America the healthiest country on earth. The nation's death rate is ten percent lower than ever before," she told an audience in Thief River Falls, Minnesota. Another time she said that "young people are drinking less all the time," and that the drunkest people at college football games were not students, but "old grads." These statements *deserved* to be true, she believed, so she had no qualms about asserting them.

Ella was far from the only one who wanted Wadsworth crushed. Women across the state were out for his "scalp," as one newspaper put it. The New York Republican epitomized the type of wealthy, entitled aristocrat that progressives abhorred. An avid foxhunter, he was pale, slender, and balding, and he spoke in a clipped, impatient voice. He'd been Skull and Bones at Yale and owned a 13,000-square-foot mansion and vast lands in the verdant Genesee Valley upstate that his family had cleared in colonial times. Republican politics had been bred in his bones. His grandfather had helped found the party in 1854, and his father had served nine terms as a US congressman after fighting for the Union in the Civil War. Wadsworth's marriage to the daughter of John Hay—Abraham Lincoln's private secretary and later a secretary of state under William McKinley and Theodore Roosevelt—deepened the tie.

Wadsworth's wife, Alice, opposed suffrage even more virulently than her husband. The senator had fought passage of the Nineteenth Amendment on the basis of states' rights, the same grounds on which he'd opposed Prohibition, arguing that these issues should be decided locally. He feared federal intervention in the private lives of Americans and believed the US Constitution existed only to limit government power and protect citizens' rights. Alice's abhorrence of women voting stemmed from her fierce belief in "True Womanhood," that creaky nineteenth-century WASP ideal of domesticity, which relegated women to their separate sphere of home and hearth, while celebrating their piety, purity, and submissiveness. As president of the National Association Opposed to Woman Suffrage (NAOWS), Alice Wadsworth did nothing to hide her militancy. She deplored not only the idea of suffrage but the very word itself. It "will no longer be dignified" by such a "high sounding name," she announced to a reporter. "A spade will be called a spade, and the doctrine of 'sex equality' will be recognized for the unnatural, abnormal thing it is."

Alice and other antis broadcast their toxic views in the *Woman Patriot*, a cranky bimonthly newspaper that published from 1918 to 1932 and spewed harsh and often defamatory false accusations and lies. A frequent target of the paper's rants was Carrie Catt, whom the *Woman Patriot* accused during World War I of inciting treason and threatening democracy by her militant advocacy of woman suffrage. Such invective reflected the antis' desperation, for with the passage of suffrage, their ranks were thinning. Many antis, in fact, had come to believe that voting wasn't such a bad thing, after all. In New York, they'd been casting ballots in local and state elections since a 1917 suffrage referendum pushed them to register to vote as their civic duty. What's more, their experiences working on relief efforts and war preparedness during the Great War kindled their desire for a say in public policy.

Of course, some antis would be using their votes precisely to defeat Ella and reelect Wadsworth. So important was his ouster to New York's Drys and Suffs, that the League of Women Voters ignored their bipartisan mandate and openly supported Ella, going so far as to arrange for her petitions to be available at several locations throughout the city to make it convenient for New Yorkers to sign them, then lending her their office to verify them. The effort paid off. By five p.m. on August 17, Ella had 3,330 signatures, 330 more than the required number. A member of the League sped by car to Albany, where she hand-delivered the petitions to the Board of Elections in time to meet their midnight deadline, thus securing Ella a place on the ballot.

The next day, Ella launched an aggressive campaign with the slogan "Send a Mother to the Senate." If she defeated Wadsworth, she would triumph over one of the most powerful men in New York politics. From her headquarters at 156 Fifth Avenue, an army of volunteers had hundreds of leaflets announcing Ella's platform printed up and distributed throughout the state. Two male supporters donated $500 to pay for a professional campaign manager, who organized for Ella a speaking tour of all fifty-seven New York counties. She set off by train at the end of the month, carrying only one tattered carpetbag and a big black purse. A billfold tucked inside the purse held recipes for non-alcoholic drinks, which Ella collected from supporters at every stop. One favorite was a ginger-ale-based mint julep, which, like all her mocktails, was "attractive to the eye, refreshing to the spirit," and had only "good effects the morning after."

Speaking in the rich alto that had made her a compelling orator since winning debates in college, Ella urged audiences in churches and town halls and at county fairs to vote for her, "the unbossed candidate." She railed against Wadsworth and the forces of the "machine": Tammany Hall—the corrupt, Irish immigrant-dominated organization that had controlled New York City politics since the mid-nineteenth century, delivering votes to reward its chosen candidates for offices from district and precinct leaders to city hall, the statehouse, and all the way up to the US Congress and the presidency.

At every stop, she warned audiences of the dangers of the 2.75 percent beer bill, then before the New York State legislature, which she argued would lead to the return of the saloon, that evil "center of degeneracy in every community," as she put it. At saloons, men spent their paychecks, met up with prostitutes, and stayed out all hours. Saloons were also where corrupt party bosses solicited votes from foreign-born immigrants, which meant Catholics and Jews. Appealing to the era's reflexive bigotry, the Suffs had argued that enfranchising women would help counter immigrant votes. Ella, however, avoided saying anything directly anti-Catholic, anti-Semitic, or anti-immigrant. She stressed her support for increased pensions for ex-servicemen and their preferential appointment to civil service positions, stiffer laws against child labor, legislation that would allow an

American woman to keep her citizenship if she married a foreigner, and the creation of a federal department of education. She called on "every man and woman in the state" to join her fight by contributing twenty-five cents to her campaign, "the price of a sundae or a tip," Ella noted. "We have no political machine to run this campaign. We have no wealthy backers," she added. "The contribution of small sums by the thousands of men and women in this state who want to restore government by the people and do away with government by the bosses will be an object lesson to the entire country." Ella believed the Lord himself had called her personally to the sacred mission of keeping America Dry. She declared war on all Wets who opposed her, promising to outlive them, outtalk them, outpray them, and outvote them.

She came by such zeal naturally. Born on July 26, 1858, in the prairie town of Van Wert, Ohio, to Colonel Isaac Newton Alexander, a prominent lawyer who served as the US Attorney for the Northern District of Ohio, and his wife, Rebecca, Ella was schooled early in social activism. When the Civil War broke out, Isaac Alexander left to fight for the Union army, returning four years later an ardent advocate of the rights of freedmen. He also became a passionate Dry, having witnessed rampant alcohol abuse among soldiers. Isaac passed on his abhorrence of drink to his family, including Ella and her two younger sisters.

As a girl, Ella's entire world existed within a half mile of the family's stately red brick home. On Sundays she walked to the nearby First Presbyterian Church and during the week to school. At the lunch recess, she saw scores of children carrying pails to the town saloons to be filled with beer for their fathers. For most men in Van Wert, drinking was a part of life, as routine as it was for Ella to romp across the neighborhood lawns with her friends and wade in the creek behind her house in the summer.

Ella was in high school during the Woman's Crusade of 1873–74, a series of anti-liquor protests that started in Ohio and spread throughout the United States, during which women prayed and sang outside saloons, exhorting the men inside to stop selling and drinking alcohol. Though most of the active protesting in Ohio occurred far from Van Wert—in the cities of Xenia, Columbus, and Charleston— Ella attended weekly Crusade prayer meetings in her hometown and considered them her own first inspiration for temperance work, following the Dry spark ignited by her father. The Woman's Crusade, which eventually spread to more than nine hundred communities in thirty-one states, gave women a chance to enter the public sphere and, while fighting for temperance, to advocate for their own rights with growing confidence and conviction. It culminated in a call for a national temperance convention in Cleveland in November 1874 that resulted in the formation of what became the Woman's Christian Temperance Union.

The convention elected Annie Wittenmyer, a Methodist charity worker, as the group's first president. In coming up with a name for the new organization, it was decided to include "woman" in the moniker, thus barring men whose aggressive nature Wittenmyer feared would push women to the background and deny them power. There was also some question about whether to include "Christian" in the group's name, and if they should "shut out the Jews." A vote was taken at the convention, and it was decided that since "there was no creed test, this result need not be feared." It's unknown how many Jews joined the WCTU in its early years, but it's clear that Jews were never given leadership roles in the organization, whose members were overwhelmingly Christian. The WCTU declared as its purpose to "moderate" the "use of all things good" and promote "total abstinence from all things questionable or harmful," including alcohol and tobacco. Succeeding Wittenmyer as WCTU president in 1879, Frances Willard expanded the organization into political involvement and built it into the nation's largest women's organization.

Growing up in the temperance movement meant that Ella also came of age with the push for woman suffrage. The two causes are impossible to separate, as women began clamoring for the vote in large numbers only when the temperance crusade changed from one of moral suasion in the early decades of the nineteenth century to a political movement in midcentury that shut them out. Temperance reform, one of America's most popular and long-standing social movements, became dominated by women in the 1850s, as they demanded a more active participation in efforts to rid the nation of intoxicating drink. At the time, women were perceived as "angels in the house," whose chief role lay behind the scenes, steering their families toward righteousness. So-called moral suasion had been the chief tactic of male temperance activists, too, but in the mid-nineteenth century, the movement evolved into a push for legal Prohibition, which meant changing laws. Now, women were left with no meaningful role, as they had no place in the public sphere. Rules of propriety barred them from speaking in public, and, most crucially, they couldn't vote.

The transformation of the temperance movement into a legal crusade coincided with a huge influx of German and Irish immigrants to America's shores. Most of these immigrants lacked the Puritan strains that ran through many American communities, and thus many newcomers found wine, beer, and spirits complements to meals and socializing. Reformers started to believe that the only way to stop their drinking was to halt the manufacture and sale of liquor. "Almost overnight the temperance cause became a movement for prohibition and therefore, inevitably, a political movement," as Jed Dannenbaum noted.

In 1851 Maine passed the nation's first law banning the manufacture and sale of intoxicating drink, and soon other states took on campaigns to ban liquor, organizing political rallies and public referenda. Women were blocked from these activities entirely. The desire to have a voice, gain access to public platforms, and influence events drew converts to the emerging women's rights movement. As the great orator and Black abolitionist Frederick Douglass wrote, "The very moment woman rises in public to protest against the blighting traffic in rum, just so soon is raised the question of women's rights."

After the success in Maine, male temperance reformers had

trouble getting more state prohibition laws passed. By 1913 just nine states had statewide prohibition, though thirty-one others had local option laws that allowed a county or town to go Dry if that's what its citizens wanted. Male temperance reformers needed all the help they could get, and they began to think it would be a good idea to let women vote. Anti-immigrant prejudice also played into their support of woman suffrage. Newly enfranchised male immigrants flocked to saloons, of which there were thousands in the decades before the Civil War, where machine politicians doled out favors and angled for votes. What's more, distilling and beer making had become big business, and many of the distilleries and breweries were owned by the foreign born.

With the proliferation of saloons, male drinking became a firmly established part of community life in America's cities and towns. Women everywhere felt an increased threat to the sobriety of their husbands and the peace and safety of their homes and children, and in retaliation, some of them resorted to militant vigilante justice. Decades before the ferocious Prohibitionist Carrie A. Nation took a hatchet to the liquor supplies in saloons in Kansas and Missouri, women across the Midwest had performed their own "hatchetations" in local drinking spots. Bands of male supporters often helped, rolling caskets of alcohol into the street, where they were emptied. Prohibition sentiment ran so high in many communities that women were seldom jailed for their destruction of saloon property. Their actions were seen not as crimes, but as righteous moral protest. In 1854, when nine women in Marion, Illinois, were tried for smashing up the town's saloons, their lawyer Abraham Lincoln successfully claimed the Boston Tea Party as a moral precedent for their violence. That same year, the Lady's Temperance Army—a group of fifty women in Winchester, Indiana—stormed the town's saloons, demanding that the proprietors pour their liquor and beer into the street. All complied, except one. The women pushed past the saloonkeeper, who stood in the door with a shotgun trying to block their way, and proceeded to break every bottle of liquor inside. The women were arrested on charges of vandalism but acquitted at trial in a unanimous verdict.

The Civil War markedly increased drinking among young, middle-class men and accelerated not only women's anxiety about their loved ones' alcohol abuse, but also their frustration and rage over being denied access to political solutions. The nonviolent protests of the Woman's Crusade after the Civil War marked the start of a new period in the temperance movement that dovetailed with the suffrage battle and led directly to the Eighteenth and Nineteenth Amendments fifty years later.

FROM ISAAC ALEXANDER, Ella had also inherited a fierce conviction in the power of law to effect reform. During Reconstruction, Isaac edited a free-soil newspaper, which he used to advocate for the rights of freedmen. All men were equal in the eyes of the US Constitution, which Ella believed had to be upheld at all cost.

At sixteen she enrolled in Wooster College, in Wooster, Ohio, where she studied Latin, Greek, math, and natural science, and was one of three women in a class of thirty-one and the youngest person ever to receive a degree from the school. She also won several regional oratorical contests. During one in her junior year, she beat out eight boys from nearby colleges. After graduating in 1878, Ella returned to Van Wert to teach high school at her alma mater, where she developed a reputation for inspiring her students with her eloquence and deep knowledge. "I first discovered my talent for public speaking there, when I found that I had the gift of making my pupils enthusiastic, whether we were discussing cube root, ancient history or natural science," she said. "During that period, I formed a large collection of insects. Natural science has always been my hobby."

Tall and sturdily built, Ella had a round face and bright hazel eyes behind rimless spectacles. She seemed uninterested in marrying until she met the temperance agitator Reverend William H. Boole, a twice-widowed evangelist thirty years her senior, at a religious conference in Indiana. Boole had served as a pastor for the Union army during the Civil War and shared Ella's belief that alcohol was "the arch enemy of the human race." When he proposed, Ella accepted. Their 1883 wedding, as one newspaper put it, was less a romantic coupling than "the marriage of a cause." After her marriage, Ella became stepmother to Boole's two grown children by his first wife and his infant daughter, Emily, left motherless by the death of Boole's second wife in childbirth. Just twenty-four when she married the fifty-four-year-old Methodist minister, Emily F. Robbins lived but a few hours after the birth of her baby and namesake.

Ella, William, and little Emily moved east, settling in Manhattan's rough Bowery District, where Rev. Boole became pastor of the Willett Street Methodist Church. "The neighborhood simply reeked with saloons. There Mrs. Boole . . . organized the first chapter of the WCTU ever to exist in that section," according to one magazine profile. When Ella became pregnant, the couple built a clapboard house in Prohibition Park, the new temperance Valhalla on Staten Island, where on February 4, 1887, Ella gave birth to a daughter, Florence. Though she had two small children to care for, Ella found time to deliver fiery sermons on the evils of alcohol at frequent temperance meetings in a huge tent erected in the community park.

Nine years later, in 1896, Rev. Boole died of a heart attack at sixty-eight, leaving Ella with just twenty dollars in the bank. She returned to the Presbyterian faith of her childhood, and for six years supported her daughters with a job as corresponding secretary of the church's Board of Home Missions. But temperance remained her passion. In 1898 she became president of the New York State WCTU and built it into the largest of the organization's chapters. She had a gift for recruiting new members and stirring them with her eloquence. Meantime, she traveled widely throughout the state on speaking tours. In March 1906, she found herself in Rochester several days after the death of the great suffrage leader Susan B. Anthony and felt honored to attend her funeral. In December 1913, Ella took part in a demonstration at the Capitol in Washington, DC. The event was inspired by a huge suffrage parade several months earlier when more than five thousand women escorted by marching bands and extravagantly decked-out floats strode down Pennsylvania Avenue to demand the right to vote. An angry mob of boys and men, outraged by the women's public display, had pulled them off the floats, ripping their banners and clothes, while the local police stood idly by, failing to intervene. Eventually, federal troops arrived to quell the riot.

In the December march, about two thousand women participated. They reached the steps of the Capitol without incident, perhaps because they were accompanied by a large contingent of men from the Anti-Saloon League. Ella, one of three women speakers (members of the ASL also spoke), argued passionately for a prohibition amendment in a speech from the steps of the Capitol that combined her natural fluency with careful logic. Prohibition "is a proper subject for Constitutional Law," she said, "for the liquor traffic interferes with life, liberty and the pursuit of happiness, accorded under the Constitution to all citizens. . . . Modern methods in medicine and philanthropy emphasize the necessity for the removal of preventable causes of disease, poverty and crime. We present this bill commending national prohibition of the liquor traffic as typifying the removal of the greatest preventable cause of intemperance, disease, vice and crime."

Throughout the Great War, Ella traveled the nation, preaching the Gospel of Temperance. She warned audiences that there were many sins being committed in the name of patriotism, including measures before the New York State legislature that would legalize prize fighting and allow the showing of movies on Sundays as long as the proceeds went to the armed services. She also fought an effort by the owners of restaurants and bars—whose staffs were decimated by the loss of men to the military—to overturn a New York State law forbidding women to sell or serve liquor unless they were a member of the proprietor's family. She pointed to the great need during wartime for all Christian people to stand by Christian ideals.

Ella visited the army's temporary training camps, pleased that they were all in Dry states. It also cheered her that throughout her

14 CHAPTER ONE

tour, she saw only one soldier under the influence of liquor, and he was on a train coming from New York. At Ella's direction, the WCTU supplied ten thousand comfort bags, including toiletries, Bibles, and prayer books to soldiers and sailors. WCTU volunteers also stood guard outside army camps to keep away innocent young girls and protect them from dangers they hadn't a clue about, presumably seduction by lonely men.

By 1913 the path to Prohibition had been cleared with passage of the Sixteenth Amendment instituting a nationwide income tax. Until then, America had depended on the alcohol excise tax, which accounted for about 30 to 40 percent of federal tax revenues. Not surprisingly, the most ardent supporters of the income tax, as Daniel Okrent noted in *Last Call*, were "the House and Senate sponsors of the Eighteenth Amendment, Richmond Hobson of Alabama and Morris Sheppard of Texas; Senator Wesley L. Jones of Washington, who would later take credit for the most punitive enforcement code enacted during the entire reign of constitutional Prohibition; and, from Yellow Medicine County, Minnesota, a lugubrious small-town lawyer named Andrew J. Volstead."

The WCTU had advocated for a federal income tax as far back as 1883, when the editors of the *Union Signal* wondered how citizens would support the government if the sale of liquor was prohibited, and then answered their own question: by instituting an income tax. But the Great War gave the final push to Prohibition becoming law. A "no compromise" fighting spirit engulfed the nation, which already was largely Dry by local option and state law. Liquor was believed by many citizens to be a hindrance to America's combat strength, and a wartime Prohibition act was set to take effect on July 1, 1919. Not only was there hostility toward American breweries because they were run by German immigrants, but also because they were using up valuable grain supplies that could be feeding the starving people of Europe. Meanwhile, the Eighteenth Amendment, making Prohibition a permanent part of the Constitution beyond the war, had been passed by Congress in 1917. Nine weeks after the Armistice, on

January 16, 1919, the required thirty-six states had ratified it, and it went into effect on January 17, 1920.

THROUGHOUT THESE YEARS, Ella supported herself and her daughters on her modest salary as state WCTU president, supplemented with lecturing fees and a small inheritance from her father. Neither daughter, Emily or Florence, married. Florence rose to be principal of a boys' high school in Brooklyn, supervising an all-male staff. Emily—remembered by friends as "small, slender . . . pretty and vivacious"—taught Spanish and English at the Manual Training High School in Brooklyn, an institution of last resort for boys on the verge of dropping out. She had been prone to depression since childhood, and though under the care of two doctors, neither they nor her family seemed aware of her deepening pain and gloom as she entered her thirties.

On Saturday, July 6, 1918, Emily had dinner at home with her mother and sister, then left the house saying she would spend the night at the home of a female colleague with whom she often had weekend sleepovers. She never reached her friend's house. Instead, carrying a loaded revolver and a dagger-size letter opener, she went to the annex of the Manual Training School on the corner of Prospect Avenue and Reeves Street in Brooklyn, which had been closed for the summer, climbed a fire escape outside the red brick building to the second-floor teachers' lounge, and let herself in through an open window. Once inside, she latched the window and locked the door, stuffing paper underneath it to block all the air and light. Then, at some point during the night, she turned on the gas jets in the room and lay on the couch with her gun.

A janitor making his rounds on Sunday morning smelled gas outside the teachers' room, forced open the door, and found Emily's body on the couch. Her gun had not been fired; perhaps she'd brought it and the letter opener as a backup plan had the gas jets been disabled. A subsequent coroner's report concluded that Emily hadn't been dead long when she was found. On the floor by the couch, the janitor discovered an oddly bloodless note, giving no hint of Emily's motivation or state of mind, just the names and contact information of those to be informed of her death:

> Notify Mrs. Ella A. Boole, 1429 Avenue H: Telephone Kenmore 1279; or Dr. Nathan Thayer 1433 Avenue H: Telephone Kenmore 617; or Dr. Burton Mosher, 164 Joralemon Street; Telephone Main 7511.

Ella told the *Brooklyn Eagle* that her daughter had been "mentally sick" for some time, due to overwork. In addition to her teaching duties, Emily had undergone a time-consuming training course in first aid to work in an overseas YMCA canteen that provided meals and medical care to soldiers on their way to or from the front.

When Emily died, Ella was in the middle of delivering a talk on "Women in the War" at the Wells Memorial Presbyterian Church in Brooklyn, just a few blocks from the scene of her daughter's death. The news rocked Ella to her core. She told a reporter she had no inkling of the depths of Emily's despair. Perhaps she had been too busy to notice. Or perhaps she didn't want to know. The pastor of the Immanuel Union Church on Staten Island in what had once been Prohibition Park, where Emily had lived with her parents as a child, conducted a private funeral service for Emily at the Boole women's home. Apparently, at the time, there was a ban on full church funerals for suicides. (Prohibition Park had not been a temperance community since 1907 and was now part of the Westerleigh neighborhood). After the service, Emily was buried next to her father in the nonsectarian Cypress Hills Cemetery in Brooklyn. She was thirty-six. As perhaps a sign of Emily's descent into despair, a few weeks before her death, she had made out a will, witnessed by two friends, leaving her meager savings to Ella and Florence. It might not have been so odd, however, that a young woman would worry about death in the aftermath of a world war, as the deadly Spanish flu also raged. Indeed, it's very possible that the horrors of a shattered world had deepened Emily's mental distress.

Ella never spoke about the tragedy and tried to smother her grief with work. She traveled the nation and the world, from Europe to Australia to China, preaching the temperance gospel at colleges, town halls, high schools, and churches. "The voice of Mrs. Boole has been heard in the Swiss Alps, across the bleak, foggy moors of Scotland, and in many other places where she has found situations that cried for remedy," wrote the editor and writer Stanley Walker in a 1930 *Outlook* profile. "Her messages, trenchant and eloquent, have had their audiences in the port of Sydney, in the broad wheatlands of Saskatchewan and among the hard-drinking Nordics along the fjords. A woman to be scoffed at? Not by a million jugsful. . . . [T]o millions of women she is a champion of sobriety, if not actually a prophet of the millennium."

Though Ella kept an office at WCTU headquarters on lower Fifth Avenue in Manhattan, she often worked out of her home in Flatbush, where she had moved after William Boole's death. There she presided from a sturdy oak chair with arms carved into lion's heads, her Maltese cat Peter curled in her lap, as a stenographer buzzed around her, taking dictation and typing up her letters and speeches. Florence cooked, kept house, managed her mother's wardrobe, organized her schedule, and changed the ribbons in Ella's typewriter, all the while holding down a full-time teaching job. Prohibition was in the Constitution, yet Ella knew it wasn't a completely settled issue. Some lawmakers and citizens opposed it violently, and enforcement was weak and underfunded. She wouldn't ignore the Wets who flouted the law or those who were determined to chip away at the Eighteenth Amendment with bills for 2.75 percent beer.

Most of Ella's speeches were pure propaganda, the same propaganda found in WCTU literature. According to one pamphlet, a single drink could turn you into a blubbering alcoholic. Ella never mentioned this kind of nonsense from the podium, but neither did she stop her troops from repeating misinformation favorable to her cause or printing baseless warnings about alcohol in the *Union Signal*. "The moderate drinker is weakening himself to an extent that his children may be born without a fair physical or mental chance in life," a Detroit physician was quoted as saying. "Such children die at the first attack of disease." Never mind the distress this statement caused parents. In Ella's view, almost any means were justified to rid the world of intoxicating drink.

AS A CANDIDATE for the Republican nomination for New York senator, Ella kept up her manic campaigning, crisscrossing the state to deliver her message, expressed succinctly in political ads that blitzed the state's newspapers:

> *If you believe in government that represents ALL the people.*
> *If you believe in supporting the Constitution of the United States.*
> *If you want a Senator that knows the people in every corner of the state.*
> *Come hear Ella Boole!*

An urgent message aimed directly at women screamed from between the lines of the ads:

> *If you believe Wadsworth needs to be punished for his sins against Suffrage and Prohibition, slaughter him at the polls.*

TWO

◇

PAULINE'S WAY

T HE BEAUTIFUL SOCIETY HOSTESS Pauline Sabin had no
qualms about supporting her old friend, Senator James Wadsworth. She had grown up with an intense interest in politics
and had already made herself a rising Republican operator. Pauline
believed fervently that to gain political power, women had to work
within the system, not attack it from the outside. Managing men was
simply women's role in life. Pauline wanted to borrow men's tools,
not bash them over the head with them, and she warned women
against joining feminist movements. "I think those of us who are
really Republicans have been very wise in not organizing a feminine
bloc," she said. "I believe the greatest good can be accomplished by
the women cooperating with the men."

To win a spot for herself and others of her sex in the hierarchy of
the GOP—to be in the room where it happened—Pauline believed
she had to prove to the men in charge that she could be trusted.
That meant not rejecting "Jimmy." Both Pauline and Wadsworth
hailed from the same world of wealth and privilege, of grand houses,
vast estates, liveried servants, bespoke clothes, and luxury cars. As a
girl, Polly (as Pauline's intimates called her) spent every summer in
Europe, one month in Versailles and another in Florence, where her

Pauline Sabin in 1927—the feminist answer to Daisy
Buchanan. Edward Steichen, Vogue © Condé Nast.

mother had rented villas. On these continental sojourns, Polly met
royalty and developed a deep knowledge of French and Italian art.

Like Wadsworth, Pauline had politics in her DNA. Born in Chicago in 1887, her paternal grandfather was J. Sterling Morton, a governor of Nebraska, secretary of agriculture under Grover Cleveland,
and the founder of Arbor Day. One of Pauline's earliest memories
was of going to the White House as a four-year-old and peering into

the bassinet of pink swaddled Ruth Cleveland, the first of five children of the president and First Lady.

Pauline's father, Paul Morton, after whom she was named, was head of the Equitable Life Assurance Society and secretary of the navy under President Theodore Roosevelt. As a teenager in Washington, DC, Pauline befriended Alice Roosevelt, the president's rebellious eldest daughter and the most famous girl in America. Alice shocked the press by jumping fully clothed into swimming pools, smoking in public, and carrying a live snake in her purse. Pauline, meanwhile, defied convention by dragging her escorts from debutante balls and the theater to listen to all-night debates in the Senate chamber. Years later, she would sneak into the so-called Board of Education, a secret room beneath the Capitol dome, which was stocked with liquor to grease the wheels of political compromise. The room got its name because it gave freshmen congressmen "an education." Texas representative John Nance Garner explained: "Well, you get a couple of drinks in a young Congressman and then you know what he knows and what he can do. We pay the tuition by supplying the liquor." The Board of Education became a favorite haunt of Ohio representative Nicholas Longworth, Alice Roosevelt's husband and a frequent guest in Pauline's home. A notorious alcoholic, Longworth had voted against the Eighteenth Amendment, unlike many of his drinking colleagues, a hypocrisy Pauline found intolerable. "I've always thought that a man who's a hypocrite about one situation can be counted on to be equally insincere about everything else," she said.

After graduating from finishing school in Boston at eighteen, Pauline "came out" to society at a grand tea party at her parents' Washington mansion. Carriages lined up for blocks along K Street, as hundreds of guests, including congressmen, senators, and President Roosevelt himself, stepped to the curb. "It's a powerful lot of fuss about a little cup of tea," one Black coachman was overheard shouting to a colleague from his perch behind a team of gleaming horses. A few months later, Polly Morton married J. Hopkins Smith Jr., a Groton- and Harvard-educated banker with a passion for yachting.

She quickly gave birth to two sons. But the marriage was unhappy, owing to Pauline's refusal to fit the mold of docile, subservient wife. "He didn't want a wife with a restless drive and ambition. He wanted a beautiful, traditional woman, which she was on the surface but not underneath," says her great-granddaughter Wendell Smith Livingston. Still, Pauline would have stuck it out had she not caught her husband on Fifth Avenue one day in 1914 arm in arm with another woman. A navy lieutenant who'd been serving abroad, he had slipped into town on leave without telling her. Pauline left him and, as a woman "on parole," the era's parlance for a divorcée, started a decorating business with a friend that brought her an income of $4,000 a year, though she had an inheritance from her father and didn't need the money. Drawing on her artistic eye and deep knowledge of European art and culture, Pauline created colorful, elegant interiors that were often featured in glossy magazines. Two years later, in 1916, Pauline married Charles Hamilton Sabin, the dashing head of the Guaranty Trust Company, who was twenty years her senior and astoundingly rich. "She flourished in her marriage to Sabin," says her granddaughter Sheila Morton Smith Cochran. He was a devoted, indulgent husband, a huge success in his world of high finance, and "he didn't feel threatened by her" drive and ambition to be a political influencer, adds Mrs. Cochran.

The couple built Bayberry Land, a lavish 314-acre estate in the Shinnecock Hills of Long Island's South Fork. At the end of a nearly mile-long pebble drive lined with a gatehouse, a guest house, a gardener's cottage, a hunting lodge, and formal gardens sat a large stucco house with a spectacular view of the bay beyond. The Sabins employed thirteen house servants and eighteen gardeners to maintain the estate's extensive grounds. To ensure they had enough topsoil for their elaborate plants, trees, and flowers, the couple bought a nearby farm, removed all its topsoil, and had it trucked to Bayberry Land.

Pauline and Charlie threw brilliant parties that became legendary for the opulent setting, full orchestra dance music, and abundant food and drink. Charlie Sabin was a committed Wet, and during Prohibition he installed a hidden door in the library disguised as a bookcase that swung open to reveal a large stash of liquor and wine. Charlie made sure his bartenders knew how to make all the latest cocktails—sidecars, southsides, bee's knees, old-fashioneds, and hanky-pankys—but for Pauline, sparkling conversation provided the most important element of their parties. "My grandmother didn't suffer dullards lightly," said another granddaughter, her namesake, Pauline Sabin Smith Willis.

Her granddaughters marveled that Pauline had great style in everything she did and irresistible charm. "Her face was constantly expressive," said Mrs. Willis, who fondly recalled Pauline's mannerisms. "Sometimes, when enthusiastically pleased while sitting in her chair, she would give her right heel a little bang on the carpet. Displeasure turned her chin a little to the right, while both eyes turned left with a doubting stare." Even as a small child, Mrs. Willis was aware of her grandmother's effect on people. Everyone "fell all over themselves for her," she said. Whether it was the mayor of Southampton, whom no one had ever bothered with among the summer residents because he was just a little local fellow, or the president of the United States. "They were all eating out of her hand for whatever she wanted to do," Mrs. Willis added. Pauline was also given to displays of generosity. She was famous for tipping extravagantly. Wrapped in a fur coat, a little dog tucked under each arm, she'd roll up to the Ritz in New York for lunch in her big black Packard. The doorman who'd worked there for forty years and knew her father would open the door, and as Pauline stepped out, she'd always place a wad of bills in his hand. Such noblesse oblige went hand in hand with a fierce sense of social justice and an open and welcoming demeanor. "She loved and cared about people and could talk to anyone from any walk of life," said Mrs. Willis.

Her wit and self-deprecating humor disarmed people who expected such a wealthy, beautiful aristocrat as Pauline to be haughty and imperious. "I was never very bright or even able at school," she once told a reporter. Indeed, she confessed, the only prize she ever got at boarding school "was for being on time every day for breakfast."

DURING WORLD WAR I, with Pauline's sons at boarding school, the Sabins swung into action. They donated generously to the Red Cross and, with other titans of Wall Street, Charlie raised more than a billion dollars in war bonds. Parties at Bayberry Land and at the couple's home in Manhattan raised money for hospitals, refugees, and disabled veterans and their families. In 1918, Pauline became involved with the Republican Party, the party of her father and grandfather, though not of Charlie Sabin, a firm Democrat. As Pauline observed, "Women tend to vote with their fathers, not their husbands."

Pauline had first become interested in politics as a companion to her father, traveling with him at seventeen to the 1904 Republican convention in Chicago to see President Theodore Roosevelt nominated for a second term. She had been attending Republican conventions ever since. The vacuous high-society life of charity balls, dinner parties, teas, and dress fittings bored her immensely. Membership on charity boards also left her cold, though she confessed, "I got my first inspiration to go into politics seriously when I found that on charity boards in New York City you had to have political pull to get things done."

After the war, in 1919, Pauline visited the headquarters of the National Republican Committee in New York as a volunteer and quickly raised $176,000 for Warren G. Harding's presidential campaign. That year she joined an internecine GOP squabble by running against two men for a seat on the Suffolk County Republican Committee and beating them both. It was the only time she ran in an election. As a divorced woman, Pauline had little chance to win public elective office, such as congresswoman or senator, and it doesn't appear she ever considered it. But there were other channels to power working behind the scenes. She thought women were naturals at the game of politics. "Politics is wooing voters and who

Pauline Sabin at Bayberry Land with her sons.
Courtesy of Sheila Morton Smith Cochran.

should know more about wooing and about how to be wooed than a woman?" she once told a reporter. Pauline herself loved the game passionately and quickly mastered the art of political organizing, honing her skills to razor sharpness.

In the late spring of 1919, Pauline became pregnant and eagerly awaited the birth of her first child with Charlie. On January 29, she entered the hospital and delivered a girl. But her joy quickly turned to sorrow. The infant was a "blue baby," born with health problems caused by the incompatibility of Pauline's and her infant's Rh factors, the inherited protein found on the surface of blood cells. Nothing could be done. The Rh factor and its consequences for mothers and children wouldn't be known for seventeen more years. The poor baby lived only one day.

The loss shattered Pauline, but she vowed to rise above her grief and get back to work. That meant taking up arms in the Wadsworth

war. Battle lines had been clearly drawn in the Republican Party with
Ella Boole's champion Mollie Hay leading the anti-Wadsworth faction during the 1920 Senate primary campaign.

MOLLIE HAY'S STORY illustrates the post-suffrage tensions among
women and shows how loyalty to Suff principles often clashed with
women's membership in America's political parties, impeding their
rise to positions of power and elected office.

Born in 1857 in Charleston, Indiana, Hay came from a long line
of politically active Republicans. Like Ella Boole, she'd become an
ardent Prohibitionist as a girl. After graduating from the Western
College for Women in Oxford, Ohio, she worked for the WCTU in
Indiana, where her brilliant organizing skills drew her into the suffrage fight. She moved to New York, where she met Carrie Catt and
worked side by side with her to build the suffrage juggernaut. After the
death of Carrie's husband, George, in 1905, Hay moved in with Catt,
eventually settling with her in a home in New Rochelle, New York.

During the last push for suffrage ratification in 1919, Hay had
organized a house-to-house canvass of nearly every voter in New
York City. She also found a solid place in the Republican Party, serving as chair of the Republican Women's National Executive Committee and working closely with Will Hays, a longtime suffrage supporter, to give women an equal voice with men in party affairs. Short
and stout, with a nimbus of white hair haloing her round face, Hay
strode into backroom meetings, a carved ivory elephant charm on a
black grosgrain ribbon around her neck, impressing everyone with
her sharp intelligence, while annoying some people with her blunt,
abrasive manner.

No sooner had the Nineteenth Amendment passed than Hay's
loyalty to women's causes began to collide with her fealty to the GOP.
She was outraged that her party challenged her opposition to Wadsworth, a man who had worked against suffrage. "The men thought
that because this was a Presidential year they could 'put him over'
with the rest of the ticket. The bosses thought we women would

vote, not as our consciences dictated, but as the party whip dictated. I rebelled," she told the *New York Herald Tribune*. Women aren't fomenting a "sex war," she declared, but men are, by keeping the GOP "a man's party." She complained that men held secret conferences to decide policy and then called meetings to tell "women what to do." The party leaders wouldn't tolerate such protest and removed Hay from both the state and national Republican women's committees and stripped her of her delegate-at-large status for the upcoming 1920 National Republican Convention in Chicago.

In the meantime, Pauline Sabin continued to support Wadsworth and stayed in the game. In February, she was one of only three women on the Republican New York State Committee who met at GOP headquarters on Thirty-Ninth Street in Manhattan to select delegates to the June convention. Then, in mid-May, she organized a rally of Republican women at the Waldorf Astoria to discuss the importance of party loyalty. Before the rally, in an effort to reassure the Drys and Suffs who were reluctant to support him, Wadsworth issued a statement that he accepted the Eighteenth and Nineteenth Amendments as law and would do everything in his power to uphold them.

After the rally, Pauline traveled around New York State, holding classes to educate women on the important issues and the candidates' positions, hoping to persuade her audiences, many of whom were uncommitted, to join the GOP. When Prohibition came up for discussion, she agreed it was a good thing for everyone, especially women and children. On a personal level, she thought the liquor ban would set a good example for her sons, now entering their young adulthood. However, her speeches dealt only glancingly with Prohibition. Rather, she emphasized the necessity of voting for Wadsworth so Republicans wouldn't lose control of the Senate. At stake, Pauline explained, were those bedrocks of Republicanism, small government and lower taxes.

In contrast, Ella Boole wanted government to become involved more heavily in a host of progressive causes, from outlawing child

labor and overseeing factory safety to ensuring rights for workers
and women. Of course, she also thought government should vigorously enforce Prohibition. Ousting the states' rights fanatic Wadsworth was just a first step in forming a better union that would work
toward improving the lives of all citizens—women and children,
especially. The doubling of the electorate gave Ella hope that she'd
prevail, as she expected women to vote as a bloc. Also, she had solid
backing from thousands of members of the New York chapter of the
WCTU, as well as members of the Anti-Saloon League, the League
of Women Voters under Mollie Hay's leadership, and the Suff chief
herself, Carrie Catt. "Mrs. Boole is and she would be head and shoulders above the men who are in the Senate now," Catt told reporters.
Wadsworth, she added, is "a reactionary," "a foe of the plain people,"
and is "too small a man to represent the greatest state in the union
in the United States Senate."

But the support of influential organizations wasn't enough to
push Ella ahead of the senior senator from New York. As it turned
out, women did not rush to the polls, and those who voted, did not
do so as a bloc. Wadsworth easily won the Republican primary. Ella
polled 90,491 votes (or 22.26 percent) to Wadsworth's 270,084
(or 66.42 percent). A third candidate, George Henry Payne, who
opposed Wadsworth's record on agriculture issues, received 46,039
votes (or 11.32 percent). The resounding defeat did not force Ella out
of the race, however. Urged on by her supporters, she accepted the
nomination of the Prohibition Party and, riding their ticket, vowed
"to stick it out to the end."

Founded in 1869 to campaign for legislation to ban the manufacture and sale of intoxicating drink, the Prohibition Party relied on
most of its support from rural and small-town evangelical churches.
Its national clout peaked in 1884 when its candidate for president polled 1.50 percent of the popular vote, and declined significantly with the passage of the Eighteenth Amendment. Still, Ella
believed she had a chance to win, which would make her the first
woman elected to the US Senate. As the Prohibition candidate,

Ella supported the same progressive causes she'd pushed running in the Senate Republican primary. But the party's "supreme" goal, "the great issue" that mattered above all, according to a 1920 WCTU press release, was to support and maintain "the entire extinction of the liquor traffic." The odds were deeply stacked against her. Mollie Hay and the other Suffs had switched their allegiance to Wadsworth's Democratic opponent, New York Lieutenant Governor Harry Walker. Hay and the others thought Walker had the best chance of defeating Wadsworth.

As Election Day neared, Hay and Catt organized an anti-Wadsworth rally in the venerable Great Hall at the Cooper Union in Manhattan, where Abraham Lincoln, Mark Twain, and Henry James had spoken, and where the first public meeting of the National Association for the Advancement of Colored People had convened in 1909. Banners on either side of a large truck parked at the curb outside announced "We Want a New Senator in Washington" and "Wadsworth's Place Is in the Home." Loud military marches played by the New York City Seventh Regiment Band filled Cooper Square as women passed out anti-Wadsworth flyers. Among those streaming through the doors was Mrs. James Wadsworth herself, a handsome, expensively dressed matron, flanked by her sister on one side and a friend on the other. Mrs. Wadsworth told a reporter they had dropped in "to see" what the Suffs "had to say against the Senator," adding that she had no doubt her husband would win.

Five-minute speeches followed from a series of women representing teachers, welfare workers, war veterans, and the League of Women Voters. A collection was taken up for candidate Walker. Then Carrie Catt took the podium. In a long speech, during which several men in the audience walked out, Catt reviewed Wadsworth's entire political career, explaining why she thought he was utterly unfit to be senator.

In the end, Ella ran a distant third in the Senate race, though as the *New York Times* noted, she made "a remarkably strong" showing—winning 159,623 votes, significantly more votes than the

Prohibition candidate garnered in the previous Senate race two years earlier. Walker came in second with 901,310 votes, and Wadsworth won with 1,434,393 votes. William H. Anderson, superintendent of the New York Anti-Saloon League, blamed Ella's huge loss on her entering the race too late and without the necessary funds "to make a real fight."

The defeat, however, did not mark her exit from the public stage. Indeed, her life in the political spotlight had only begun. Just a month after the election, Ella traveled to Washington, DC, for a meeting of reformers at the Metropolitan Church on Pennsylvania Avenue SE, a few miles from the White House, where Warren G. Harding would soon take up residence as the nation's twenty-ninth president. A small-town newspaper publisher from Marion, Ohio, the handsome, affable Harding was, as one biographer described him, "a weak and colorless and mediocre" man who "never had an original idea." Nonetheless, he had risen swiftly through the ranks of the Republican Party, becoming a US senator in 1915 and then president, easily defeating Democrat James M. Cox, the Ohio governor.

At their three-day meeting, Ella and the other reformers passed resolutions condemning a host of "immoralities" they saw plaguing the nation, including "screen vampires," "close dancing," Sunday baseball games, cigarettes, and "joy rides," which Wilbur F. Crafts, founder of the International Bureau of Reform that sponsored the conference, said "often proved a ride of lifelong shame and woe," presumably because girls with boys in cars often led to petting and sex. Their chief concern, however, was fear that the Volstead Act wouldn't be vigorously enforced. They had reason to worry. Despite Prohibition, the corridors of power in Washington, DC, sloshed with booze, starting at the top. When Harding moved into the White House on Inauguration Day on March 4, he had $1,800 worth of liquor that he'd purchased before Prohibition transferred from his home to the president's private quarters. He kept a house near the Chevy Chase Club, which his manservant Taylor stocked with beer and scotch. Harding's attorney general, Harry Daugherty, the man ultimately responsible for enforcing the law, had large quantities of liquor delivered by Justice Department employees to his infamous den of backroom deals, the Little Green House, a limestone residence on K Street.

Though the public rooms on the ground floor of the White House stayed Dry, upstairs in the president's private quarters, the liquor flowed at card games and cocktail parties. One evening during an official reception downstairs, Alice Longworth slipped upstairs to Harding's study, where the president was entertaining a group of his cronies. The air was "heavy with tobacco smoke," and trays were laid out "with bottles containing every imaginable brand of whiskey," Alice recalled. Most of the nation's senators and representatives were as dripping Wet as the president and his cabinet. William Slayton, a US Navy captain and head of the Association Against the Prohibition Amendment (AAPA), caught the mood on his many lobbying excursions to Capitol Hill. "The truth is, the number of congressmen who wanted to take a drink with you or find out the name of your bootlegger was very much greater than the number who sought to browbeat you," he told the writer H. L. Mencken.

If the president refused to stop drinking, what hope was there for the War on Liquor?

The answer proved to be a prim thirty-two-year-old woman, just five years out of law school, who'd been plucked from a public defender's office at the far end of America and put in charge of enforcing Prohibition.

THREE

THE ENFORCER

MABEL WALKER WILLEBRANDT grew up an only child in a nomadic life on the Midwestern frontier. She'd been born in a sod shelter dug into the side of a hill on May 23, 1889, in Woodsdale, Kansas, where her parents, Myrtle and David Walker, had a homestead claim to farm a small acreage. From there, the family moved by covered wagon around the Midwest, chasing opportunities that never quite panned out. At various times, David Walker ran a newspaper, worked in a factory, farmed, and owned a small-town bank. The bank failed. Both Walkers taught school intermittently, their only reliable source of income.

They doted on Mabel, once halting their wagon journey across the prairie to retrieve a bright flower the little girl had spotted in the distance. In Blackwell, Oklahoma, the family lived in a small tent. David Walker edited a newspaper, the *Blackwell Times*, out of a second tent pitched next door. Mabel was alone with her mother one day when a flash flood ripped through the flimsy canvas structures. Mrytle saved Mabel and the family printing press by setting them both on an overturned kitchen table and holding on until the water subsided. Soon, the family moved on, first to Kingman, Kansas, to stay with David's oldest brother, then to an eighty-acre farm near Powersville, Missouri, this time to be close to Myrtle's relatives.

Mabel learned how to milk cows and care for chickens and often walked behind the plow with her father as he cut furrows in the soil, talking "man to man" to him about crops, business, and politics.

As far back as she could remember, Mabel wanted to have a career. The traditional housewives she knew did what men expected. If she worked and earned her own money, she reasoned, she could do what she wanted. Her mother always worked and set an example of resourcefulness. At one point when the family funds were particularly low, Myrtle Walker completed a correspondence course in optometry and went door to door fitting glasses. Mabel's father took pleasure in his daughter's fierce intelligence, but his discipline could be cruel and coarse. As a homeschooled child living in the middle of nowhere, Mabel's sole companions were a mother cat and her seven kittens. Once in a fit of anger, Mabel bit the ear of one of the cats, and in response her father bit *her* ear. The lesson was less about respecting animals than about restraining one's emotions. David treated Mabel no differently than he would have a son. But he pushed her to act tougher and more mature than any child, boy or girl, should have been expected to act. When seven-year-old Mabel's pets killed the Walkers' chickens, David gathered up the cats to drown them in a stream. Mabel sobbed uncontrollably, as she begged her father to spare their lives. "'Stop it! You're acting like a child. Go to your room until you can control yourself!'" her father said, "with his blue eyes flashing and with Jehovan sternness," Mabel recalled. Rather than resenting her father or becoming bitter over his harshness, she loved and admired him more for giving her a high standard "to live up to." Although not as severe a disciplinarian as her husband, the deeply religious Myrtle also expected much from Mabel and developed in the little girl a strong sense of Christian charity and rectitude. Mabel's parents basked in her intelligence and encouraged their daughter's love of reading and writing. Mabel "was always interested in words," David recalled, "and we always tried to be sure she knew the meaning of each new one she met."

As Mabel entered her adolescent years, her life changed

dramatically. Her parents sold their farm and moved to a small house in Kansas City, Missouri, so Mabel could start sixth grade in public school and have the stimulation of association with other children. Soon after they arrived, a flood hit Kansas City at the same time Mabel came down with whooping cough. She felt dreadful to be sick "because she couldn't go to the bluff and see the houses and things floating down the river," her mother recalled. Around this time, the Walkers took in a foster child from a Chicago orphanage, a sweet, gentle fifteen-year-old girl named Minnie Hickstein. Soon afterward, the family gained another child when Mabel brought home from school a ragged, but intelligent girl, Maud Hubbard, whom Mabel wanted to rescue from her own impoverished, neglectful parents. Now Mabel had two "sisters" that she would remain close to for most of her life.

In 1906, Mabel and Maud applied and were accepted to the academically rigorous Park Academy in nearby Parkville, Missouri. A year later, Mabel—ever the independent, confident thinker—argued with the principal on the doctrine of the virgin birth (she didn't believe in it) and was immediately expelled. Still, she completed enough coursework to get a teaching job in the timber town of Buckley, Michigan, where her parents had moved to care for David Walker's aged mother. Maud stayed behind, eventually graduating from Park Academy, becoming a poet, and marrying a Christian missionary.

One day while walking home from the school in Buckley, a forest fire trapped Mabel for hours. Another time, during winter, she was lost for hours in a blizzard. Her students were as unruly as the weather, and she had no qualms about employing physical punishment when necessary. After a boy she failed threatened Mabel with a knife, she grabbed the weapon, then gave him a good thrashing, she later recalled. Her pluck and fortitude drew the attention of the young school principal Arthur F. Willebrandt. Mabel was flattered that this tall, handsome man found her attractive. When she looked in the mirror, though, she saw a pudgy nose, fleshy cheeks, a too-wide mouth, and a strong chin with a masculine cleft. She also wore hearing aids, necessary because she was partially deaf. She hid the clunky devices by carefully arranging her dark blonde hair over her ears before gathering it into a knot at the back of her head. Sometimes, on evenings out, she would stash the devices in her brassiere.

Mabel's character, too, seemed to embody all that was thought to be unfeminine: she was argumentative, ambitious, and a workaholic, and she didn't have one submissive bone in her body. The idea of being bound to a husband forever seemed outrageous to Mabel. But she knew her parents expected her to marry. So, when Arthur fell ill with tuberculosis and asked Mabel to be his wife and move with him to a sanatorium in Arizona, she accepted. Mabel was just twenty and Arthur twenty-one. They traveled by train with a weak, wheezing Arthur on a stretcher in the baggage car and wed during a stop in Grand Rapids, Michigan.

While Arthur slowly recovered in Arizona's warm, dry climate, Mabel completed college at Temple Normal School in Phoenix and took a teaching job. What started out as a romantic adventure, however, soon turned into a dreary slog. Mabel resented being breadwinner, housekeeper, *and* nurse, and the marriage floundered. Then she became pregnant. She professed in a 1928 article for *Good Housekeeping* that motherhood had been her "most cherished hope," but years later told her adopted daughter that she'd considered an abortion. She didn't say why—whether because she felt she couldn't cope with a baby at the time, or because she didn't want a child with Arthur, or another reason entirely. She claimed to have sent Arthur out to find an abortionist, though this seems unlikely, as Mabel was too sensible to risk the kind of dangerous "back alley" procedures that were the only ones available at the time to women who wanted to end their pregnancies. Desperation might have driven Mabel to take the terrible risk, though her deep Christian faith more likely would have prevailed in moving her to accept her condition. In the end, though, she had a miscarriage, which turned out to be a tubal pregnancy. The subsequent surgery left her permanently infertile.

With no child tying her to Arthur, Mabel might have considered divorce, though a scandalous act at the time. In the end, she decided to remain with her husband, at least for the time being, and when Arthur's health improved, she moved with him to Los Angeles, where Arthur's mother joined the couple in a small house in Buena Park. Mabel got a job as the principal of an elementary school in Pasadena, and she and Arthur enrolled in the College of Law at the University of Southern California. They agreed that Mabel would follow a part-time course load while working the first year. The next year Arthur would work so Mabel could attend school full-time. But this never happened. Exhausted and fed up with Arthur's exploitation of her—she supported the household while also doing all the cooking and cleaning— Mabel moved to an apartment with a woman law school classmate.

During her last semester of law school in 1916, Mabel began taking pro bono cases in the Los Angeles courts and immediately stood out for her tireless work, exceptional intelligence, and devotion to social justice. As the city's first female public defender, she represented prostitutes, junkies, abused women, and single mothers, eventually trying two thousand cases. Outraged that men were rarely arrested in prostitution cases, she pioneered a procedure that enabled her female defendants to request jury trials, thus forcing their johns to testify. She helped some of her clients give up prostitution, including one madam to whom she lent money to encourage her to retire.

Mabel wanted judges and male attorneys to take her seriously, and she was desperate to break down their skepticism about her ability. She felt she had "to walk the tight-rope of sexlessness without the loss of her essential charm," she later wrote in an article for *Smart Set*. To this end, she adopted a practical, no-nonsense uniform of plain tailored suits, crisp white blouses, and low-heeled shoes. For photographs, she made sure she smiled with her mouth closed.

After earning her law degree in June 1916, Mabel opened a practice on Spring Street's "attorney row" in downtown LA with two classmates, Fred Horowitz and John S. Shepherd, whose lawyer father furnished the offices with desks, chairs, conference tables, and a library of reference books. With her unshakable sense of duty, devotion to public service, and workaholic temperament, Mabel thrived on eighteen-hour days. She continued to help women victims in the public defender's office, while teaching English at night to Mexican immigrants. She also found time to study for her master's of law degree. Her only relaxation came on the weekends when she hiked and camped in the Sierra Mountains with Fred and John. Mabel fell madly in love with the tall, square-jawed John Shepherd, who was as handsome as a movie star. It seems their relationship never progressed beyond friendship, though it might have if America had not entered World War I in 1917. John was drafted into the Ninety-First Division of the US Army, the same division in which Arthur Willebrandt reluctantly served. Arthur had asked Mabel to use her political connections to win him a draft exemption. Appalled by this latest example of his weakness and selfishness, she refused, telling Arthur that if his TB had been cured, he'd have to serve. Despite his medical history, Arthur passed his physical and was sent to France, as was John Shepherd. Fred Horowitz, meanwhile, received a military exemption for disability; as a child, he'd been hit by a car and forever afterward walked with a limp.

At the end of the war, Arthur returned home. John Shepherd, however, was killed fighting in the Argonne Forest on October 1, 1918. Mabel was devastated. He was "the only man Mabel ever really loved," said Fred, who stepped in to console her. Fred wanted to marry Mabel if she ever got around to divorcing Willebrandt. But Mabel could never muster an attraction to him. Fred's looks were ordinary; he hobbled and suffered from asthma. Perhaps because Mabel lacked confidence in her own physical attractions, she had a weakness for exceptionally handsome men. She yearned to feel a stirring of passion, and that was missing with Fred, despite his complete devotion, not only to her, but also to her parents. After the failure of David Walker's latest venture, a small bank in Buckley, Michigan, that specialized in farm loans, Mabel bought property for her parents in Temple City outside Los Angeles, where they raised chickens.

Fred helped arrange a loan for the couple to build a small house. He visited them frequently to help with chores, even plucking chickens, though the poultry fuzz caused his asthma to flare up. "He is so thoughtful of us," Myrtle reported to Mabel. "I just want to baby him."

Fred delivered Mabel's soiled laundry and worn stockings to Myrtle for washing and mending. Once, during a severe flood when the telephone service went out, Fred hired a car to drive to the Walkers' home to check on them. "That is the kind of friend Fred Horowitz is," Myrtle wrote her daughter. Myrtle didn't care that Fred was Jewish, and she deplored the visceral anti-Semitism and racism of rural America, the idea "that all good Jews are like good Indians—dead." She loved Fred like a son.

Proud as she was of Mabel, Myrtle worried that her professionally ambitious daughter was neglecting her relationships and spiritual life. It was true; Mabel had little time for anything but work. Her fame was spreading as a savior of underprivileged women, and she became a sought-after speaker at Los Angeles women's clubs. In 1920, the Women's Legislative Council, which represented almost 200,000 newly franchised female voters in California, hired her as their legal adviser. The next year, after Warren Harding took office, California Republican Senator Hiram Johnson recommended Mabel for the post of assistant attorney general, a job that had gone previously to a California woman, Annette Abbott Adams, appointed by Woodrow Wilson in the last year of his administration. In the manner of political tradition, that gave a leg up to another California woman. But the other California senator, Samuel Shortridge, wanted the job for his sister. Clara Shortridge Foltz was the first woman admitted to the bar in California, a single mother of five, and a suffragist of the first hour, who'd worked tirelessly for the passage of the Woman Lawyer's Bill in the California state legislature, giving women of the state the right to study law. Foltz had also invented the concept of public defenders, when she proposed the idea to the Congress of Jurisprudence and Law Reform at the 1893 Chicago World's Fair.

But Foltz was seventy-one in 1920, and though she would live for another fourteen years, she couldn't compete with Mabel's energy and youth. Nor could she match Mabel in the number and passion of her supporters. Mabel's were legion, and they fought hard for her, blitzing Harding's attorney general, Harry Daugherty, with telegrams extolling the young woman's virtues. "She is one of the most unselfish and hard-working attorneys I have ever met, and if you make her a member of your staff you will have a live wire who will stay awake nights trying to think up new ways of giving more credit for the office," read a telegram from one of Mabel's police court colleagues. The job, though, wasn't exactly a plum. The new assistant attorney general would be in charge of enforcing Prohibition, already recognized as an impossible task that no one wanted. So, of course, as one of Mabel's friends remarked, they gave the job to a woman.

IN AUGUST, DAUGHERTY CALLED Mabel to Washington to meet President Harding. She left Los Angeles on August 17 for the four-day journey on the Southern Pacific Railroad. As the train rattled across the nation along 2,600 miles of track—past cities, towns, farms, and open country—Mabel poured out her fears in long letters to her parents. She worried about being wrenched from her California life, about giving up her new law practice, and, mostly, about being so far from her mother and father, who had loved her "so hard" and who she depended on for unfailing emotional support. She pitied adults who didn't remain close to their parents and would desperately miss "those evening confidences that have always meant so much in my life when we three have talked over intimate things." She would be uprooting her life for only $110 a month, the assistant attorney general's salary, which was just $10 more than she had earned as a school principal. Even worse, Mabel feared, she would be a token woman in an "inconsequential groove," in a constraining government post.

Mabel arrived at the White House for the most important interview of her life on a blazing hot day. Flowers wilted in the parkways, and the Capitol's marble monuments looked bleached against the white sky. With her simple outfit and scrubbed-clean face (she never wore makeup), she looked more like a schoolgirl than a hard-charging prosecutor. Harding, who had an eye for attractive women, took one look at her and shook his head. "You are splendid," he said. "But I'm afraid you're much too young!"

Mabel leveled her gaze at the president and replied in a firm voice, "I promise to outgrow it."

Harding smiled. "In that case, you've got the job."

FOUR

AMERICA'S MOST POWERFUL WOMAN

T HE ANNOUNCEMENT OF Mabel Walker Willebrandt's appointment, accompanied by a photograph of her looking fetching in a
tailored jacket and white blouse, appeared in newspapers across
the country. She moved into an apartment in Meridian Mansions, a
luxury building on Sixteenth Street in the Adams Morgan neighborhood that was popular with diplomats and congressmen, and she
reported to work on September 27, 1921, immediately following her
swift confirmation by the US Senate.

The Prohibition Bureau, an entirely new unit, had been created
under the auspices of the Treasury Department but was housed in
the Department of Justice building. Mabel oversaw all Prohibition
cases, and also those involving income tax violations and the federal
prisons. During her tenure, she supervised the establishment of an
institution for young male offenders at Chillicothe, Ohio, and a wom-
en's prison at Alderson, West Virginia, and she enlarged the industries at federal prisons across the nation to provide work and wages
to prisoners. She was enormously proud of these accomplishments,
though putting bootleggers out of business and prosecuting them
would occupy most of her time.

When Mabel took office, Prohibition had been in effect for nearly
two years, enough time for the difficulties of enforcement to be

Mabel Walker Willebrandt, the most powerful woman in the
US government, at work in Washington, DC. Library of Congress
Prints and Photographs Division, LC-DIG-ds-00643.

abundantly clear. Liquor flowed into the United States by ship, car, and plane from Canada, Bimini, Barbados, Cuba, Scotland, and England. Almost immediately, bootlegging became big business and sparked waves of violence as gangsters battled to control the illegal trade. Meanwhile, enforcement cost a fortune, and America had neither the will nor the funds to successfully implement it. Congress allocated a paltry $4.75 million budget to Prohibition enforcement in its first year. (The Volstead Act had charged the Bureau of Internal Revenue, the forerunner of the IRS, in the Treasury Department with enforcing the Eighteenth Amendment, and therefore the bureau had been set up under the BIR.)

Uncle Sam got little help from the states. Only eighteen of them had set aside any money at all for enforcement, and these were meager sums, a fraction of what was spent to enforce fish and game laws.

To make matters worse, Prohibition agents, who were exempt from civil service standards and received small salaries, were notoriously incompetent and corrupt—"as devoid of honesty and integrity" as criminals, Mabel noted. Often, they used their jobs as a kind of bootlegging school before going into business for themselves.

After just a few weeks in Washington, Mabel started to feel that she was the only government official who took Prohibition seriously. Andrew Mellon—the immensely wealthy secretary of the treasury, whose department oversaw the agents charged with discovering violators of Volstead—despised Prohibition and never missed a chance to express his disdain for the law. He didn't object when his son Paul and a group of the young man's friends from Yale had a roaring booze party one winter night at the Mellon home in Pittsburgh. The treasury secretary asked only that the students not toss their empty bottles out the window, lest the neighbors see them when the snow melted.

Mellon's deputy, Prohibition Commissioner Roy Haynes, was weak and ineffectual, and Attorney General Harry Daugherty, Mabel's immediate boss, regularly flouted the law with Harding's Ohio Gang of hard partyers. In contrast to Mabel's simple, plain attire, Daugherty was a peacock who stuffed his portly body into dapper three-piece suits and accessorized his silk ties with a pearl stick pin. As a key member of the Ohio Republican machine (five of the ten preceding presidents, including Harding, hailed from Ohio), he epitomized the "boss" who treated politics as a game and government service as an opportunity to enrich his bank account. Daugherty rarely went to the office and paid little attention to enforcement. He liked and admired Mabel, however, and she remained loyal to him— she owed him her job—when he later faced corruption charges. But he made her work that much harder by ignoring the grafters, extortionists, and thieves who hung around her office, polluting the force of federal agents.

Still, Mabel wouldn't admit to herself or anyone else that Prohibition couldn't be enforced, and she found a hint of hope wherever she could. In the fall of 1921, a Hollywood rape and murder case provided it. Roscoe "Fatty" Arbuckle, a beloved silent film comedian, had been accused of raping and murdering showgirl Virginia Rappe during a drunken bacchanal in a San Francisco hotel. Every lurid detail of the events leading to Rappe's death had been covered in the press, shocking the public. "If the facts are correct, they show how far the present disregard for the law, especially for the prohibition law, has been carried," Mabel told a reporter in one of her first interviews after her appointment. "What is encouraging is the shudder of horror which has apparently been aroused throughout the country. The pendulum has swung so far that public opinion is shocked at last. These revelations about what has been going on in the breaking of the prohibition laws has awakened public conscience. . . . [T]here is no doubt but that these revelations in the Arbuckle case, whether true or not[,] will make prohibition enforcement easier. The national conscience has been shamed."

READING THESE WORDS in the newspaper, Ella Boole felt cheered. She knew she had a staunch ally in Mabel, and she wasted no time calling on the new assistant US attorney general at her office in room 501 of the Justice Department at Vermont and K Streets. The "Queen," as Mabel's staff affectionately called her, sat behind a big mahogany desk piled with papers, files, a signature stamp, and a candlestick phone. She hid her smoking habit from outsiders as carefully as she concealed her hearing aids, and she had stashed her cigarettes and ashtray in a drawer. Still, a stale, fumy odor filled the air.

Ella assumed that good Christian Mabel abhorred liquor as much as she did. The *Union Signal*, the WCTU's weekly newspaper, noted proudly in an item announcing Mabel's appointment that her mother, grandmother, and great-grandmother had all "worn white ribbons." According to the *Los Angeles Evening Post-Record*, Myrtle Walker took Mabel to her first Prohibition meeting "where she had the white ribbon pinned on her" when she was just three years old. Ella would have been horrified to know that before Mabel took office, she served wine at dinner parties and enjoyed a glass or two of bourbon herself. Though Mabel had belonged to many clubs and civic organizations in California, she had never joined the WCTU or the Anti-Saloon League, and she had not participated in the fight for a Dry law in California.

Nor did Mabel tie Prohibition to women's rights, as did Ella and other older activists such as Mollie Hay, Carrie Catt, and Jane Addams. Mabel didn't think banning liquor and outlawing saloons would significantly help women. She believed that without striking at the foundations of inequality, without abolishing laws such as the ones that denied married women the right to own property or failed to protect them from abusive men, society would continue to treat women as second-class citizens. It's unknown if Mabel supported the proposed amendment to the US Constitution that suffragist Alice Paul, with the backing of the Woman's Party, introduced to Congress in 1923. Supporters argued that the Equal Rights Amendment, which came to be known as the ERA, would end legal distinctions between the sexes in property ownership, divorce, employment, and other matters that held women back and relegated them to inferior status. But many working-class women who toiled in factories, hospitals, and offices opposed the amendment on the grounds that it would end their special protections for employment hours and working conditions. To this day, the ERA has failed to achieve ratification.

SOON AFTER ELLA RETURNED to New York after visiting Mabel in Washington, an item about the new assistant attorney general appeared in the *Union Signal*. "Protection of Prohibition laws against all legal attacks will be one of [her] major tasks," the paper reported, adding that Mabel's appointment "is regarded as the highest recognition President Harding has made of the ability of [a] woman to fill 'a man's job.'" Mabel felt intense pressure to be a model for her sex, to prove that a woman could, indeed, perform "a man's job" and do it brilliantly. If she failed, she would be failing not only herself, but all women. It seemed every time a question that related to women came up, reporters called Mabel. Her opinions on topics from politics to the law to women's rights and the idea of salaries for wives—she favored them—were quoted extensively in the press. She also found herself in great demand as a speaker for organizations from the American Women's Bar Association and the National Woman's Party to the Boston Chamber of Commerce and the Women's Republican Club. In May 1923, she told her parents that she spoke to "three or four hundred" members of the League of Women Voters in Pittsburgh, adding, "I'm getting so spoiled. . . . I resent being called to speak before less than a thousand or so!"

Invitations to Georgetown dinner parties poured into her office. Sometimes she was the only woman on the guest list. At a dinner at the home of Solicitor General James Beck, who was famously anti-suffrage, she joined twelve male colleagues from the Justice Department, but no wives. "It was a stag party and I was the only doe," she wrote in her diary. No doubt Beck had felt obliged to include her, never expecting that she'd actually show up.

The press thrilled at Mabel's youth, intelligence, and femininity. The last was a key component of her celebrity. "She must always be the alert, skillful, resourceful lawyer and somehow she manages also to be always a gracious, charming woman," one writer noted. Unlike her predecessor, Annette Abbott Adams, whom Mabel's secretary described as "rather masculine and so terribly cold," Mabel was warm and empathetic. She came by these virtues naturally and never felt she had to act like a man to be taken seriously. She was always and utterly herself. The scrupulous equality of the prairie had been bred in her bones. She never put on airs or demanded special privileges, surprising everyone with her down-to-earthness. Her staff "expected a large, loud wail," one newspaper wrote, when the federal budget chief ruled there weren't funds to print stationery with her name embossed on the letterhead, but Mabel contented herself with the Justice Department's generic stock. Her staff responded to her kindness and fairness with undying loyalty, and they became an island of comfort in the sea of corruption, graft, and incompetence that roiled around her.

As the most powerful woman in the US government, Mabel had the added vexation of constant scrutiny of her looks. "Mrs. Willebrandt presented a picture of handsome young womanhood, unexpectedly girlish . . . as she sat at her imposing desk. . . . She has well-molded features, wavy chestnut hair, a fresh complexion, expressive gray eyes and a slender, graceful figure," read a typical description in one paper. Mabel was embarrassed by such attention to her appearance, especially since she herself gave it so little thought. She didn't worry about her clothes or hair (except as it successfully hid her hearing aids), all the "girlie-girlie" stuff reporters focused on when describing women. Fashion didn't interest her, and, anyway, she didn't have time for it. Still, historians and biographers are glad to have these descriptions for the vivid picture they offer of how women looked as they moved through the world. Clothes are rarely just clothes. They offer clues to personality and cultural currents, and they have great symbolic power. Mabel adopted a uniform of dark tailored suits and white blouses to signal her no-nonsense professionalism. Even more importantly, she did not cut her hair into a fashionable bob, as did many women her age, lest anyone think her a flapper, that Jazz Age ideal of feminine sex appeal and rebellion.

Mabel worked long days that stretched into the night, as did many members of her staff, driven by loyalty to "the queen" and an eagerness to emulate her work ethic. The "other asst. a.g.'s say they can't get any stenographic help at night. . . . *My* girls come *any* time I ask," Mabel boasted to her parents. No one was more devoted to her than her secretary Margaret Smith. "I am so very proud of her and everything she does. . . . [I]t is so much fun being her secretary and I wouldn't have missed knowing her as I do for anything," Smith wrote Mabel's mother. "Everybody loves her and she is held in such high regard by the Attorney General and all the other Assistants. It is so interesting to hear the remarks the men make as they come out of her office and a great number of them come over to me to tell me that she is not only an extremely smart woman but a charming one."

It didn't take long for Mabel to realize the impossible challenge she faced. Illegal liquor flushed throughout the United States in an unstoppable flow from outside and within the nation's borders. Bootleggers everywhere thrived. The term had originated in the 1880s in the Midwest, when White traders concealed flasks of liquor in their boot tops while negotiating with Native Americans. Now, women hid flasks in their garters, barbers stashed liquor in bottles on their shelves, and tailors poured liquor into the hollows of dressmaker dummies. Homemade liquor was cheap and easy to produce, and stills had dotted the backyards of rural areas for generations. Prohibition just made amateur liquor production more lucrative by opening up opportunities for wider sales to far-flung locales. Suddenly, stills sprouted in yards and wooded areas nationwide.

The open flouting of Prohibition laws by Washington officials astounded Mabel. Once during a session of Congress, she saw a senator who was so drunk, "he had to hold [on] to his desk to keep himself upright." Colleagues tried to persuade him to leave the chamber, but he refused. The spectacle, Mabel wrote, "was apparent to every member of the Senate and to hundreds of people in the galleries." But the senator, himself, apparently, felt no shame.

A great paradox of Prohibition was that never before in America had liquor been so glorified. The orgy "began with a whoop" at the stroke of midnight 1920, wrote F. Scott Fitzgerald. Drinking became ultra-cool, a way for men to thumb their noses at the establishment and its prissy reformers and for women to express their independence. Lois Long, who typified the Jazz Age flapper and chronicled nightlife for the *New Yorker*, regularly got so drunk while reporting that she'd go back to her office and throw up before sitting down to write.

In the meantime, competition among bootleggers and mobsters gave rise to a vicious new type of gangster. Mobsters in Chicago and New York had expanded their criminal enterprises from gambling and prostitution to large and lucrative cartels with extensive networks to distribute illegal liquor, and they regularly murdered their rivals in blasts of machine-gun fire.

The relentless workload often overwhelmed Mabel. "Each month seems crammed so full that the next *must* hold less, but when it comes its capacity outdoes all that has gone before," she told her parents. In November 1921 alone, during her first year in office, she had three cases to present to the US Supreme Court. Though Mabel had gained confidence in her first months in Washington and confided to her diary that she no longer felt "the inward terror at the magnitude" of her job, arguing before the Supreme Court scared her. At such times, she found herself up against some of the nation's most prominent attorneys. In one case in which she argued that bootleggers' customers could be prosecuted if no records were kept of the illegal sale, she was up against John W. Davis, a former ambassador to Britain and sometime presidential candidate, who represented the defendants. Mabel marveled at Davis's "polish, beauty of diction, clearness and scholarly presence. His name draws a crowd. To put me opposite him . . . felt like matching a Ford car with a Pierce Arrow," she wrote. Nevertheless, she won the case.

Hoping to fit in as much as possible at the Supreme Court, Mabel had bought a black pin-striped suit, "the uniform" of the male lawyers arguing before the nine justices, though Mabel's suit, of course, had a skirt instead of trousers. It did nothing, however, to deflect attention from her gender. One of the justices, James C. McReynolds, abhorred women attorneys and was known to leave the bench in a great huff if a woman attorney appeared to argue a case. Even more than McReynolds, however, Mabel feared that her performance at court would be hindered by "the dread shadow of deafness." She became skilled at reading lips, but when a speaker was too far from her, she sometimes had to ask for a repetition of what was said, or guess. On her staff, only her secretary Margaret Smith knew about her hearing loss. Whenever Mabel received a compliment, she thought to herself, "'Damn, you think that *good*, do you know what then *could* I do if I weren't struggling under the most horrible handicap that you do not guess?' In other words, if I could use in intellectual energy that extra attention and nerve and willpower that I *always* exert to even keep the drift of what's going on what couldn't I do? It cuts so deeply to be thought stupid or appear so because you haven't heard & can't therefore make the connection."

Despite the limitations caused by her hearing loss, Mabel would go on to win nearly every Prohibition case she argued before the Supreme Court. The bigoted McReynolds stayed seated, though occasionally he'd turn his back on her, as he did whenever the Jewish Justice Louis Brandeis spoke.

AS THE 1922 CONGRESSIONAL campaign season began, Republican officials tapped Mabel to deliver speeches across the nation. Two years after suffrage, the women's vote was still an uncertain, perplexing element in elections, and the GOP thought Mabel could shore up its appeal to female voters. California Senator Hiram Johnson was among the first politicians who asked for Mabel's help in his reelection bid. At first, she demurred because of overwork, but when he and his cronies pressed her, she agreed to do it. She traveled to the West Coast in August and September to deliver a series of speeches to women's clubs and stopped to visit her parents.

On November 3, a few days before the election, she spoke at a large rally in Zanesville, Ohio, "the finest, biggest meeting yet," she wrote in her diary. As always, when she stood at a podium, she wore her "good luck" opal pendent. "Hundreds turned away from the door. At least 200 standing in the rear," Mabel noted. She chastised herself for not speaking "as smoothly as usual" and compared herself unfavorably to Republican Representative Simeon D. Fess, who was running for the Senate and "quite overshadowed" her. Most likely, she was being unduly harsh on herself. In any case, the next day, Fess handily won the Senate seat.

Campaigning had left her physically and emotionally exhausted. She found it extremely difficult to balance the public's often-hostile perceptions of a woman in power and her obligations to the GOP and the men to whom she owed her job, with her need to be true to herself as a high-achieving public servant. She wrote "blue" letters to her mother, who in response sent Mabel Bible verses and a few of her own inspirational poems, which Myrtle called "the children of my mind." She worried that her daughter was spiritually malnourished and urged her to find time to read her Bible. But Mabel had little time to read anything that wasn't a legal brief, a letter, or an official document.

IN HER FIRST YEARS IN OFFICE, Mabel's chief goal was to take down the nation's biggest suppliers and distributors of illegal alcohol. She paid less attention to shutting down speakeasies, which thrived in the great urban centers. By some accounts, the word came from nineteenth-century Ireland, where illegal bars were called "speak softly shops" because voices were kept low to avoid detection from outside. Trying to stomp them out in Jazz Age America, Mabel knew, was like trying to eliminate mosquitoes from a swamp: kill a few, and twice as many returned in their place. In the mid-1920s, there were around five thousand speaks in Manhattan alone, most concentrated between Thirty-Eighth and Fifty-Ninth Streets and between Fifth and Ninth Avenues. According to *Variety*, the city's entire theatrical district was "dotted with establishments of this nature. They nest in empty lofts, former dancing studios, the lower floors of old English basements and high stoop houses, in flats and wherever one can imagine." At the high end was the 21 Club on West Fifty-Second Street in Manhattan, which had a button behind the bar that when pressed dropped the bottles of liquor on the back wall down a trapdoor through glass-shattering grates, and then onto a pile of rocks in the basement. A single Midtown apartment building might have three speaks. Some of them catered to very specific professions or social groups, such as lawyers, college students, writers, artists, teachers, or commercial airline pilots. Some blocks in Midtown housed so many speaks, that residents had taken to posting signs on their doors: "No Liquor Here."

To own a speak, especially a swank one, became an underworld status symbol and gave a nightclub an exciting aura of outlaw chic.

Gangsters such as Arnold Rothstein, Owney Madden, Dutch Schultz, and Larry Fay all had stakes in Manhattan speaks. Thugs will always be thugs, however, no matter how bespoke their suits and expensive their shirts and watches. Prostitution, brawling, drugs, and murders were almost as common at the gangster-controlled speaks as the watered-down booze. Regulars at the speaks routinely saw cops, magistrates, and federal agents getting drunk and walking out without paying their tabs, which added to a pervasive cynicism about Prohibition.

New York's most sophisticated publications treated the Eighteenth Amendment with derision. Dorothy Parker complained in *Vanity Fair* that one of Prohibition's worst effects was that it had ruined Broadway's cabarets and revues by causing them to be overrun with bad Prohibition jokes. Ella and Mabel were often singled out for special ridicule. A *New Yorker* writer conjured a new board game in which a certain throw of the dice would result in several imagined disasters: the defeat of Zachary Taylor in the Mexican-American War, the return of Louisiana to France, and the appointment of Mabel Walker Willebrandt to the Supreme Court. A cartoon in *Vanity Fair* depicted Ella sitting at a nightclub table commiserating about Prohibition with New York's most famous speakeasy hostess, the former silent film star Texas Guinan. "Just suppose the Eighteenth Amendment were finally repealed," says Texas. "We'd both be out of a job."

FIVE

QUEEN OF THE NIGHT

I F MABEL WALKER WILLEBRANDT was the face of Prohibition, then Texas Guinan was the avatar of rebellion against it. A vaudeville and silent film star, Tex, as she was known to intimates and strangers alike, was already famous when she landed in New York in 1922 and embarked on a career running a series of notorious speakeasies: El Fey, the 300 Club, the Salon Royale, Club Intime, and Club Argonaut. In a business known for flamboyance and boisterous fun, Tex surpassed all other hostesses in her ability to create an atmosphere of liquor-fueled excitement and bawdy camaraderie. A big bottle blonde swathed in finery and glittering with diamonds, Tex greeted guests warmly wherever she happened to be hostessing and made them feel privileged to pay an exorbitant $9 or so cover charge. Once inside, Tex handed them red, white, and yellow noisemakers inscribed with "Texas Guinan and the Gang," which they waved frantically as absurdly young showgirls clad in bits of silk cavorted onstage, then shimmied between tables to drop cherries in the mouths of inebriated men. Tex popularized the phrase "butter and egg man" to refer to the typical out-of-town businessman who liked to overspend at her clubs. The phrase became the title of a popular 1925 play (and later movie) by George S. Kaufman.

Tex delighted audiences with her witty banter. Many of her quips, however, which Walter Winchell and the other columnists who were regulars at her clubs often printed, were rehearsed. Tex passed the time between waking at 3 p.m. and going to work at midnight by coming up with wisecracks with the help of several members of her staff. Stenographers would write them down on scraps of paper and collect them in baskets with words of "advice" and other "laugh provoking nonsense," her manager/publicist John Stein recalled. When one of the girls came onstage to dance with an eight-foot boa constrictor draped across her shoulders, the audience exploded in cheers. More cheering rang out as Tex belted in her raucous voice, "If they padlock this place, I'll open another!" She made good on the boast. Every time Mabel's "dry snoopers" shut down one of her clubs, Tex would spring back in another location. She favored hotels, as hotels with fifty rooms or more were permitted to keep their doors open around the clock, beating the 3 a.m. curfew.

TEX WAS BORN Mary Louise Cecilia Guinan in 1884 to Irish immigrant parents in Waco, Texas, where she later claimed the family's next-door neighbors were Myrtle and David Walker and their little girl Mabel. Mayme, as Tex was known then, recalled the future assistant US attorney general as a meek weakling whom tomboy Mayme enjoying taunting, teasing, roughing up, and sending home in tears. The fact that the Walkers never lived in Waco didn't concern Tex. She held the cynical view that people are gullible, and they'll believe what you tell them if you sound sincere. Her experience as a young woman in a traveling vaudeville show where she regularly encountered a "whole caboodle of petty conmen" taught her that "the average citizen is a sucker." Tex was an expert confabulator, and it amused her to make up stories about Mabel, "that mean, measly reformer."

It was difficult to discern where Tex's lies ended and the truth began. But this much is known: Her father worked as a grocer in Waco; her mother gave birth to nine children, only four of whom survived. Mayme attended the Sacred Heart Academy in town, where she was known as a prankster who talked back to the nuns and daydreamed through the lessons. Early on, she fell under the spell of the painted heroines and villains in the traveling troops performing melodramas at the gingerbread-trimmed Waco Opera House. Mayme "was always hungry for the limelight," her publicist later said.

At home, she wrote and performed plays with her siblings in which she starred as the heroine who always saved the male lead from death and also paid off the mortgage. She grew up with a sharp fear of poverty due to her father's struggles to make a living in the grocery business. By 1910, Michael Guinan had washed up as a grocer. The descendants of his business partner told one of his daughter's biographers that Guinan had embezzled money from the store, leaving it in ruins and causing it to go bankrupt. Whether or not this was true, the family moved to Denver, where the Guinans had relatives and Michael held a series of jobs as a salesman, real estate agent, and cotton broker. He may have had a small plot of land in Denver, but it was hardly the lush 50,000-acre spread Mayme claimed as the scene of her great feats roping cattle and breaking broncos. Somehow, though, she learned to ride. She also developed a flamboyant persona, showing up for mass at the Church of Immaculate Conception in a semiformal black lace gown with a plunging neckline, her head covered in a black plumed picture hat.

One summer at the home of a cousin, she met John "Jack" Moynahan, a stocky, dark-haired cartoonist for the *Rocky Mountain News*. In 1904, when Mayme was twenty and Jack was forty, they married and moved to Chicago, where Jack took a job at the *Chicago Examiner*. The union didn't last a year. Marriage cramped Mayme's fierce ambition. "If you became a model wife, you just stayed home and vegetated and perhaps birthed a few brats. But if you were a good actress, you became a star. Your name went up in big electric lights . . . newspapers ran your picture and people made a fuss about you," she recalled. Chasing her dream of a show business career, she moved to New York, settling in a studio flat in Greenwich Village. She remained friendly with Jack, who sent her money to pay the rent, while she haunted the dusty offices of Broadway agents. Finally,

Mayme landed a spot in a vaudeville show and went on tour. She started calling herself "Texas," a new name for a new life that bound her to the romance of the Wild West.

Tall and buxom with coarse features and a thick figure, Texas knew she couldn't rely on her looks. Nor did she have much talent, though she could sing a little, dance a little, and act a little. Her chief asset as an entertainer was her willingness to flout conventional feminine style. Cowboys and cowgirls were the superheroes of early mass entertainment, and Westerns were the most resonant expressions of American boldness, courage, and strength. Onstage, Tex tamed men as easily as she broke horses and made a joke out of the idea of a damsel in distress. Audiences thrilled at her aggressive, born-to-be-bad persona.

Then, in 1913 she lent her name to a huckster promoting a weight loss elixir, and she claimed to have used the potion to reduce from 204 pounds to 125. When the promoter was tried and convicted of mail fraud, a slew of damning articles about Texas appeared in the press. "Actress Quack Plays Fat Lady to Get the Money" blasted one headline in the *Chicago Tribune*. To escape the notoriety, she fled across the country to Los Angeles. At the time, Hollywood welcomed vaudeville stars who could transition to film, and it wasn't long before Triangle Studios discovered Texas. Casting her in a series of silent two-reel Westerns, she played a tough, gun-slinging rebel. In one of her first pictures, *The Gun Woman*, she killed the man she loved because he cheated on her. "Never jilt a woman who can shoot" read the title card at the end of the scene.

Next, Texas signed a contract with Reelcraft Pictures, where she was not only the star, but head of the unit that produced the movies. It was the golden age of Westerns, and Tex's athleticism and daredevil moxie made her an ideal cowgirl. She could swim, ride, lasso, and twirl a revolver on her index finger better than anyone on-screen. Her fame grew and drew the attention of the Republican Party. In August 1920, she joined the Harding and Coolidge Theatrical League, a collection of seventy Hollywood stars led by Al Jolson that toured the country with the candidates. Texas became a favorite of Harding and stood next to him at campaign events to remind him of the names of people who greeted him. After his election, he gave her a bronze tablet of himself inscribed "To Texas Guinan, whose friendship is as staunch as the redwood trees of California."

Tex, as she often was called, returned to Hollywood, where she formed her own independent film company, Texas Guinan Productions. As a producer, she was tireless and innovative. Rather than hiring stock companies, she cast the films herself, oversaw distribution to theaters, and supervised aggressive publicity campaigns that incorporated live skits and tie-in products, including Texas Guinan postage stamps and balloons featuring her image on horseback. Later, when her publicity tour to promote her film *Spitfire* played in Washington, DC, Harding attended a theater performance that consisted of her acting out scenes from the movie. At the climax of the twenty-two-minute act, Tex rode across the stage on her horse Waco and saved a post office from being robbed. When it was over, the president stood in his box and announced to the audience that he hoped he would be as good a president as Texas was an entertainer. In addition to *Spitfire*, Tex made at least two silents with her company: *The Code of the West* and *Texas of the Mounted*, in which she played the dual roles of brother-sister twins. As the brother, a member of the North-West Mounted Police, Tex is murdered by an outlaw. Afterward, as the sister, she hunts down her brother's killer.

In 1921, Texas moved back to New York, explaining that she was "tired of kissing horses in horse operas." Truth be told, at thirty-seven, she was aging out of films, which favored actresses in their teens and twenties. She'd always had trouble controlling her weight; as she approached forty, her body grew bulkier, and the athletic horseback riding that had marked her early success became difficult. Her chain-smoking, something she had in common with Mabel, didn't help. As the columnist Walter Winchell noted in his memoirs, "You couldn't put [a cigarette] between your lips and light it without Tex taking it."

New York was a logical place for Tex to land. She'd fallen in love with the city the moment she'd stepped onto Broadway a decade earlier, and she forever considered Manhattan her spiritual home. "I would rather have a square inch of New York than all the rest of the world," she told a reporter. Specifically, a square inch of the Great White Way, so named for the area's brightly lit theater marquees, which extended along Broadway from Times Square at Forty-Second Street to Fifty-Third Street. Plush-seated, gilt-ornamented theaters where the leading actors of the day performed live shared the district with gaudy movie palaces featuring the hottest Hollywood stars, horse-betting parlors, call girl apartments, and the music publishers of Tin Pan Alley. Hundreds of speakeasies also turned the area into the Great Wet Way and the command center of America's bootlegging network of liquor producers, financiers, and distributors.

One evening Texas found herself at the Café des Beaux-Arts on West Fortieth Street, a popular haunt of the theater crowd. The scene was sedate and quiet until someone noticed the film star in the crowd and asked Texas to sing. She didn't need much coaxing. After her song, she stayed onstage, wisecracking in an impromptu stand-up routine that had everyone in the club laughing and applauding. The next night, the owner of the Beaux Arts hired her as mistress of ceremonies. Soon however, she was lured away by the manager of the Old King Cole Bar at the Hotel Knickerbocker on Forty-Second Street.

In her new role as club hostess, Texas dyed her hair a lighter shade of blonde and swathed herself in sequined gowns and furs. On some nights, she wore a necklace of tiny gold padlocks and a diamond bracelet dangling a police whistle. She rented a seven-room apartment at 17 West Eighth Street in Greenwich Village, where she installed two Pekingese, two canaries, a squawking parrot, and a revolving cast of lovers. (At the end of her life, she claimed to have had three husbands, but actually she was married only once, to Jack Moynahan.) Tex, who was even more unlucky in love than Mabel, seems to have had a different man for every phase of her career (and some in between). During her vaudeville days, her chief beau was the theatrical producer John Slocum. In Hollywood, she fell in love with the slick, dashing Julian Johnson, an influential drama critic, until she became smitten with George Chesebro, her handsome leading man in her first film, a short called *South of Santa Fe*. A notorious philanderer, Chesebro's attentions to Tex didn't last long. After she moved to New York, she became romantically involved with night-club manager Al Kerwin.

The apartment where she lived until the end of her life was ridiculously cluttered with heavy brocade and silk covering the walls and ceilings. Lamps, dolls, pillows, pictures in silver frames, and tchotchkes crowded the tables, cabinets, and sofas, some of them lifted from hotels and restaurants. Tex had a "kleptomania" habit, according to her manager/publicist, and often took butter plates, silverware, towels, mugs, and other items from the establishments she patronized. Tex employed two maids and a chauffeur who drove her dark gray Excelsior, a Belgian luxury car that she'd acquired from Larry Fay. The mobster had tricked it out with a bulletproof chassis, a shatterproof windshield, and, in the rear, a radio mounted on a device that had once supported a machine gun. Nils Thor Granlund—a Broadway producer who was best known by his initials, N.T.G., and whom Tex had met while touring the nation with the Harding and Coolidge Theatrical League—had introduced her to Fay. Soon, she left the Knickerbocker and joined forces with Fay, a onetime taxi driver who discovered rum-running after transporting a rich customer 365 miles to Canada. Fay used his bootleg profits to buy a fleet of taxis and soon controlled the cab stands at Grand Central and Penn Stations. He quickly joined forces with super gangster Owney Madden, dubbed the "killer" by the press for his quickness to murder anyone who got in his way.

Growing up in the Irish ghetto of Hell's Kitchen, Madden had been a gang leader who, after getting away with several murders, finally served time in Sing Sing for knocking off a rival. After his release in 1923, he hooked up with the Combine, a gangster-owned network of illegal breweries and distilleries, booze-smuggling operations, and speakeasies. With backing from his partners in the

Combine, Madden owned the Cotton Club in Harlem, the flashiest of New York's speaks. With their late hours, available girls, loud jazz, and flowing booze, nightclubs had many things mobsters loved, and owning a piece of one became a status marker for the underworld. Fay put Texas in charge of El Fey Club, the spelling change meant to mask his ownership, which he shared with Madden and other mobster silent partners. A narrow, shoebox room in a red brick townhouse on West Forty-Sixth Street, El Fey sat only eighty patrons and drew the top celebrities of the day, including Babe Ruth, Charles Lindbergh, Charlie Chaplin, Rudolph Valentino, Clara Bow, Gloria Swanson, and the Prince of Wales. Reached by climbing a steep flight of stairs, the club had a door with a peephole and, inside, blue silk walls, velvet banquets, and a small stage. Bottles of liquor were stashed at the barbershop next door and passed to the bartender through a hole in the wall disguised by a removable brick. As the audience knocked back outrageously priced cocktails, threw confetti, and blew noisemakers, showgirls undulated past the tables, stopping occasionally to sit on men's laps, while the waiters, getting into the act, sang and bantered with Texas. Anyone caught with their hands under the table pouring liquor from their own hip flask into a glass would be thrown out by the bouncers. This went on from midnight until five a.m.

After the police padlocked El Fey in 1926, Tex moved a few blocks uptown and opened the 300 Club on West Fifty-Fourth Street with backing from Madden and the gangster Arnold Rothstein. One young regular of the club told Tex's biographer, Louise Berliner, that the gangsters mostly kept a low profile, preferring to play poker upstairs rather than partying downstairs with the club patrons. As business partners, the gangsters were totally unreliable. Even worse, the possibility of violence hung in the air whenever they were around. Nils Granlund remembered that four of his mobster employers were killed, one of the girls in his shows was shot, and "another was with a gangster when he was bumped off."

Tex lived on high alert, always looking out not only for misbehaving mobsters, but also undercover cops. Though she joked about being shut down and padlocked, she felt constantly stressed by the threat of raids. Adding to her woes was keeping on the good side of the vicious men who paid her bills. For Tex and her beloved brother Tommy—who worked for her and Owney Madden and at various times operated his own clubs—the excellent money went a long way toward compensating for the stress and danger. It's unknown how much Tommy earned, but Tex received 50 percent of the club's $5,000 weekly profits; the gangsters divided up the rest between them. Tex cultivated the crème of the underworld, often feeding tips about their activities to influential columnists and displaying gifts from mobsters in her home, including candlesticks and hand mirrors from the Gangster King himself, Chicago's Al Capone.

Soon, the 300 Club became *the* Manhattan speakeasy, featuring the best bootleg liquor, the prettiest showgirls, and the most glittering clientele. Tex loved to bait her rich and famous customers, calling out "Hello, Sucker" to each one as they entered her smoky, dimly lit lair. "You may be all the world to your mother, but you're just a cover charge to me." Speakeasy showgirls were often expected to perform sexual favors for high-rolling customers. Texas bragged about protecting her girls, some of whom were as young as thirteen, from sexual harassment and abuse, though the very act of employing scantily clad adolescents in an illegal speakeasy was exploitive in itself. She treated the girls well in her fashion, however, or so she boasted. In summertime, she took them on excursions to Coney Island and let them bunk with her when they fought with their parents and boyfriends. She paid them a decent wage, loaned them money on occasion, and urged the customers to tip them generously. She promoted the girls who had talent, letting them sing solos, and shouting out at the end of each performance, "Give her a great big hand!" Some of them went on to grander success. Singers Ruby Keeler and Lillian Roth and film star Barbara Stanwyck all got their start in Tex's clubs. John Hylan—the New York City mayor until he was defeated in 1925 by the flamboyant speakeasy regular Jimmy Walker—reviled Tex's dancers as a little gang of prostitutes. Tex herself undoubtedly knew that some of them moonlighted for Polly Adler, a friend of hers and a notorious madam, whose parade of "prostipretties," as Walter Winchell called Polly's stable of whores, were regulars at Tex's clubs.

Tex endured endless raids and overnight jail stints. When agents padlocked the 300 Club in 1927, she moved four blocks away and opened the Salon Royale on West Fifty-Eighth Street. Her blatant defiance of the Volstead Act with few serious consequences showed that law enforcement was no match for New York's devotion to speakeasies. During every raid, Tex had her band play "The Prisoner's Song" as police carted her off to jail. She accepted these regular interruptions as part of her job, but she also saw them as excellent publicity opportunities, especially when US senators and Hollywood stars were in the house. Her clashes with the law, her love affairs, and her rumored facelifts all made front-page news. Reporters could always count on Texas for a colorful quote. "I like your cute little jail," she said after one night in the West Thirtieth Street station house. "And I don't know when my jewels seemed so safe."

SIX

◇

A TRUE HANDMAIDEN OF JUSTICE

W
HILE TEX RELIED ON HER MOB associates to keep her in business by paying off corrupt policeman, judges, and federal agents, Mabel Walker Willebrandt concentrated on going after the nation's largest suppliers of illegal booze. She enlisted the help of colleagues throughout the nation, bombarding federal district judges and prosecutors everywhere with letters and pep talks over the phone. She also organized her own battalion of righteous, whip-smart lawyers to replace inept and corrupt US attorneys. Occasionally, she'd even assign a notably Dry judge from a parched southern state to preside over cases in Wet strongholds like New York. Dismissing the Volstead Act as "puerile," "puny," and "toothless," she pioneered the use of tax laws to broaden her authority and had great success going after bootleggers for their tax dodging. In 1931, after Mabel left office, prosecutors would use this innovative tactic to put away Al Capone.

Mabel first employed the strategy in 1922 to break one of the nation's most notorious bootleg rings, the so-called Big Four Savannah, which was led by a former grocer named Willie Haar. His fleet of boats picked up liquor on ships coming into the Savannah Harbor from the Bahamas, Cuba, France, and Scotland. Then it was packed in fruit and potato crates; loaded on trucks, cars, and trains; and transported to fifteen states across America. Haar bribed police, judges, and Prohibition agents to ignore his bootlegging. Mabel's investigation revealed that the Haar ring, which had earned millions of dollars, owed close to $2 million in unpaid income taxes. She sent sixty agents and three lawyers to Savannah to put the case together and traveled to the city herself to oversee the issuing of indictments against Haar and seventy-two of his men. In September 1923, as the date of the trial approached, she sent an additional fifty-eight agents to keep tabs on jurors and witnesses. On November 24, Willie Haar and his gang were found guilty, a great win for Mabel and proof, she believed, that the law could be enforced with a determined leader in charge. On his way to jail, one of the Haar brothers said that his gang had "everybody in Washington fixed but one man and that 'damned woman.'" Mabel didn't know which man he meant, but clearly the woman was herself. She considered it "some of the highest praise I have received."

She used the tax law strategy again to break the King of Bootleggers, George Remus. A Cincinnati lawyer and onetime pharmacist, Remus had purchased fourteen licensed distilleries with bonded liquor intended for medicinal and industrial use. He also bought a pharmacy in Covington, Kentucky, which he used as a front to receive the whiskey he owned for the medicinal market. Then he staged a series of hijackings of his pharmacy's trucks, diverting the "medicinal" liquor to the bootleg market. Eventually, Remus branched out into stealing directly from the Jack Daniel's Distillery, using a system of pipes and hoses to drain whiskey directly into his trucks. To keep his operation running smoothly, Remus also set up a vast and complex scheme of bribes that included payoffs to politicians, police, lawyers, Prohibition agents, and even corrupt cronies of President Harding.

Remus made $25 million a year in illegal income on which he paid no taxes. Mabel charged him with two counts of tax evasion and three counts of violating the Volstead Act. He was convicted at trial and drew a sentence of two years in a federal prison on the tax charge and a one-year sentence for maintaining a nuisance at his Death Valley Farm northwest of Cincinnati, so-called because of the gun-toting thugs who patrolled access to it. Remus appealed and so did Mabel, arguing that the judge's ruling that the Volstead statutes in the case superseded the stiffer IRS statutes was wrong. The case went all the way to the Supreme Court. Mabel won in an opinion delivered by Justice Oliver Wendell Holmes, "whom I love dearly— from afar," she told her parents, adding that "since everyone was convinced I couldn't win" using the tax evasion charge, "it is regarded as a great victory and congratulations have just been pouring in."

Many of those congratulations came from members of the WCTU, Mabel's most impassioned supporters. WCTU state presidents and legislative directors chipped in to buy her an enormous silver loving cup engraved with the inscription "to a true handmaiden of justice." Groups of white ribboners often showed up at the trials of those who'd been charged with violating the Volstead Act, and the *Union Signal* regularly and enthusiastically promoted Mabel. They published her speeches, ran features on her, frequently quoted her, and reprinted articles about her that appeared in the mainstream press. On September 11, 1924, the *Union Signal* ran an ad directing readers to a profile of Mabel in *Collier's* that recounted her success in prosecuting Willie Haar and George Remus. "This story of the big battle staged with bootleggers and their ilk by Assistant Attorney General Willebrandt will stir your fighting blood, and show how bootlegging in every phase can be abolished. Circulate this publicity sheet by the thousands. Order it in [the] thousands. It is worth thousands." The paper urged readers to do this "good publicity work for prohibition and silence the cry, 'It can't be enforced!'"

The WCTU also gave money whenever it could. After the Pennsylvania state legislature refused to fund a state enforcement law, the WCTU donated $250,000 to Governor Gifford Pinchot "to use as he saw fit for enforcement purposes," Ella Boole wrote Mabel. "Feel assured that back of you, you have the prayers and good wishes of the thousands of women who belong to the Woman's Christian

Temperance Union and you have only to ask us for what is needed
and we will be ready to help." Mabel appreciated the WCTU's support; indeed, she counted on it. But the organization's hero wor-
ship of her greatly embarrassed Mabel. "If you could see how I am
received" by WCTU audiences, amounting "almost to reverence,"
she told her parents, "[y]ou would understand that your daughter
is in greater danger" of growing conceited "than any other harm or
disgrace."

Publicly, Mabel praised the WCTU for its integrity and lack of
hypocrisy. "Their consecration is sincere, unwavering and utterly
unselfish," she wrote. "You seldom find them voting for a carousing
public official solely because he voted for a dry law." She never dis-
paraged the organization nor Ella Boole directly, though she told the
New Yorker she was "repelled by the *fanatics* with whom she had to
work." And no one was more fanatical than Ella Boole.

TO ELLA, "SISTER MABEL" EXEMPLIFIED "True Womanhood,"
that outdated but potent nineteenth-century idea of women's purity
and special status as keepers of moral authority. Ella believed fervently that all America needed was to keep Prohibition strong, and
from there would flow the dismantling of toxic male culture and the
abuse of women. In this sense, suffrage was not so much a right as an
obligation conferred on women by their superior natures. This idea
gave urgency to the WCTU's increasing politicization in the early
1920s. The organization paid a full-time lobbyist in Washington and
maintained a national network of activists who deluged congressmen and senators with letters and petitions. Ella and her lieutenants
also testified regularly before congressional committees investigating
the Prohibition laws.

Ella could not face the reality that Prohibition was impossible
to enforce. She refused to be discouraged even at efforts in her own
backyard to weaken the law. In 1923, after New York Governor Al
Smith repealed the state's Mullan-Gage Act, which had made the
federal violations outlined in Volstead also state crimes—a law that

had resulted in only eighteen convictions out of thirteen thousand indictments—the WCTU vowed to mobilize American women to insist that the federal law be enforced. "Women all over the country have been watching the action of Gov. Smith and few have taken any stand but to denounce it," said Mrs. Lenna Lowe Yost, the national legislative chair of the WCTU. "Many of them have come to me and asked how they can help Prohibition along. They had thought it able to stand upon its own feet, but now see that as voters they must watch carefully the efforts of those who would take us back to the days of intoxicated men upon the street, poverty and unhappy homes."

Then Yost delivered a warning to the rest of the nation:

> Every state that threatens to act similarly to New York is only adding fuel to the flame of indignation that is growing among women voters of this country. This fall will see thousands of women flocking to Washington to legislate for various bills in which they are interested. But I would predict that every one of them will gladly cast aside for the moment their separate interests to legislate against the monster that is threatening to destroy the effectiveness of the Eighteenth Amendment. . . . So, politicians had better beware the feminine anger against their efforts to destroy law enforcement in relation to Prohibition. The majority of women see in such action only the selfish interests of men who would use such actions for their own interest. Woman now is a power in the land and she means to make her vote count for right.

Ella completely misinterpreted Mabel's zeal to enforce the law as passion for a liquor-less America, and she would have been shocked by how little enthusiasm Mabel actually felt for the cause of Prohibition. Mabel shared with Ella, however, a conviction that Prohibition was here *to stay*. The Eighteenth Amendment "was ratified by more states than any other amendment that has ever been adopted—by forty-six of the forty-eight states," Mabel noted. Since Prohibition is "probably permanently embedded" in the Constitution and unlikely ever to be repealed, it *had* to be enforced. Mabel had a sense of

calling, an "uncanny feeling" that God had marked her as his instru-
ment "to step into a crisis" of some kind. If it hadn't been Prohibition,
it would have been something else. As she told her parents, "It seems
that it may . . . cause me agony of heart, but I can't escape it. With
recurring frequency I have had the feeling so often, all my life, since
I was a very little girl. Lately, I've quit fighting it, and that in itself
helps me to ward off the terrible fits of depression I've always had."

She also felt twinges of guilt for being so fiercely ambitious, which
the culture told her was unseemly in a woman. She did not want
to appear, or to feel, selfish and unfeminine. Everyone who knew
her well, though, knew that ambition defined her character and that
what she wanted more than anything was something few women had
ever aspired to before: she yearned to be a federal judge. A judgeship, Mabel believed, suited her type of legal mind, which was "judicial," not "an advocate's." In 1923 her prospects for a judgeship looked
good. While traveling with Harding on a tour of the West Coast, the
activist and Republican Party Executive Committee vice chair Harriet Taylor Upton (the first woman ever to hold this post) urged the
president to appoint more women to federal posts, and Harding
promised he would when he returned home. Upton believed Harding was on board to give Mabel a post on the federal bench in California, when a spot opened up. For Mabel, returning to California
would mean being close her beloved parents and also escaping the
corruption and scandals of Washington that reached to the Oval
Office. Harding himself disgusted Mabel. He had fathered a child
with one mistress and paid $5,000 a month in hush money from the
RNC to another woman to whom he wrote steamy love letters. Mabel
said she wouldn't campaign for him if he ran for a second term, even
if he did make her a federal judge.

Meanwhile, Harding's secretary of the interior, Albert Fall, was
under investigation for accepting bribes from oil companies in
exchange for exclusive rights to drill for oil on federal land, including a site near a teapot-shaped dome in Wyoming. Also, Mabel's
boss, the notoriously anti-labor Attorney General Harry Daugherty, faced impeachment in 1922 for abridging the rights, including

the freedom of speech, of striking railroad workers. When 400,000 of them walked off their jobs, Daugherty called their strike "a conspiracy worthy of Lenin" and obtained an injunction prohibiting them from appearing anywhere near the railyards or talking about the strike. Mabel testified on Daugherty's behalf before the House Judiciary Committee and assisted in cross-examining witnesses who were called to provide evidence supporting his impeachment. Afterward, she wrote in her diary, "I believe I was clear. Naturally now there are many things I think of and regret not saying." In the end, the committee rejected the charges against Daugherty, and the impeachment didn't go forward. Daugherty's lawyer Paul Howland was a bitter anti-suffragist, but during the hearings he had been "very lovely to me," Mabel noted. And why wouldn't he be? She was a sterling character witness for his less-than-sterling client.

Indeed, among Daugherty's associates Mabel, was probably the only upstanding citizen. The attorney general surrounded himself with sleazy, bribe-taking miscreants. He "seemed to ignore their activities and, in effect, use his office to protect them," according to one of his biographers. Mabel tried to have as little to do with Daugherty's friends as possible, although she couldn't avoid Jesse Smith, who used an office next to hers. A onetime owner of a dry goods store in the small town of Washington Courthouse, Ohio, where he first became close to Daugherty, Smith idolized the politically savvy attorney general, who was thirteen years his senior, and followed him to Washington after Harding's election. A big, awkward man with a doughy complexion and pale blue eyes, the divorced Smith served as Daugherty's factotum, a combination of "secretary, greeter, go-between, valet, odd-job man and foil," as one historian wrote. Smith made Daugherty's travel arrangements and accompanied him to White House dinners and other official functions, while Daugherty's wife Lucy remained mostly bedridden with arthritis at home in Ohio. For a while, they lived together in a suite at the Wardman Park Hotel. They "were the most intimate friends," Smith's ex-wife Roxie Stinson recalled. People whispered that the men were lovers.

Mabel was never sure about their true relationship. Nor did she know exactly what Smith did all day, except stink up the office with his Cuban cigars. "Don't pay any attention to Jesse," Daugherty urged Mabel. If he had any directions for her, he said he'd call her on the phone himself. Sometimes Jesse had visitors, sketchy types such as Thomas B. Felder, a notorious con man who propped his feet up on Smith's desk, pushed his hat back on his head, and settled in for a good long schmooze. Mabel found Smith weak, flighty, and emotionally unstable. Whenever he entered her office, she stood up as if she were on her way out, to encourage him not to remain. He often seemed depressed. Still, she was shocked when Smith committed suicide in the apartment at the Wardman Park Hotel he shared with Daugherty. At 6:30 a.m. on May 30, 1923, William J. "Billy" Burns, the director of the Bureau of Investigation who lived one floor below the men, heard a gunshot and snapped awake. Rushing to the scene, Burns discovered Smith in his bedroom in pajamas and a robe, dead with his head in a wastebasket and a pistol in his hand. The bullet that killed him had smashed though his right temple and lodged into a door frame. Before dying, Smith had burned some incriminating documents. Nevertheless, it would soon come out that he'd been taking bribes from bootleggers, including George Remus. Mabel had put up with Smith to humor Daugherty. What she knew about his crimes and when she learned of them can't be discerned, though as one investigating US senator noted, it was impossible to work in the Justice Department and not know about the corruption.

Mabel told her parents that when she saw Daugherty two weeks later, he was "looking better than I found after the blow of Jesse Smith's death." But the attorney general's life was a mess. His wife was in "fearful pain constantly." Daugherty had brought her to Washington and moved her into the apartment he'd shared with Smith, and "he is with her all the time," Mabel wrote the Walkers. To "cap the climax" of Daugherty's season of disaster, his son Draper—a ne'er-do-well with a penchant for running up debts and sleeping with tawdry showgirls—had escaped from the sanatorium where he was being treated for alcoholism, an event that made headlines across the nation. Daugherty insisted he wasn't going to resign "unless I completely collapse," and he implored Mabel to stay by him. "You've done so wonderfully so much better than I believed anyone could do that no one would fill your place," he told her. She was hands down "the *best* appointment he had made." She appreciated the compliment. Nevertheless, she couldn't wait to depart Washington and its cesspool of political scandal.

But her hopes that Harding would send her back to California as a judge ended on August 2, 1923, when the president died suddenly of a heart attack in a San Francisco hotel room. At the time, Vice President Calvin Coolidge was visiting Vermont, his home state. Before dawn the next morning, Coolidge's father, a notary public, swore in his son as the nation's thirtieth president. Coolidge was on the record saying that he didn't think the world was ready for a woman on the federal bench. Still, when an opening came up in the Northern District of California in November 1924, Mabel hoped he might bow to pressure from Harriet Taylor Upton and others to appoint her. But Coolidge appointed a man, Adolphus Frederick St. Sure. Mabel felt crushed. "Tho outwardly I showed no disappointment, and at first wouldn't confess [it] to myself, really at heart I care terribly—For I feel it was a sign from God that my life's work and field of service lie in different ways than I hoped or desired," she told her mother. "If this had come, the future was so beautiful—and all mapped out. Now in my heart I feel I may stay East and *possibly* never come back. I'm plunged into doubt again and a feeling that destiny is a thing one's desires cannot deflect nor toy with as perhaps I have tried to do unwisely." Myrtle felt Mabel's disappointment as her own. She herself had worked tirelessly at a variety of difficult jobs and had ambitions that were never fulfilled. She had thrilled at Mabel's early success; it was a vindication of her own years of struggle without reward, and now she suffered with her daughter. But she reassured Mabel that there would be other judgeships down the road. Mabel just had to be patient.

EIGHT MONTHS LATER, Mabel was still on the job and still thinking about resigning. Daugherty had finally resigned himself at the end of March 1924, and Mabel had a new boss, the widely admired law professor Harlan Fiske Stone, who less than a year later would be appointed to the US Supreme Court. Her task was simply too big and unmanageable, and she had to make it up as she went along. No one had ever before held her position. She worked for an entirely new office—the Bureau of Prohibition—that was charged with enforcing an entirely new law.

The nation's force of fifteen hundred agents were underpaid, often incompetent, and frequently corrupt. (Their income from bribes often exceeded their $1,200 yearly salaries.) Congressmen and senators secured the appointments of hundreds of these "Mabelmen," as the press dubbed them, though some of them were women, based on recommendations from ward and county bosses. Frequently, Mabel wrote, becoming an agent was reward for "stealing ballots" and "slugging" the opposition poll watchers on election days. Forerunners of FBI "G-men," Prohibition agents were responsible for investigating Volstead violations of which there were legions. What's more, anyone charged with breaking these laws was entitled to a jury trial. In eight years, Mabel's office handled 160,000 cases that jammed the courts. Mabel worked with local US attorneys in the states and attended the more important trials herself, sometimes coaching fearful witnesses and escorting them to court. Close to three hundred of these cases reached the Supreme Court; Mabel argued about forty of the most important ones—with one exception: *Olmstead v. United States*, the so-called "whispering wires" case.

Roy Olmstead was the owner of Seattle's first radio station and a former policeman who ran a thriving bootleg operation transporting liquor from docks in Canada down the Pacific coast to Los Angeles. Most of the government's case against him came from wiretaps placed on his phones. Some of these taps picked up children's stories his wife read on Olmstead's radio station at night, which Mabel and her agents and investigators concluded were really "code signals" to the bootlegger's boats advising them where the Coast Guard was likely to be and "when the coast was clear."

After Olmstead was convicted in February 1926 of conspiracy to violate Prohibition laws and sentenced to four years in prison, he appealed. The case went all the way to the Supreme Court. Mabel recused herself from arguing it, as she "thoroughly disapproved" of wiretapping and, given her beliefs on the subject, said she could not in good conscience represent the government. Solicitor General William D. Mitchell brought in attorney Michael J. Doherty from Mitchell's old law firm in St. Paul, Minnesota, and Doherty argued the government's case in Mabel's place. In 1928, the Supreme Court decided five to four against Olmstead, upholding the legality of evidence obtained through wiretapped conversations. Echoing Mabel's views on the subject, Justice Brandeis's dissenting opinion referenced a constitutional "right to be let alone," a fundamental privacy implied in the Fourteenth Amendment that the court acknowledged forty-five years later in protecting abortion in *Roe v. Wade*.

As the historian Jill Lepore has argued, the US Constitution was never meant by the founders to be "frozen." They expected it to change over time, and they conceived of amendments as the best way to achieve political settlement of conflicting views on social issues. In 1920, the two big national dramas of Prohibition and women's suffrage ended in amendments. Three years later, in 1923, the ERA amendment was introduced and failed, as it would forty-nine years later in 1972, aggravating a period of political instability in American history from which we have yet to recover. Overturning *Roe* in 2022, the justices not only ended a woman's constitutional right to control her body, but called into question all other Supreme Court decisions that related to privacy. This threat would have appalled Mabel, a fiercely private woman who herself had considered abortion during a low point in her life. That a court at the time with three female justices could issue such a ruling would have further dismayed her. Mabel expected more from women. Like Ella Boole, she believed her sex superior to men—at least when it came to the public sphere.

Women were "always the wielders of the soap" in cleaning up corrupt politics, Mabel told the League of Women Voters. Though she knew her own record was untarnished, she felt tainted by her association with so many unscrupulous government officials, as if some of their dirt had landed on her. If she resigned, however, "the Drys will say I am untrue to the duty of my work in this Election Year, [and] the Republican organization will discount the sincerity of my motives," she told her parents. "But all their respect is not worth the loss of my own self-respect, and the question I am pondering and have not yet answered is whether I can keep it and remain." A quick return to California seemed less and less likely. "I might as well kiss [a judicial] appointment good-bye," she complained. Mabel was frustrated because she knew she'd be a good jurist and "could do real, constructive service" on the bench. Whereas, she could "do little real good this election year I fear in Prohibition Enforcement where I am with all the political pulling and fixing."

At the same time her job got much more difficult with the escalating carnage caused by the illegal liquor traffic, as criminal syndicates grew in size and organization. A description she gave her parents in April 1924 of "an ordinary day" in her life reveals her crushing routine:

> I have to appear before the investigating Committee on Prohibition Enforcement . . . at the Capital at 11:30. Before that dictation at 8 a.m. and a conference with 2 detectives making a big case at 9:30. Noon Supreme Court for an hour and a half.
>
> Afternoon a conference with officials of Treas. Dept. on undercover operations to go into making certain smuggling cases on the New Jersey coast. . . . See 3 attys applying for positions in my dept. Meeting attys my division and probably 4 or 5 out of town officials who'll "drop in" then to be chinked in between—besides mail and office routine! Then at night I go to Louisville, Ky where Congressman Langley whom I indicted is to be on trial.

Often Mabel worked until midnight, returning to her rooms at the Hamilton Hotel, where she lived in the mid-1920s, to listen to classical music on the radio through headphones before falling asleep for a few hours. Many nights, she slept in a train berth as she traveled across the nation to oversee investigations, confer with US attorneys, attend trials, and give speeches. She'd taken the night train to Lexington, Kentucky, for example, for the trial of the Dry Republican John Wesley Langley, who was convicted of taking $115,000 in kickbacks from bootleggers and bribing a Prohibition agent. (He was sentenced to two years in the Atlanta penitentiary.) On the other hand, a perk of her job was meeting some of her heroes. At the World Conference of Social Workers in Toronto in June 1924, she sat on the speaker's platform next to the venerable reformer Jane Addams, whom Mabel thought "the foremost woman" of the day, and was thrilled when Addams praised her speech.

Mabel's travel schedule escalated as the 1924 presidential campaign speeded up. She couldn't accept all the requests that poured into her office, but she took on as much as she could. She acted out of a sense of loyalty to the Republican Party, not out of any enthusiasm for Coolidge, whom she found a typically cool, flinty New Englander, whose "lack of virility" marked "his every utterance." In Chicago, where she spoke at a rally with the former Governor Frank Lowden, two secret service men followed her wherever she went, because she'd received death threats from "some bootleggers," she told her parents. "It makes me feel like the president's wife. She always has two shadows—even when she goes shopping!" Her pace was so frantic and her schedule so grueling that while sitting on the dais at conferences and official gatherings she often felt at the point of collapse. At times, every moment speaking was "physical exertion" and she could "hardly sit up" while others were talking.

Mabel's breakneck life allowed her to avoid hard decisions about her personal life. Her divorce from Arthur Willebrandt went through quietly in 1924 with no notice from the press. A lawyer friend of Mabel's had managed to avoid all publicity by filing the complaint in Los Angeles using the couple's middle names, "Frank" and "Elizabeth." Myrtle Walker worried about Mabel being alone and hoped she would remarry, but not to an aristocrat who would change her into "a cold eastern woman who loved to wield power." If Mabel would be happy in an atmosphere of wealth and elite social position, Myrtle assured Mabel, "I would rejoice in your happiness; but if your heart was in the west, if the west called you, it seems foolish for you to attempt to make *yourself* over, to 'change inside.' Back here among your friends who really love you for yourself might bring you more real happiness."

Among the dearest of those friends was Fred Horowitz. Myrtle wasted no opportunity to praise Fred's loyalty, integrity, intelligence, professional success, and looks, though Fred's appearance was plain and ordinary. Knowing her daughter had a weakness for exceptionally handsome men, however, Myrtle extolled Fred as "a magnificent looking man. Tall and big [with] his dark hair and eyes and his fine sensitive mouth. He is tanned now and it is really becoming." She imagined Mabel smiling at these words and saying "'Mama is sure dippy about Fred,'" and admitted, "I guess I am but so is your Papa." Reading Mabel's diary and letters, it's easy to conclude that the marriage she and Fred considered was primarily one of convenience. They loved each other in a platonic way, but there doesn't seem to have been any romantic spark between them. Mabel's divorce was not yet public. She was still "Mrs. Willebrandt," a respectable married woman in the eyes of the world, so she didn't "need" to remarry.

It seems Fred, however, felt some urgency to wed to affirm his stability, trustworthiness, and masculinity. In 1920s America, a single man above the age of thirty or so was almost as suspect as a single woman. At the time Mabel was stalling about marrying him, Fred began courting their mutual friend Winnie Ellis. Winnie had attended law school with Fred and Mabel, and played tennis on the amateur circuit. She had already been married once, at seventeen, to an older man, Walter Ellis, who had left his banking job when World War I broke out to join the army, though he was above draft age. In October 1918, he died of pneumonia while at an infantry training camp in Arkansas. Myrtle Walker wrote to Mabel that Fred had begun romancing Winnie, who worked as a law librarian in Los Angeles. One night when Mabel was with Winnie in California, Winnie confessed that Fred had told her he'd grown to care for her and asked her to marry him. Winnie said "she couldn't decide for physically he was repulsive to her—tho he didn't know it," Mabel noted in her diary.

Unsurprisingly, Winnie turned Fred down. As if to justify her own failure to return Fred's affection, Mabel found fault with him, blaming her trouble summoning romantic feelings for him on his emotional remoteness. "My nature with my dear friends is garrulous. I open the door and invite them right into my thoughts and heart. He doesn't. He locks his closest friends outside and when outside one wonders what goes on within," she told her parents in her Christmas 1922 letter. Later, she wrote her mother that she "always knew" Fred would make "lots of money, but *is* he storing up things in his personal and intellectual and spiritual life to 'retire' on when he gets old besides money?"

Once Fred sent Mabel a book of poems with a typed note inside: "Dearest Mabel—Not long ago I read a poem in the Literary Digest that I thought was very beautiful. It is out of the collection I am sending you." Mabel's only comment on the thoughtful, romantic gift was a terse comment in her diary: "I wonder why Fred types his personal notes." And yet, she continued to let Fred hope she'd eventually marry him. Meanwhile, Fred grew impatient to settle his future. Knowing that a union with Mabel was unlikely, especially as she and Fred lived on opposite sides of the continent, Myrtle tried "to point" Fred "to his stenographer, who is wholesome" and "wonderfully bright." But Fred demurred. He said his stenographer "was too good an office girl to lose." The Walkers warned Fred that "someone else would marry her and he would lose her, anyway. He said no, he would keep raising her salary and she would not leave. He talks of everyone else marrying and having a family but insists he cannot find anyone for himself."

What he really wanted, and had never stopped wanting, was

Mabel. Though she'd strung Fred along for years, it seems she was offended when he pursued other women. The sparse evidence for this is a cryptic note left in her papers that she wrote at three in the morning in October 1924 after an overwrought phone call with Fred, apparently never sent. "Oh, I've just finished talking to you and the world is all black and bitter. I mustn't write now. I'll say terrible things. . . . You made your situation shutting me out of your life—not I and . . . you are just a year late in coming back—why didn't you try it in 1923."

Nevertheless, Fred did try to win Mabel back in 1924 and traveled to Washington in November to press his suit in person. Mabel took him to a party to celebrate Coolidge's recent election and introduced him to the president. Perhaps her intention was to humanize herself in the president's eyes. As she once explained to her parents, Coolidge is "abstract in his thoughts of women unattached to some man"—in other words, he didn't trust single women. Coolidge admired Mabel's intellect and achievements, but he had no intention of making her a judge, as he still didn't think the time was yet right to appoint a woman to the federal bench. Mabel urged Fred to take a job as a prosecutor in the Justice Department. If they were in the same city, they could spend more time together, and Mabel could better make a decision about their future. But Fred was not about to give up his lucrative private practice. Before he boarded the train for the long journey home, he told Mabel he'd give her a year to finally and definitively make up her mind about marrying him.

She spent Christmas Day with friends and New Year's Day at the White House, as she had the year before. Mabel had complained then about President and Mrs. Coolidge, who tried "to be very gracious." Only Mrs. Coolidge succeeded in Mabel's view, though the First Lady was "a little tense and strained." As for the president,

he gave a limp hand, and was manifestly indifferent. He gives the impression he not only does not care a hang about the person before him, but wishes the whole world would leave its favors on the doorstep without ringing the door bell. A vast difference between this White House and two years ago at New Year. This year even the guards had caught the changed and impersonal atmosphere and were abrupt and surly. President Harding's great strength (and weakness, too) was an irrepressible friendliness. He and Mrs. Harding were tall, benevolent, interested and gracious. Mrs. and Mr. Coolidge were two New Englanders quite simply and honestly doing their Christian duty.

No doubt, the Coolidges seemed even more subdued on New Year's Day 1925, as they were grieving the shocking death just six months earlier of their sixteen-year-old son from a case of sepsis that developed after a minor foot injury. Mabel would have been sensitive to their lack of holiday cheer considering her own fierce bond with her parents. They were her greatest source of support, strength, and comfort, as she remained theirs. Though a continent separated Mabel from her beloved "Mama and Papa," she wrote them long, heartfelt letters in which she poured out her feelings about her life. Myrtle Walker had been studying Christian Science and Mabel relied "hard" on her mother's healing thoughts and prayers. She carried a picture of her parents at all times and worried about their health and finances. She sent them $100 or $200 every month and felt like "such a rotter" for not managing her finances better so she could send more.

Mabel tried to embrace Christian Science herself, particularly as a way of coping with her hearing loss. She attended a few Christian Science meetings with friends and noted in her diary that she was learning to tap "the love that unlocks the infinite power of God," to overcome her deafness. If she could fill her heart with love, she reasoned, she could create "channels of trust" with people around her who, without knowing exactly what they were doing, would *enable* her to hear better. She confessed in her diary that this happened "for a bit" when she argued a case before the Supreme Court, and "the Justices just helped me," even the rude bigot James C. McReynolds.

The Christian Science faith didn't help as she struggled with a decision about marrying Fred. Mabel yearned for love and companionship, but disliked the institution of marriage. This presented an impossible dilemma for her as an American woman in the 1920s. "Why should society be so cruel?" she confided in her diary. "Why should I care what it thinks. Is that strength or numbers? Why should I so fiercely refuse at slavery. Why when I'm so tired and perplexed at the world so yearn to yield my wrist to manacles I so fiercely hate." Despite her mother's fears, there was little chance Mabel would become romantically involved with an eastern aristocrat. She didn't trust such people to look past her humble beginnings, believing that wealthy easterners thought themselves superior, which "put me into a perfect complex of inferiority. Their imported clothes, their soft voices, always repressed and proper, their scholastic conversations distress me so—and prevent all my best qualities from showing."

PAULINE SABIN WAS EXACTLY the sort of wealthy, glamorous, socially prominent woman who made Mabel "stutter and want really to get in bed and cover up my head." Had they met in 1924, they would not have been drawn to one another. Pauline likely would have thought Mabel a drab, government workhorse; while Mabel no doubt would have seen Pauline as one of life's "petted darlings," a spoiled socialite who had been born to money and position and never had to work a day in her life. It's possible, in fact, that they did meet in June 1924, at the GOP convention in Cleveland, Ohio. One thousand women attended, including four hundred delegates and alternates, a showing that would test for the first time the power of women in national politics. Though not a delegate herself, Mabel had "an immense influence" working behind the scenes at the convention, as one reporter wrote. But she was completely overshadowed in Cleveland by Pauline, the envied "Leader of Women at the Convention," as one headline announced.

For reporters who covered politics, Pauline stood out for her beauty and wealth. It was impossible not to notice her chauffeur-driven

Packard as she rode through town or her exquisite silk dresses as she glided across the floor of the newly built Public Auditorium, her hair expertly coiffed and strings of priceless pearls dangling from around her neck. Pauline participated in "all the important conferences," in Cleveland, and advised the men not only on how to capture the women's vote, "but also on matters affecting the whole party." She fought off opposition from a group of anti-suffrage members of the rules committee and saw through a resolution that she had longed struggled to impose to have fifty-fifty representation of men and women on the Republican National Committee. She received a standing ovation every time she spoke and was the only woman who had a "say so" with William M. Butler, President Coolidge's campaign manager. In the past, Pauline had worked behind the scenes. Now, the convention served as "a great coming out party" for the glamorous beauty, when her "political astuteness" and "extensive talents" were finally revealed to the world, after her years working behind the scenes.

Her rise signaled a new era for women in politics. When the famous suffragist Harriet Taylor Upton resigned from the Republican National Committee to run for Congress on June 4, a battle ensued for her successor, with Upton pushing for a member of the old guard of Suffs who'd worked tirelessly for decades to win women the vote. (In the Republican primary in August, Upton had lost her bid to become a representative from Ohio.) These women, now in their sixties and seventies, "held some negative connotations, more harmful than helpful to the party," one Republican observer noted. That is, they were perceived to be old, frumpy, stern, and rigid. In contrast, Pauline and her friends were young, pretty, lively and modern. "Doesn't [Pauline] just look as though she put the 'pep' into politics?" gushed one reporter. "Mrs. Sabin is so pretty that it often deceives people into thinking she can't be more than ordinary clever," swooned another. Women reporters described her outfits in ridiculous detail—her silk gowns, delicate T-strap heels, satin wrap trimmed in ermine, and smart little black lace hat. At a ball, the first in convention history, Pauline, in a shimmering blue silk gown from

the Parisian House of Worth, led the dancing with Senator Wadsworth spinning her onto the floor, then arching her backward in a
move partygoers dubbed "the GOP dip."

HAD PAULINE AND MABEL TAKEN the time to talk to one another,
they would have seen they had much in common. Both were fiercely
intelligent, independent, and driven, with reputations tarnished by
divorce. Both struggled to achieve their goals in a political system
dominated by men who wanted women's votes but didn't want them
to have real power.

Pauline was disappointed that in four years of suffrage, women
had not turned out in greater numbers at the polls. Voting is a habit,
and it took a while for women to develop the same practice of casting
ballots on Election Day as long-enfranchised men. As Christina Wolbrecht and J. Kevin Corder noted in *A Century of Votes for Women*, in
a social context where "political activity is expected of men but not
of women, men will feel compelled to vote even when not particularly interested in politics, while women who lack political interest,
will feel less social pressure to participate." Women who came of age
before suffrage had been taught to consider themselves unsuited to
politics, and that voting places, which were often in saloons, were
rowdy hangouts, where men gathered to smoke, drink, and argue, and
where they sometimes came to blows. Still, as Wolbrecht and Corder
discovered, in states such as Wyoming and Utah, where women were
enfranchised to vote in local elections long before national suffrage,
and where barriers to voting were low, women's turnout relative to
men's "was quite high." In contrast, "states . . . with the most stringent voting laws also had the lowest levels of turnout among women.
Massachusetts and Connecticut required voters to take literary tests.
Connecticut and Virginia had long residency requirements. Virginia
levied a poll tax, among other discriminatory practices directed at
African Americans and poor whites. . . . [R]estrictive state election
laws were directed particularly at African Americans in the South
and immigrants in the Northeast."

In general, women tended to support the same candidates as men, though as studies of voting patterns in the first decades after suffrage have shown, not because their husbands, fathers, and brothers told them to do so, and not because they voted as part of a "women's bloc." Eleanor Roosevelt came to the same conclusion after her long observation of women and politics. "I think it is fairly obvious," she wrote in 1940, "that women have voted on most questions as individuals and not as a group, in much the same way that men do, and that they are influenced by their environment and their experience and background, just as men are."

PARADOXICALLY, THE PASSAGE of suffrage had coincided with the appearance of a new, apolitical feminine ideal—the flapper. With her bobbed hair, short skirts, rolled stockings, and hip flask filled with bootleg tucked in her garter, the flapper cared above all about pleasure and freedom. She danced all night in jazz clubs, smoked cigarettes, and slept with whomever she pleased. Epitomized by the silent stars Clara Bow, Louise Brooks, and Colleen Moore, the flapper's exploits were chronicled obsessively in the media, notably in a regular column in the *New Yorker* by the twenty-something Lois Lange, writing under the pen name "Lipstick." Flappers made the Ella Booles and Mabel Willebrandts of the world seem hopelessly out of touch. The term "flapper" derived from English slang, first used as far back as 1631 to refer to a prostitute, then, later, a young girl whose braided pigtails "flapped" on her back. In the early twentieth century, fashion copywriters adopted it to describe a gawky teenager who required dresses with long, straight lines to cover her awkwardness and not-yet-blossomed curves. Stores labeled these garments "flapper" frocks.

The flapper was a type, perhaps mostly a creation of the media, but her presence in the culture reflected the reality of changing social mores, if not an actual discernible population. It's impossible to know how many young women identified themselves as flappers or lived the flapper life. Bobbed hair alone, the most obvious symbol of flapperdom, was considered a scandal in many places outside America's urban centers. The newspapers were filled with stories about young women who'd been fired as nurses, teachers, or shopgirls for bobbing their hair, though by 1925 *American Hairdresser* reported, 90 percent of American women under thirty had cut their tresses, banishing from their daily toilettes unwieldy side combs, nets, and hairpins.

The flapper dominated discussions in the press about the avalanche of social changes that had accompanied suffrage—the entrance of women in the workforce in greater numbers than ever before, the loosening of sexual mores, and the growing prevalence of the automobile. The changes extended even to religion, when in September 1922, the House of Deputies of the Convention of the Protestant Episcopal Church voted to take "obey" out of the marriage ceremony.

PROHIBITION MARKED THE END of the male-only saloon and the explosion of speakeasies, where the sexes mingled and drank together. Many students, working women, wives, and mothers dabbled in flapperdom by visiting the "speaks" on glamorous nights out. Even Mabel, though she would not take a drink (at least publicly) or cut her hair while in office, occasionally visited clubs where illegal liquor was served. One night after delivering a speech to the Women's Bar Association, a group of friends took her to the Plantation, a popular Harlem speakeasy that was decorated to look like the rural South with a hen roost and a Mississippi flatboat at the end of the dance floor. Mabel had two "fat dances" with one of the men who'd brought her (a senator), shook a noisemaker to the beat of a "colored" jazz orchestra, ate a plate of southern-style ham and eggs, and heard some "lovely negro singing." She was home by 2:30 a.m., however, a ridiculously early night for a true flapper.

Despite her herculean workload and often overwhelming fatigue, Mabel found time and energy to go to the opera and to the theater in Washington, DC. She accepted as many theater invitations as she could fit into her schedule and even attended a prizefight. She also was a frequent guest at receptions, musical evenings, teas, and dinners at the White House and occasionally was invited to meals at the homes of Supreme Court Chief Justice William Howard Taft and Justice Louis Brandeis.

When she traveled, she usually went by night train, sleeping in berths that were converted from seats, so as not to waste any precious waking hours that she could be working. Sometimes, she donned a one-piece aviator's suit to ride on a government mail flight. On one 500-mile trip to Boston, her airplane almost ran out of oil. As the plane approached the East Boston Airport at dusk, the oil pressure gauge plummeted toward zero. Though the pilot feared they'd crash, he managed to land the plane safely. As Mabel left the cockpit, photographers snapped her in her flight suit, her goggles pushed up to reveal her shining eyes. Underneath her flight suit, the *New York Times* reported, she wore knickers, gray golf stockings, a black knitted jacket, and black pumps. Rather than discouraging Mabel from flying, the experience left her hungry for more. "I'm so happy flying," she wrote her father. "Soon it will be the way I'll always go." She had been more exhilarated than scared while in the air, mesmerized by the beautiful views and feeling a lightness of being. It wouldn't always be so.

Once, Mabel flew to Oakland, California, to address the American Bar Association and then traveled by train to Seattle. During her return to Washington, DC (via Chicago), on Boeing Air Transport, she sat next to the company's owner, William Edward Boeing. At five thousand feet above a jagged mountain range, the engine suddenly stopped. Boeing went "white as a sheet," Mabel recalled, though he told *her* not to worry, that the pilot would be able to land "somewhere." After gliding twenty miles, the pilot landed the plane in an open field, repaired the engine, and took off again. An icy fear coursed through Mabel, as the plane bumped through the clouds on two cylinders, eventually arriving safely in San Francisco. She felt ashamed that she hadn't be able to control her terror like a stalwart westerner. Instead, she had behaved like a gutless "caution artist" who was allergic to physical risk, a type of person, she told her parents, who was usually an easterner and often from Boston.

Wherever she ventured, Mabel took time to visit the sites. Though she was the most powerful woman in the US government, she was still young, energetic, and eager to experience life. At the same time, she was always conscious of propriety and careful of her image. Once, while on "a lovely moonlight ride" in an open roadster through Atlanta with local officials, she refused the mint juleps her hosts offered her from their flasks. It wasn't against the law to *drink* alcohol, only to buy and sell it, but Mabel knew better than to risk her reputation by imbibing liquor in public. Soon enough, her behavior would spark a fire of scorn and smash her life to ruins. When this happened, though, it would have nothing to do with Prohibition.

SEVEN

THE MORAL NAPOLEON

THE WCTU ELECTED ELLA BOOLE president by a unanimous
vote at the organization's annual convention in Detroit on November 17, 1925. Supporters of the Eighteenth Amendment already
knew her as the group's dauntless leader, its "guiding prophet" and
"moral Napoleon" whose name was known to every congressman,
senator, and newspaper editor in the nation. To her detractors, however, she was a stereotypical Prohibitionist, "a scorned, white, protestant, evangelical, Midwestern woman," as political scientist Mark
Lawrence Schrad has noted. The misogynistic stereotype derived
from the most famous Prohibitionist of all, Carrie A. Nation, who
notoriously led troops of women into Kansas saloons, where she
smashed liquor bottles with a hatchet while singing hymns and quoting the Bible. Nation became a celebrity who supported herself in
later life by sermonizing on the vaudeville circuit and selling photographs of herself and souvenir miniature hatchets. She died in 1911,
nearly a decade before the Eighteenth Amendment became law. Ella
shared Nation's zeal for abolishing liquor, but not her gimmicky tactics and unhinged mind.

Still, the Wet press often treated Ella as Nation's heir apparent,
the perfect example of what was frumpy and nutty about women who
insisted that Prohibition was a success. Five years in, it was clear the

opposite was true. Drinking had not disappeared; it had just gone underground, launching an explosion of violence and carnage associated with the illegal liquor trade. Meantime, enforcement of the Volstead Act was a joke. As Fiorello La Guardia, the very Wet Democratic representative from New York and future mayor of the city, quipped, "It is impossible to tell whether Prohibition is a good or a bad thing. It has never been enforced in this country."

No one exemplified official indifference to Prohibition more than James J. Walker, "the Jazz Mayor" of New York City, as the newspapers called him. The wisecracking, womanizing Walker, elected the same year as Ella ascended to the WCTU presidency, partied all night at speakeasies "and slept half the day," *New Yorker* writer Milton MacKaye wrote. Jimmy Walker "drank too much and steamed out at health resorts, he praised his [Catholic] Church and ignored its commandments, he bought diamond bracelets at $15,000 a crack and would not pay his bills. Yet the city loved him."

Ella fought against such thrilling flamboyance and pushed relentlessly to win people to *her* side. She followed the advice of the former WCTU president Frances Willard to "do everything" in the battle against liquor—to preach, teach, pray, publish articles, and petition lawmakers. Ella bombarded the nation with radio addresses, editorials, and newsreel spots extolling the Eighteenth Amendment as the savior of society, women and children in particular. Looking fierce in a black dress and pearls in one clip shown before the feature film in theaters, Ella urged audiences to pay attention to the fact that "women are relieved of the fear of a drunken husband, children no longer hide with terror as they see their father reeling home."

At the same time, she was aware that the forces against her were mounting, and in response, she escalated the WCTU's lobbying efforts in Congress. It was here, as "an applier of pressure where pressure will do the most good that her talents begin to show the hallmark of genius," wrote Stanley Walker in *Outlook*. Ella's deputies and the WCTU's full-time Washington lobbyist kept close tabs on the nation's lawmakers, taking their temperatures on Prohibition and pushing those officials whose support for the Eighteenth Amendment seemed to waver, "just verbal pressure, friendly pressure," Ella claimed. But lawmakers knew the WCTU members would try to vote them out of office if they didn't comply with the group's demands.

Hand in hand with WCTU lobbying efforts was an intense drive to attract new converts and increase the organization's membership rolls, including in African American communities. The Black clergy and many of the nation's Black intellectuals supported Prohibition. They believed temperance gave their community a chance to prove its respectability to White people and that the Eighteenth Amendment bolstered the landmark Fourteenth and Fifteenth Amendments, which extended civil rights to African Americans and voting rights to Black men, but were mostly ignored in the South. In the early nineteenth century, temperance advocates had worked side by side with abolitionists and suffragists against America's deep-rooted systems of subordination and domination. Consequently, nearly every major Black abolitionist and civil rights leader before the First World War—from Frederick Douglass, Martin Delany, and Sojourner Truth to Frances Ellen Watkins Harper, Ida B. Wells, and Booker T. Washington—endorsed a liquor-less society. In his autobiography, *Narrative of the Life of Frederick Douglass*, as historian Lawrence Schrad has noted, Douglass wrote about his "firsthand knowledge of how masters would strategically intoxicate their slaves to keep them stupefied, divided and disorganized. Liquor, he wrote, 'was the most effective means in the hands of the slaveholder in keeping down the spirit of insurrection.'"

In New York, Harlem's so-called Black Victorians—the old elite of civic leaders, intellectuals, ministers, and reformers—had been ardent supporters of Prohibition since the earliest days of the Dry movement. During Prohibition, Black Victorians condemned Black people who refused to abide by the Volstead Act as "race traitors," singling out women who drank as particularly culpable. In a column for the African American newspaper *Amsterdam News*, the influential Black intellectual and Howard University professor Kelly Miller wrote that "any Negro woman" who failed to support Prohibition is "against both her race and her sex."

Frances Ellen Watkins Harper—a poet and the first Black woman to publish a short story, which appeared in 1859 in the *Anglo-African Magazine*—had been tapped by Frances Willard in 1866 to become national superintendent of the WCTU's division of "Work Among the Colored People" after speaking at the National Women's Rights Convention in New York City with suffrage leaders Susan B. Anthony and Elizabeth Cady Stanton. Harper denounced White women who bemoaned their own oppression and disenfranchisement, but were complicit in denying rights to their Black sisters. "Talk of giving women the ballot box?" she exclaimed. "I tell you that if there is any class of people who need to be lifted out of their airy nothings and selfishness, it is the white women of America."

Ella believed her organization was doing just that. The WCTU endorsed a model of womanhood that fit many Black women's own ideals, uniting Christian values to activism. It promoted racial uplift and gave women a chance to be useful, to "build a Christian community that could serve as a model of interracial cooperation" on many fronts, "a place where women might see past skin color to recognize each other's humanity," as Glenda Gilmore writes in *Gender and Jim Crow*. At least in theory. One thing was sure: the WCTU and Black women reformers shared a belief that women, as wives and mothers, were better equipped than men to give future generations the skills, education, and respectability that would enable racial progress. It was a worldview that harked back to nineteenth-century notions that saw women as morally superior and men (Black and White) as easily waylaid from their responsibilities to home, family, and community by demon rum.

Yet Prohibition also was often associated with White supremacy. In the South, Drys had forged alliances with the Ku Klux Klan, who believed that America was under siege by Catholic immigrants, whose drinking and saloon culture threatened their Anglo-Saxon ideals. A "high official" of the Klan once paid a visit to Mabel Walker

Willebrandt's office and, as she reported to her parents, offered to "serve me in certain states where I was having a good deal of difficulty on liquor cases, but I refused his tender of help, telling him quite frankly that I did not think, as a government official, I should deal with a secret organization."

Ella, meantime, abhorred the Klan's activities as unchristian and disastrous for the coalitions she was trying to forge with Black women leaders. Some historians have long dismissed the WCTU as racist, owing partly to remarks Frances Willard made disparaging Black men and her failure to publicly support activist Ida B. Wells's anti-lynching campaign. The WCTU also came under fire in the late nineteenth century for treating Black women as second-class citizens, for separating them from Whites in special "negro units," and denying them leadership roles in the organization. Starting in 1883, many states had a WCTU superintendent of Work Among the Colored People, invariably a White woman. In 1895 the British journal *Anti-Caste* chastised the WCTU for condoning "the drawing of a colour line" by allowing the group's state organizations to organize these separate Black and White chapters. Apparently unaware that most of the northern chapters were also segregated, the journal wondered, "How long will the Northern members of the WCTU fail to see that the insistence on Caste separation on the part of their white sisters at the South is not only an infliction of personal humiliation and injustice on every coloured woman against who it is applied, but an attempt to evade and repudiate the very principles and spirit of Christianity."

Not surprisingly, Black women balked at being relegated to units overseen by Whites, and in 1890, five years before the *Anti-Caste* article, Black women in North Carolina seceded from the national organization and formed their own group. The new African American WCTU held separate statewide conventions in several states in 1890 and 1891 and received organizational status equal to the national White WCTU. Afterward, Black WCTU unions were formed in several other southern states. For many Black women in the segregated

WCTU chapters, more was at stake than control. Separation, they felt, allowed them dignity and self-respect. As educator Charlotte Hawkins Brown told a group of White people in Greensboro, North Carolina, "I will be separated, but never segregated." That is, she would accept the racial distance only if it was of her own choosing, not if it was imposed from outside.

By the late 1890s, however, the separate Black WCTU was defunct. It's difficult to know how many Black chapters (or unions) existed under the umbrella of the main organization during Prohibition, how many members were enrolled, and who were the leaders. The Frances Willard House Museum and Archives in Evanston, Illinois, has embarked on an ambitious project to document Black women's involvement in the WCTU, but progress is slow due to sparse and scattered records. Though the evidence is sketchy in the extreme, researchers have uncovered a murky picture that unsurprisingly hints at tensions between Black and White women in the organization, a lack of sufficient funding that impeded the establishing and running of Black unions, and a reluctance of Black women to be part of yet another group that relegated them to inferior status.

The deep racism Black women faced was reflected in the noxious catchphrase "free, white and twenty-one" that became popular in the 1920s and 1930s with young White women who wanted to assert their power and independence. The phrase appeared in newspaper and magazine stories and in movies, a casually tossed, but potent public insult to Black people. Hollywood sirens like Norma Shearer used it on-screen to declare their right to do as they pleased. "I'm free, white and twenty-one!" Shearer, playing a sexy glamour girl in the talkie *Strangers May Kiss*, tells a lover who objects to her many affairs. For Black people sitting in the audience, such words were "repulsive," a painful reminder of Whites' intractable feelings of superiority, as Walter L. Lowe, a prominent African American insurance broker, noted in the *Chicago Defender*.

It seems that many Black WCTU chapters were short-lived, owing to the difficulty in finding women who were willing to serve as leaders. Eva Dean, a Black WCTU organizer from Urbana-Champaign,

African-American Department
Service of Triumph
FOR

LIEUTENANT VIOLET HILL WHYTE
1897 - 1980

Bethel African Methodist Episcopal Church
Druid Hill Avenue and Lanvale Street

TUESDAY, JULY 22, 1980
12 Noon

Dr. John R. Bryant, *Minister*

After Repeal, Violet Hill Whyte, a popular WCTU organizer, became the first Black police officer in Baltimore, Maryland. Courtesy of Enoch Pratt Free Library, Maryland's State Library Resource Center.

Illinois, noted in her annual report of 1924, "The problem is to secure presidents to carry on the work after it is organized." The Ida Gill Union in Dean's home city of Urbana-Champaign presented a rare example of longevity, owing to the leadership of Mrs. H. J. Wells (her first name is unknown), who was president for thirty-three years from 1917 to 1950 (and possibly longer). It's also difficult to know any details about individual Black WCTU members, though the few whose lives have been documented offer insights into the type of Black women who gravitated to the WCTU and the role Black women played in the organization. One of the few who became a leader was Violet Hill Whyte, a teacher and wife of a school principal who went on to become the first female police officer in Baltimore, Maryland.

Whyte had been born in Washington, DC, on November 18, 1897, the eldest of ten children of the Rev. Daniel G. Hill, a pastor of the Bethel African Methodist Episcopal Church, and his wife, Margaret Peck, a devoted temperance advocate and founder of Baltimore's Black WCTU chapter, which had been named in her honor. As a child, Violet's life centered on family, school, and her father's church, which was a short walk from the family home on Druid Hill Avenue, in West Baltimore, within an all-Black enclave of middle-class and wealthy citizens—pullman porters, waiters, teachers, doctors, lawyers, politicians, and a young Thurgood Marshall, who would grow up to be America's first Black Supreme Court justice.

Petite, pretty, and soft-spoken, Whyte had a serene, calm manner. Even as a girl, she showed a fierce work ethic and a talent for public speaking. She had been drawn into WCTU work to help her mother, Margaret Peck Hill, who was singled out in 1914 by a Black WCTU superintendent as a "wide-awake city organizer." (More than a century before "woke" became a contentious polemical adjective, "awake" and "awoken" signaled alertness to social justice in Black vernacular.) Hill's daughter, Violet, quickly drew the attention of WCTU leaders, and by 1922 her integrity and devotion to uplifting the Black community had made her "a national character," according to one African American newspaper. She had worked as a public teacher until her marriage in 1916 to George Sumner Whyte with whom she raised four children, two biological and two adopted. Thereafter, she became a full-time organizer for the WCTU, which paid her a small salary, rising in 1931 to National Secretary for Negro Work.

In the summer of 1922, the WCTU sent her out across America as a "national department field worker" to organize Black unions and give temperance talks in churches and schools, where she charmed audiences, both Black and White, with "her versatility," "earnestness," and "easy flow of excellent English." All offerings at the churches where Whyte spoke went toward WCTU programs in the Black community.

Her work was supervised closely by White WCTU superintendents, who found it unfailingly excellent. Mrs. Josephine Buhl, the state WCTU president of Oklahoma, told the *Evening Journal* in Saline, Kansas, "She has just finished a month's work in Oklahoma. I want to assure you that Mrs. Whyte is an excellent worker among her people and is a most conscientious Christian woman. She is a great credit to our cause. I am very glad I can most heartily recommend her to your state." The *Union Signal* reported that her work in a school in Oklahoma "was especially noteworthy. She is said to be a veritable encyclopedia of W.C.T.U. methods and was successful in securing many members among the women of her race." In Kansas, "she aroused the colored people she addressed to a sense of responsibility for the success of Prohibition and law enforcement, and created a keen interest in the W.C.T. U."

In the Black community overall, however, it's unclear how much enthusiasm there was for Prohibition among women *and* men. The very Dry Kelly Miller thought the majority of Black people were uninterested in the issue, a fact he deplored, though he claimed to understand its cause. Since the US government did so little to enforce the Fourteenth and Fifteenth Amendments protecting Black people's rights to life, liberty, property, and the right to vote, why should they care about the Eighteenth Amendment? Miller—who'd been born in 1863 in South Carolina to an enslaved woman and a White Confederate soldier—believed the only way to get Black people to support Prohibition in significant numbers was for them to form their *own* Dry organizations. As it was, he wrote, the only two Black people he knew of "who are seriously devoted to educational temperance work among twelve million members of this race" are "on the payroll and under direction" of White organizations. Apparently, he ignored the many Black women who fought for the temperance cause who were not members of White groups.

Marie Madre Marshall was among them. Born in Washington, DC, the year the Civil War ended, Marshall graduated from Howard University and Howard Law School, though she never practiced law. Instead, she worked as a teacher in a Black elementary school in Washington while taking on leadership roles in several church and civic groups. At fifty-three, she married a Baptist minister, who shared her anti-liquor convictions. Marshall was one of sixty-five women and the only Black activist who testified during Senate Prohibition hearings in April 1926. Calls for legalizing light wine and beer had been growing steadily louder that spring, as Prohibition was fiercely debated in homes, offices, restaurants, hair salons, and barbershops. The inevitable showdown between Wets and Drys played out before the Senate Judiciary Subcommittee. Starting at dawn on April 15, and every morning for nearly three weeks following, crowds lined up outside the Senate Office Building, hoping for a seat inside to find out what lawmakers were going to do about the burning issue of the day.

The committee allowed Marshall and the other women—all leaders of welfare, social, civic, and church organizations and all supporters of Prohibition—one minute each to plead for keeping the Eighteenth Amendment intact with no modifications. The women had printed their remarks on index cards, and they stood to read from them when their names were called. Most used their time to extol Prohibition's improvement in the lives of women and children, though they offered no hard facts to back up their assertions. Claiming to represent "the fifteen million colored people who have suffered from lack of enforcement" (three million more than Miller estimated), Marshall argued that Prohibition had nevertheless improved the morals of the African Americans. "We do not want liquor back, for we have better homes, better children in the schools, and the moral of the people in general has been raised," she said. Then she appealed to the White men on the committee. "We must live side by side with you and nurse your children and if our morale breaks down, yours will break down, too."

In sharp contrast to the women's testimony, a parade of Wet witnesses—all male—followed and, painted a vivid picture of Prohibition's colossal failure. Lincoln C. Andrews, the assistant secretary of the treasury, testified that authorities had been able to seize only 5 percent of the illegal booze deluging America and had shut down a mere tenth of the nation's bootleg stills. Emory R. Buckner, the district attorney for the Southern District of New York, called the government's apparatus for controlling illegal liquor a "toy" machine and noted the four-year backlog of Prohibition cases in the courts. To decrease it in his district alone, he testified, would require the appointment of eighty-five more federal judges and a huge increase in the budget.

The Drys were up next to echo and expound on the chorus of women's voices at the start of the hearings. Most of their arguments, the *New Yorker* noted, "were repetitions of the old familiar harangues." They vociferously opposed any amendment to Volstead that would bring back the saloon. To avoid being cross-examined by Senator James A. Reed, a bitterly sarcastic Missouri Democrat, Wayne Wheeler, head of the Anti-Saloon League, refused to testify, though at the end of the hearings, he delivered an hour-long summing up of the Drys' position. A parade of churchmen contended that the turmoil and lawlessness in American life was a reaction to the Great War and not a result of the liquor ban. Bishop James Cannon Jr., chair of the Commission on Temperance and Social Services of the Methodist Episcopal Church, argued that it would be absurd to end Prohibition just because the law was routinely ignored. "What community [demands] the repeal of the Ten Commandments because they are persistently violated?" he asked.

When Ella took the witness stand, she opened her testimony by reading from the WCTU handbook, describing how the organization's members believed it their duty and high privilege to educate the public on the importance of "total abstinence . . . and to unite our efforts for the enforcement of the Eighteenth Amendment." Then she read the pledge signed by all WCTU members to never touch a drop of intoxicating drink. Ella painted a rosy picture of Prohibition America, a Dry world free of want caused by drunken men. The closing of the saloon, she boomed, "has resulted in better national health, children are born under better conditions, homes are better and the mother is delivered from the fear of a drunken husband. There is better food. Savings bank deposits have increased and many a man has a bank account today who had none in the days of the saloon." The problems and failures of Prohibition, she insisted, could be remedied with improved enforcement. She urged the senators to crack down on Volstead's violators and warned them against any modification of the law to allow for the sale of light wine and beer. "We believe the Volstead Act should be strengthened, not weakened," she said.

Senator Reed scowled throughout her testimony. When Ella had finished her prepared statement, he tried to goad her into saying that it was better to have liquor produced in distilleries than to have it made in home stills. "Do you think it makes for moral advancement to have liquor manufactured in the home?" Reed asked.

"Certainly not," Ella answered.

"Is it better to have something like over 1,000,000 stills in the homes or to have the liquor manufactured outside and carried into the homes?"

"I decline to answer as a choice between two evils because our organization is against the legal manufacture of liquor in the home or elsewhere. The whole purpose of our organization is to keep the home from having anything to do with the liquor traffic in any way."

Loud clapping burst from the Dry section of the audience. "Now that applause is the best thing we could have," said Reed, his voice dripping with sarcasm. "It changes our minds up here instantly."

Mabel had declined to give testimony to the committee, but she showed up at the hearings on April 19 to answer questions. When asked about the state of enforcement, she cited statistics that showed an increasing record of improvement—38,000 convictions for violations of Volstead and $7.6 million in fines in 1925, up from 22,000 convictions and $4 million in fines in 1922. She also offered recommendations for boosting enforcement and cited the government's inability to assess penalties commensurate with the crime as the greatest deficiency in the Volstead Act. One of the most helpful measures to keep Prohibition strong, she believed, was to prosecute the legion of corrupt local and state officials who were guilty of bribery and conspiracy, or simply turning a blind eye to bootleggers.

When Ella returned to Brooklyn, she wrote a front-page editorial in the *Union Signal* concluding that the hearings were a triumph for the Drys. "The modificationists miserably failed . . . to sustain their contentions that the sale of wine and beer would solve the liquor problem," she noted. Ella also singled out Mabel as a star witness for her side, who "delighted her hearers" and challenged the Wets "to the limit." Opinion was divided on if that was true. One thing was certain to the reporters who'd attended the hearings, the women of America stood firmly behind Prohibition. Not one of them had testified for the Wet cause.

EIGHT

VOTE DRY—OR ELSE!

E VEN AS SHE YEARNED for her family in California, Mabel Walker Willebrandt was putting down roots in Washington, DC. In 1926 she moved into a spacious, beaux arts house on Fifteenth Street NW with two female friends, Annabel Matthews, a Treasury Department lawyer, and Dr. Louise Stanley, the head of the Bureau of Home Economics at the Agriculture Department. Mabel was exceptionally close to the elegant, accomplished Matthews, who was six years her senior. Matthews had grown up in Culloden, Georgia and, like Mabel, had taught school before becoming a lawyer. After moving to Washington in 1914 to work in the Bureau of Internal Revenue at the Treasury Department, Matthews attended night school at the Washington College of Law, graduating in 1921. She became an expert on tax law and would go on to be the first woman member of the US Board of Tax Appeals.

Mabel relied on Matthews for emotional support, once writing her, "I miss you dreadfully," after Mabel was gone from home for just two days. But as Mabel told her biographer Dorothy Brown, she didn't want people to think she was part of a lesbian couple. Two roommates, she reasoned, would squelch any such gossip about her and Matthews, so she invited Stanley to join the household on Fifteenth Street. Despite her unconventional living situation, Mabel entertained like a traditional Georgetown wife, hosting teas and dinner parties, and optimistically announcing in the newspaper that she would be home on Thursday afternoons to receive callers, a quaint society custom few single men would honor.

Around this time, Mabel's foster sister, Maud Hubbard Brown, became pregnant with her third child. Maud—whose tuition at Park College in Parkerville, Missouri, had been partially paid by Mabel—had married a Methodist missionary and moved with him and their two sons to China. Now she was back in California, and Mabel had considered bringing Maud and her boys to live with her in Washington, assuring her mother that she "only *desired* to do it" out of a deep longing for children. "I *wish* I could have" a baby, she confided to Myrtle Walker, an impossibility since her tubal pregnancy with Arthur Willebrandt had left her infertile. "The regret that now, at the height of my powers I cannot have one makes me tender with everyone who does." She decided to adopt a child. After visiting several orphanages and seeing many babies, she settled on a two-year-old girl who had been living on a farm in Michigan with a former client of Mabel's from her days as a public defender in Los Angeles. The woman already had a son by her first marriage, and on the eve of her remarriage to a minister, she realized she couldn't cope with the little girl, who apparently had been abandoned by her birth mother. Fred Horowitz, still hoping to marry Mabel, met her in Michigan, where they picked up the child, Dorothy, and took her to Washington. After a trial weekend, during which Mabel fell in love with the bright, adorable Dorothy, she decided to keep her. Myrtle Walker assured Mabel "you will be such a fine mother," adding that any child her own daughter welcomed would be "very, very dear to me. I love children and will rejoice" in being a grandmother.

Mabel approached motherhood as she took on all jobs, determined to excel and to raise, if not a perfect child, one who was impeccably behaved, groomed, and educated. Worried that Dorothy might have been damaged by her rocky start in life, Mabel had her examined by no fewer than five psychologists. They reassured Mabel that the toddler was "an unusual find." Perhaps recalling her father's strictness, Mabel's ideas of discipline could be harsh. Mabel sometimes took Dorothy to work and once brought her to have lunch in the Senate dining room. When Dorothy balked at eating her spinach, she later told Dorothy Brown, Mabel took her outside, talked to her about the importance of eating her vegetables, and gave her a spanking. Back in the dining room, Dorothy continued to refuse to eat her spinach, so the talk and the spanking were repeated until the spinach was eaten. Another time, after Dorothy suffered a gash on her head when a large dog knocked her down, Mabel stuck the child in the shower, and poor Dorothy began to scream as blood gushed from the wound. Mabel spanked her hard. She didn't think she was being cruel. It's how her own father reacted whenever Mabel herself failed to be stoic.

Dorothy might not have lived up to Mabel's standards of behavior, but she would be as well dressed as any Georgetown child of the elite. Mabel hired a seamstress to make dresses for Dorothy and also sent the girl's measurements to Myrtle. "I'd love her to have anything you made most of all," Mabel told her mother. She boasted to her parents that Dorothy already dressed herself and had excellent table manners—"you should see her use a finger bowl"—and confessed, "I'm just foolish about her." Dorothy, she told her parents, is "the dearest, wisest little two-year-old I ever saw, who *honestly*, no joking, looks like Papa—the same blue, blue eyes with quite a similar expression and a mouth with large full lips like all us Walkers are cursed with! And her forehead is like Mama's."

Mabel vowed to alter her workaholic life to spend more time with Dorothy, but her packed schedule had little slack. The only regular time mother and child spent together was in the morning when they had "a romp in bed," often followed by a cold bath, which Mabel believed promoted health and well-being, an idea that stretched back to ancient Greece. Dorothy's care during the day was left mostly to Rosa Gainor, her young, Black housekeeper and a mother herself. In the evenings, when Mabel was traveling or stuck at the office, Dr. Stanley filled in. The kindly home economist was more lenient

Mabel with her daughter Dorothy at home in Washington,
DC, in 1926. Courtesy of Jan Christopher Van Dyke.

than Mabel, and though Mabel celebrated Dorothy's strong spirit,
she worried about her being spoiled. Dorothy "could easily be a little tyrant," Mabel told her parents. "Dr. Stanley is inclined to stop
and listen to her demands, and you ought to see the way D will order
her around if she can—and she usually can. She has quite a different

attitude toward me. She loves me just as much—more, in fact, I think—but she doesn't try to tell me to get up when I am reading a book and go and get her a pencil, the way she demands her Aunt Louise to do. I have a sneaking suspicion that she would 'bully' her grandmother in a good deal the same fashion."

Fred had given Mabel a year to decide about marrying him, and when it had ended, she broke up with him in a letter, telling him that she couldn't risk a second marriage that might end in divorce. She feared her reputation wouldn't survive it. Fred didn't understand how hard the past year had been for Mabel, the challenges she faced daily and the constant pressures. It was different for Fred. To start, he wasn't in the public eye as she was. "To break off after five years or ten would add, not detract from your prestige and opportunities for a full life," she told him, because people would expect a career woman like Mabel to be an unsatisfactory wife and not be surprised when he tired of her. Indeed, Fred would be applauded for not putting up with a woman who didn't make him her top priority. People might whisper, "Yes, the young unknown man whom Mrs. W married, there must be more to him hidden, but of course he couldn't remain so tied." For Mabel on the other hand, a divorce would wreck "all my self-repressions and discipline and achievements so far. I'd be broken . . .—and I couldn't bear your pity."

Years later, in an article for the *Smart Set*, Mabel deplored "the cruel world" that "should exact of a girl who tried to climb up in business or profession the sacrifice of home and children." She had tried to best the system by becoming a single mother, but she could never find a husband with whom she wanted to share her life. Still, Mabel assured Fred she would always care for him with a love "that's more than possession." But that was little consolation to him. Mabel's definitive rejection after so many years "took all the buoyancy out of me," he confessed. Fred had always thought Mabel would eventually come around. When he received her breakup letter, "I couldn't believe it," he recalled. He reread it—again and again, hoping that, somehow, he'd misinterpreted the meaning of Mabel's words. But upon every reading, it said "the same thing." Even two years later, the thought of the letter rekindled his pain. He would never get over Mabel.

After her decision, however, Mabel felt "a great inner peace of mind," she told her parents, "for I know so surely what I want." That included enough money to support herself and Dorothy and possibly another child, and to guard against any future disability. Her sense of self-respect demanded that she provide for herself and not "marry that capital." She'd always had an inferiority complex about making money, and she needed to prove to herself that she could stand on her own financially. Yet she often fought loneliness "to the point when I knew I'd rather be married, no question of that, if my marriage could be a private affair in my life the way it is for a man. Unfortunately, the things I most prize are tenderness and intellectual challenges. I don't expect to find both in anyone."

Her grandsons who knew Mabel in her later years regarded her as brisk and demanding. One grandson, Jan Christopher Van Dyke, thought it "typical" of Mabel to have a relationship with a man that was more of "a business arrangement rather than a romance." Mabel's deepest emotional attachment would always be to her parents. Still, she remained close to Fred, and for years after Mabel left government, they maintained a private law practice together. Fred sometimes traveled to Washington on business, and on one trip, in the summer of 1926, he picked up Dorothy and took her with him back to California to meet her grandparents, the Walkers. When Dorothy returned to her mother at the end of the summer, Mabel saw a profound improvement in the child's character and felt that her time with her grandparents had been transforming. "You've done so much for Dorothy. I think you do not guess how much," Mabel wrote the Walkers. "Really, she's a different child—much more thoughtful, spontaneous and with so much more 'family' orientation—I couldn't put my finger on what was lacking before—tho it worried me." In California, Dorothy loved "strolling with her grandfather in the afternoons and racing in terror from the 'giant' trolley cars plunging down the street," Mabel wrote, cataloging for her parents the things Dorothy recalled about the visit, including the swing David Walker had built for the child and playing with her grandparents' chickens.

A few months later, Mabel traveled to California herself—first to San Francisco to deliver closing arguments in the trial of an IRS agent charged with embezzling government liquor, then to Los Angeles to present evidence to a grand jury in a liquor-smuggling case. The trip extended to the Christmas holiday. During the visit, she saw Fred, who helped her trim a tree at the Walker home, while Mabel's parents sat nearby, her mother sewing and her father reading a book. After Christmas Day, when she boarded the train for the long journey home to Washington, DC (it's unclear if Dorothy was with her on this trip), Mabel felt close to tears.

> Somehow I felt worse to leave you standing in the station today than I have ever for a long time. Not that I felt depressed at you. You both appeared healthier and happier than for some time past. I hope the appearance was real. But I just longed to have more time with you, when we three might sit together with time enough to say nothing for the evening or talk as we wished. But . . . this was not intended to be a visit. I came for only a business trip and if the original places had worked out I'd been back in Washington by the 15th and not really as long at home as I had as it was. And it was nice to have Christmas eve together. Nevertheless, . . . I want more of you. If I weren't such as financial nincompoop I'd have saved enough somehow by now so you folks could travel . . . and spend some time back here with me.

Mabel had not given up hope that a federal judgeship would bring her and Dorothy to California for good. Though she was still fighting the era's prevailing prejudice against women in high office, the junior California Senator Samuel Shortridge had promised to secure Mabel a judgeship in exchange for her endorsement in the 1926 election. The only problem was that Shortridge was a Wet with a reputation for dishonesty and virulent racist attitudes toward California's

Japanese immigrants. Mabel loathed him, and two years earlier, she had refused to go to him for help in obtaining an appointment to the bench. "Ten judgeships would not be worth it. I have to at least respect anyone of whom I will ask a favor," she had told her parents. But five years in Washington had toughened her to the ethically dubious exigencies of politics, and now she considered endorsing the hateful Shortridge. When California Senator Hiram Johnson, a former governor of the state, heard about the possible endorsement, he was incensed. If "she would sell her principle" for a judgeship, Johnson vowed to Mabel's mentor, the law professor Frank Doherty, he would "retract everything" that he had said about her in recommending her for her job. Johnson also excoriated Mabel to Harold Ickes, the progressive Republican political operative who would go on to become secretary of the interior. "Though she has performed the duties of her office with fair success, I know she has been more successful in obtaining publicity," Johnson wrote. He took credit for "everything politically that she is," but she had since become "a devotee of power and worships at the shrine of the prevailing dynasty."

Mabel invited Shortridge to a party she hosted in Washington for the Hollywood mogul Louis B. Mayer, who contributed large sums of money to the Republican Party. Her fame and connections in Los Angeles legal circles had drawn the attention of high-profile members of the film community who cultivated access to powerful government figures. Mabel no doubt enjoyed showcasing her far-reaching influence to Shortridge, though she never did endorse him. Nevertheless, he won reelection, while Mabel continued to hope that a judgeship was within her reach.

THE 1926 ELECTION also gave Ella Boole and Pauline Sabin a chance to flex their political muscles. The Republican Party was becoming wetter, and the dividing line over Prohibition played out in the state of New York, reflecting the national political landscape. In New York City, Ella's and Pauline's home, they got into a public fight over a statewide referendum asking voters whether a petition should be sent to Congress requesting modification of the Volstead Act allowing the manufacture and sale of light wine and beer. Ella branded the referendum "futile and pernicious" and urged her troops to vote against it in November. She insisted that the Eighteenth Amendment was here to stay; she would not have any challenge to it.

In her endorsement of the referendum, Pauline reminded voters that its success carried no mandate to modify the law, only a directive to Congress of New York's satisfaction or dissatisfaction with Prohibition. That "certain organizations"—a pointed reference to the WCTU—urged women not to support the referendum baffled Pauline. "It seems strange to me that any woman should not want to register her opinion on this vital question," she told a reporter in Suffolk County. Like many women in America who'd watched in horror the escalating violence provoked by bootlegging, she was moving closer to the views of her friend Senator James Wadsworth, who had become more vocal about his loathing of Prohibition, a stance that threatened his reelection in 1926 to a third term. Wadsworth was running on a platform of Volstead Act revision, and he might have had little trouble vanquishing his Democrat opponent, the soaking Wet New York State Supreme Court Justice Robert Wagner, had the Drys not put forth a third candidate, the arid stalwart lawyer Frank Cristman, as an Independent.

Ella saw a chance to destroy Wadsworth once and for all. In her keynote address at the WCTU convention in Niagara Falls in October, she enthusiastically endorsed Cristman, though he was shockingly unprepared to run and take on Wadsworth, admitting to a reporter that he had no clue about the senator's Prohibition record until he read "something which was handed to me" by a WCTU volunteer moments before he stepped up to the podium to deliver a speech. Back home in Brooklyn, Ella sent an election bulletin to her troops that went out over the wires and was published in newspapers across the nation: "See to it that every Dry Voter votes on election day for Dry officials. This is mandatory. Make it very clear that a vote 'no' on the referendum is not sufficient to win the fight to uphold Prohibition, but is supplementary to a vote for Dry officials."

Pauline stayed loyal to Wadsworth. She declined to run for another term as the president of the Women's National Republican Club so she could advise her old friend's campaign. One of the first things she did was suggest he move a scheduled rally from Madison Square Garden to Carnegie Hall. Carnegie would attract more people and be more dignified, as befitted Wadsworth's (and Pauline's) background. Earlier, at a luncheon of Republican women in Albany, she urged them to put aside any lingering distaste they had for Wadsworth as an opponent of suffrage. "Courage" is what women admire most in men, she told the crowd, and Wadsworth has moral courage, the courage of one's convictions. He could be counted on to do what was right concerning Prohibition, unlike most politicians in Washington who lived in fear of alienating the powerful Anti-Saloon League lobby and being lambasted publicly by its zealous leader Wayne Wheeler.

Meanwhile, at the Hotel McAlpin, where five hundred members of the WCTU had gathered, Ella called for Wadsworth's defeat. She denounced him for supporting even the smallest modification of "the divine" Eighteenth Amendment. Even if Prohibition was imperfect, she said, it enhanced America's moral leadership in the world. She wouldn't rest until she saw Wadsworth driven from office.

Another prominent woman who wanted him gone was Eleanor Roosevelt, wife of Franklin Delano Roosevelt, the Democratic politician who in two years would become governor of New York on his way to the presidency. In a series of radio debates, Pauline argued for Wadsworth's reelection, while Mrs. Roosevelt implored voters to support Democrat Robert Wagner, a Wet New York State judge. On the radio, Mrs. Roosevelt came across as shrill and strident, perhaps because in her public statements about Wagner she had to ignore her private feelings about Prohibition. Her father was an alcoholic who died at thirty-four after a seizure following a suicide attempt when Eleanor was just ten, and she had several other relatives whose lives had been wrecked by alcohol. She couldn't abide anyone who drank to excess. Eleanor deplored FDR's fondness for cocktails and never imbibed herself unless she was entertaining the hard-drinking

Tammany bosses, in which case she'd sip a bit of champagne and sar-saparilla so as not to appear too much of a prig.

Although she had supported Prohibition at its start, toward the end of the decade she thought the United States faced more critical issues than keeping America Dry. Mrs. Roosevelt "considered it just as important to enforce the Fourteenth and Fifteen Amendments, guaranteeing the vote to African-Americans, as it was to enforce the Eighteenth Amendment," wrote her biographer Blanche Wiesen Cook. At the same time, Mrs. Roosevelt tried to get agents to raid the farm of Patsy Morry, a Hudson Valley man whose home still was supplying her alcoholic uncle Vallie Hall with bootleg. After Hall's companion wrote her that Vallie had "been drinking for a month" and something had to be done, Eleanor traveled to Columbia County to investigate for herself. What she found appalled and saddened her. "I'm wondering how I can get [Patsy Morry's] place raided as not only Vallie but some young boys on the farm under 20 whom he influenced are getting drunk constantly and their mother has tuber-culosis and is at wit's end!" she confided to her friend, the Demo-cratic activist Elinor Morgenthau. "Tonight I want the Volstead law enforced unmodified and I want to get rid of all the state police who connive with bootleggers!" It's unknown if Hall's bootlegger was, in fact, raided. Hall, a onetime tennis champion, died in 1934 in his bed in Tivoli, his health destroyed by alcohol, a few hours before Eleanor arrived to visit him.

PAULINE ORGANIZED FUNDRAISERS for Wadsworth, escorted him on campaign tours, and defended him in speeches and radio addresses. She knew voters were avid to learn exactly where the can-didates stood on the Prohibition issue, and she stressed that Wads-worth supported temperance. What he objected to was the perver-sion of the Constitution that inserted a "sumptuary police statute," a "thou shalt not" of forced abstinence into America's most sacred doc-ument guaranteeing personal freedom. "Mr. Wadsworth is a leading upholder of the Constitution and has constantly protested against a further extension of Federal power at the expense of the states," she said in a radio broadcast on October 15. As always, Pauline worked hard to mobilize women voters, sending out her own bulletins urging them to vote. In one, she noted that many women were failing to register because they were afraid to reveal their ages, when, in fact, all they had to admit to was being over twenty-one.

On October 18, Pauline debated Eleanor Roosevelt face-to-face before a large audience at the Women's City Club on Park Avenue. Repeating the disdain for Wadsworth she'd evinced in her radio addresses, Mrs. Roosevelt referred to him as a type of "country squire of the seventeenth century" out of step with twentieth-century politics. She also accused him of being a hypocrite. "As I understand it, Mr. Wadsworth is personally wet . . . but in his speeches in the southern tier [of New York] where the constituency is very dry, he has been careful to say that he is always for temperance," she said. Pauline countered that Justice Wagner, Mrs. Roosevelt's candidate, had been "singularly uncommunicative as to what he would do if he were sent to the Senate. He asks voters to take him on faith," whereas "one of Mr. Wadsworth's assets is that he has been honest and sincere in his convictions and never left you in doubt where he stood."

During a rally at the home of Nicholas Butler, Pauline warned the audience, "Everyone knows Mr. Cristman cannot be elected." Though Pauline sympathized with women who felt "they must make their protest against Senator Wadsworth's stand on Prohibition," a vote for Cristman was tantamount to a vote for Wagner and "Tammany Hall, an organization far wetter than the Republican Party." As it turned out, Cristman did, indeed, split the vote. Wagner was elected, defeating Wadsworth by 116,217 votes. Cristman received just 231,906 votes; had he not been in the race, Wadsworth no doubt would have won. Cristman's showing was larger than the 159,623 votes Ella had pulled in 1920, but she had run then on the Prohibition ticket, not as an independent offshoot of another party.

Pauline blamed the League of Women Voters for turning women against Wadsworth and voting in general by juxtaposing statements from a Republican and a Democrat in their weekly bulletin right before the election that seemed to poke fun at women who got involved in politics. The first statement was by Wadsworth's wife, Alice Hay, "a woman who has never held a political position or even taken an active part in politics," Pauline noted, except to vociferously oppose suffrage. Alice Wadsworth insisted women had no influence in politics because men didn't take them seriously. "About all [the men] do is throw [women] an orange now and then," Mrs. Wadsworth is quoted saying. On the other hand, Emily Blair of the Democratic National Committee, suggested that women regarded men as ragingly competitive "gladiators" who scared women away from participating in politics.

A furious Pauline resigned from the League, accusing it of violating the organization's mandate to be bipartisan and "for being totally unfair and entirely unethical" by printing Mrs. Wadsworth's statement on the same page with Mrs. Blair's. Pauline's response seems out of all proportion to the comments and driven more by her anger at Wadsworth's defeat. She felt compelled to lash out, and the League of Women Voters made a convenient target.

PROHIBITION'S SUPPORTERS MIGHT HAVE been dwindling, but they were a loud, zealous minority. Ella had showed that the WCTU and those who supported their cause could employ pressure tactics to win elections. With Wadsworth's defeat, they proved they had the power to remove a politician from office.

The message was clear: Elected officials who wavered in their public commitment to Prohibition would soon find themselves unemployed. Many politicians continued to vote Dry, not because they believed in Prohibition, but because they feared Ella Boole and her male colleagues in the Anti-Saloon League. "While polls in the late 1920s . . . indicated that as many as two-thirds of the members of Congress privately hoped to see Prohibition modified or repealed," Michael Lerner wrote in *Dry Manhattan*, "as long as the Anti-Saloon League, the Woman's Christian Temperance Union and the Methodist Board of Temperance remained at work in a political arena devoid of any formidable wet organizations, the 18th Amendment would remain safely ensconced in the Constitution."

Ella would continue to badger politicians with threats of retribution if they didn't vote Dry on every relevant bill that came before them. Indeed, the more Prohibition was threatened, the harder she lobbied to win support for it in Washington and across the nation.

NINE

◇

CROOKED

T HOUGH MABEL WALKER WILLEBRANDT had no use for most of the dishonorable pols and hangers-on of the late President Harding's Ohio gang, she remained steadfastly loyal to a man at the center of that hard-partying group—Harry Daugherty.

During his tenure as attorney general, Daugherty had been frequently accused of corruption. Though there was no firm proof, his biographer Nathan Masters wrote, there was plenty of reason to believe he "had accepted bribes in return for a variety of favors— from liquor permits, to immunity from prosecution" to the approval of a large alien property claim. (During both world wars, the government Office of Alien Property served as a custodian of property that belonged to the nation's enemies.) Mabel disbelieved these accusations. But two years after he left office, Daugherty was indicted on charges that he and the late Jesse Smith had skimmed $224,000 from the $7 million sale of American Metal Company assets that had been seized and impounded during World War I and subsequently released.

The trial began in September 1926 and resulted in a hung jury. Emory Buckner, the US Attorney for the Southern District of New York, decided to try the case a second time, and in January, Daugherty asked Mabel to appear as a character witness. "I hate to cause you any trouble . . . but this may be an important phase of the trial at this time," Daugherty wrote Mabel. She told her parents she didn't think "any harm can come from telling the truth," and that her presence on the witness stand would actually "do much for Daugherty to lend a tone of respectability to his case. Likely I'll be . . . panned by radical editorial writers, but I'll survive that, I think, having done so at the time of the investigations twice before."

Mabel took the train to New York to testify on February 17, 1927. The press smirked at the sight of the assistant attorney general being compelled to defend a man that one of her DOJ colleagues was prosecuting. On cross-examination, Buckner asked her, "You are really one of my bosses, aren't you?"

"Well, if you mean that I pass on all you do and approve of it . . ."

Buckner shot back, "Such as this prosecution, for instance?"

The courtroom erupted in laughter, and a red flush spread across Buckner's face.

"I have nothing to do with this," Mabel said. Her voice stayed calm, but her eyes flashed anger. She and Buckner glared at one another.

Asked if Daugherty had ever interfered with her duties, Mabel said, "A peculiar characteristic of service under Mr. Daugherty was that things were not done over your head."

Next Buckner asked her about Jesse Smith's status in her department. "The best way I can describe him is that he was very familiar with the messenger boys," she said icily.

Mabel's testimony might have lent respectability to the case, but it doesn't seem to have had much impact on the jury, which voted eleven to one to convict Daugherty. One juror held out for acquittal, creating another hung jury, thus saving the former attorney general from a guilty verdict and, most likely, prison.

Mabel joked to her parents that she hoped she, too, didn't end up behind bars. So much corruption surrounded her—Senator Henry Ashurst, a Democrat from Arizona, called the DOJ under Daugherty "the Department of Easy Virtue"—that she couldn't help feeling guilty by association.

A MONTH EARLIER, IN JANUARY, Pauline Sabin had traveled to Washington with her husband Charlie in tow, for a three-day conference of Republican national committeewomen at the Carlton Hotel. Ella Boole also was in town for a WCTU Prohibition conference at the Mayflower Hotel. With Mabel a few blocks away in her DOJ office, the opportunity arose for the three firebrands to cross paths, which they did on January 12 at a White House reception hosted by President and Mrs. Coolidge to honor the federal judiciary. Though it's unlikely the three women were aware of each other's presence at the event, they were among the two thousand guests—including the nine Supreme Court justices, cabinet officials, politicians, reformers, and society figures—who mingled in the flower-bedecked state drawing rooms, as the US Marine band, hidden by a screen of potted palms, played popular tunes.

The previous evening, Ella and Pauline were guests at a dinner at the Twentieth Street home of Secretary of War Dwight F. Davis, with whom Pauline would become intimately involved in a few years after the death of Davis's wife. The soon to be ex-senator James Wadsworth invited the Sabins for drinks at his house before the dinner, where President and Mrs. Coolidge were the guests of honor. Wadsworth thought Charlie Sabin might need "a little fortifying against the strain" of what promised to be a bone-dry evening.

It was just five days before the seventh anniversary of the "Red Letter Day" of "National Constitutional Prohibition," as the *Union Signal* put it. Now, Prohibition was under siege on all sides. The country was becoming wetter. Voters in 1926 in five of the eight states that held Prohibition referenda, including New York and Illinois, had overwhelmingly endorsed some modification of the law. And in the heart of the Dry belt in Montana, voters had demanded the outright repeal of state enforcement laws. Election Day, 1926, had marked "the turning of the tide," wrote the *New York World*. "That tide, we hope and believe, will not recede until it has obliterated the intolerance and the hypocrisy and the lawlessness of Volstead prohibition."

The *New York World* was part of a growing chorus of Wet sentiment in the American press. William Randolph Hearst, once a supporter of Prohibition, had turned against it by the end of the decade and used his twenty-six or so dailies to chronicle the failures and excesses of Prohibition enforcement. In Chicago, Robert McCormick's *Tribune* regularly denounced nefariously overzealous agents and judges, once reporting the arrest and thirty-day imprisonment of a twelve-year-old girl in Greenville, South Carolina, who was found guilty of carrying a quart of liquor across the street. Another time, the paper reported on the killing of the wife of a small-time bootlegger in DeKalb, Illinois, who was shot to death by machine-gun-toting agents who'd stormed her home to collect a few bottles of liquor in the family basement. In New York, the stately paper of record, the *New York Times*, as Catherine Gilbert Murdock noted in *Domesticating Drink*, daily reserved a full page for Prohibition stories on raids, hijackings, bootleggers, and Wet and Dry speeches. Drys complained that gathering the stories in one place and giving them so much play sensationalized the issue and turned citizens against the Eighteenth Amendment.

At the start of the seventh year of Prohibition, however, Congress was still Dry. The required votes for Repeal—two-thirds of the House and the Senate followed by ratification in three-fourths of the forty-eight states—seemed about as likely as "a humming bird to fly to the planet Mars with the Washington monument tied to its tail," in the oft-quoted words of Morris Sheppard, the parched Texas senator who had authored the Eighteenth Amendment.

If only people would respect the law, Ella believed, public support for Prohibition would stay strong. At a private White House meeting with Coolidge one morning during her Washington visit, Ella urged the president to push for more stringent enforcement measures. When Coolidge announced his budget for 1927, he recommended that Congress increase funding to the Coast Guard for expanding their fleet and hiring more personnel to fight rum smuggling on the seas.

Crucially for Ella, Mabel was still on the case. Every encounter with the assistant attorney general bolstered Ella's admiration of her. Mabel thrilled Ella and her troops when she spoke at the January

1927 WCTU conference in Washington. Even more meaningful for
Ella was being invited with a few of her lieutenants to Mabel's home
for tea. When Ella returned to Brooklyn, she wrote Mabel a note:

> On behalf of the National Woman's Christian Temperance Union,
> I thank you for your fine contribution to our recent Conference in
> Washington. Your words of appreciation of our organization and of
> our representative, and your strong statements in regard to judicial
> decisions being the basis for law enforcement made a deep impres-
> sion. Added to this was the fact that our representatives had the priv-
> ilege of seeing you in your own home and seeing the dear little girl
> whom you are mothering which added greatly to our enjoyment and
> to our [a]ffection for you personally.

No amount of evidence to the contrary could shake Ella's conviction that Prohibition had had a positive effect on the nation. Pauline Sabin, however, was starting to doubt it. She had originally supported Prohibition because she thought it would be good for her sons
by removing any temptation they might have had to drink. She was
haunted by "the apprehensions" all mothers have "when their sons
leave home," she said. Of course, anything forbidden is especially
alluring to young people, and despite Prohibition, her eldest son,
Morton, had become a heavy drinker while an undergraduate at Yale.
Students had easy access to bootleggers and drank openly on campus and in the nearby roadhouses, as Morton's classmate Russell Lee
Post testified before a Senate subcommittee hearing on Prohibition
in 1926. Later, a poll conducted by the *Yale Daily News* found that 75
percent of students drank and that, overwhelmingly, by five to one,
they favored repealing Prohibition. They knew the law wasn't much
of a law, and they had no qualms about flouting it, Post testified.

Morton never did get control of his drinking problem, which
escalated into alcoholism and severely affected his judgment and stability. While a Yale sophomore in 1928, he married a seventeen-year-
old flapper named Betty Shevlin, the daughter of a wealthy timber

magnate who had been a football star and coach at Yale. Tall, dark-haired, dark-eyed, and beautiful, Betty had a taste for flashy cars and clothes. She had had her society debut at the Southampton Beach Club the previous summer after a sojourn in Paris at the school run by the Russian noblewoman Princess Meshcherskaya. The marriage produced two children, but ended after four years in a Reno divorce.

Pauline's sorrow and disappointment over Morton remained private. Not so the embarrassing arrest of her chauffeur, Samuel Carter, who was caught running a bootleg operation out of the Manhattan garage at 120 East Sixty-Sixth Street, where he parked her black Packard. Carter was arrested by the nation's most famous Prohibition agents, Izzy Einstein and Moe Smith, two New York City friends who, as an enforcement team, were spectacularly successful, claiming more than four thousand arrests by the mid-1920s under their exceedingly rotund belts.

They became famous for their elaborate, creative disguises, posing variously as laborers in denim overalls, musicians carrying trombone cases, fruit peddlers, and truck drivers. Once one of them masqueraded as an opera singer in a fur-trimmed camel coat. The pair claimed to have seized five million bottles of liquor valued at $15 million in raids across the nation. Before Prohibition, Izzy had been a post office clerk with a wife and four children, while Moe worked as a cigar salesman and the manager of a fight club on the lower East Side. But they were actors at heart. As federal agents, they brought "Vaudeville" to "Volstead," *Collier's* noted, a delicious combination that drew reporters to write in obsessive detail about their every flamboyant exploit.

They nabbed Carter, however, by sheer chance. One day in April 1924, while searching for a place to park in Manhattan, Einstein and Smith happened upon Pauline's garage and inquired about leaving their car. According to newspaper reports, a woman who lived above the garage told them there were no spots available, as the place "was full of whisky." Acting on the tip, the agents entered the garage, where they seized $12,000 worth of liquor stashed in crates. That the pinch was done by Izzy and Moe guaranteed wide coverage in the press. Carter insisted Pauline knew nothing about his bootlegging. Still, the *Long Islander*—a newspaper that was widely read by Suffolk County year-round citizens who resented wealthy summer residents like the Sabins—disparaged Pauline as "a misrepresentation of the nobler class of women," and who was, rather, a representative of the "bob-haired bandit" class of "women criminals by her avowed advocacy of opposition to the law." After a friend of the Sabins complained about this characterization of Pauline, the paper printed an apology. Pauline found out about Chester's arrest only when she read an account of it in the newspaper. She fired him immediately. To have kept him on would have seemed hypocritical. Pauline was especially worried about how it would look to the Republican women she'd so carefully cultivated if she continued to employ a bootlegging chauffeur.

ON AUGUST 2, 1927, PRESIDENT COOLIDGE announced that he would not seek reelection in 1928, a decision he had reached years earlier, in 1924, after the death of his son Cal Jr. When the boy died, "the power and the glory of the presidency went with him," Coolidge wrote in his memoirs. He lost all desire to lead the nation and couldn't wait to return to private life.

Soon after Coolidge's announcement, the popular Commerce Secretary Herbert Hoover proclaimed his candidacy for president and quickly became the front-runner. Hoover was an orphaned boy who had raised himself up from a forlorn childhood and grown wealthy as a mining engineer in Australia and China. He was widely respected as a humanitarian for his overseeing of food administration during World War I. Women also were drawn to him for his striving as commerce secretary to improve home-keeping through standardized sizes for food containers and household and building supplies. If nominated at the upcoming GOP convention in Kansas City, he would likely face New York Governor Al Smith, the Democratic front-runner, in the general election.

Ella, Mabel, and Pauline all supported Hoover, each in her own way.

Mabel had never been a fan of Coolidge's, whom she thought flinty and ineffectual. The "accident" of Harding's death had placed him in the White House, not "his own vigor, or prowess or popularity with the American people," and he did not have "the courage of his own convictions to change the trend of corruption in the Republican Party," she believed. Also, she knew she'd never become a judge while he was president because of Coolidge's attitude that the nation wasn't ready for women on the federal bench. She saw Coolidge's decision not to seek reelection as an opportunity not only for more support for Prohibition, but also for her own advancement. Mabel had come to know Hoover and his wife, Lou Henry, and did not regard him as "a spectacular man." Still, "he is by all odds nearer a man of the people than can be gotten anywhere else; and he certainly was preferable to some accidental demigod who might appear on the scene and manage to get elected," she told her parents.

Using her DOJ contacts in the South, she helped Hoover gain a foothold in this historically Democratic region. After learning that the commerce secretary had sent money to a corrupt Georgia political organizer who "ought to be in the penitentiary," Mabel complained to a member of his campaign staff. As a result, the money was redirected to a trustworthy Black Republican committeeman whom "decent white folk could work with," she wrote. Mabel was useful to Hoover in other ways as well. When a federal judge in New Jersey who'd spent a weekend at the home of J. P. Morgan Jr. alerted her to the immensely wealthy donor's tepid feeling for Hoover, she suggested that the Hoover campaign seduce Morgan by hinting that, if elected, he'd appoint Morgan's close friend Dwight Morrow as secretary of state.

Mabel had announced her endorsement of Hoover in January at the national convention of the WCTU in Washington presided over by Ella Boole. Mabel told the crowd, as she had previously assured Ella privately in a letter, "I say unhesitatingly I am for Herbert Hoover because, in my opinion, he is the answer to those who said Prohibition cannot be enforced." Reporters and Democrats seized on her comments as an admission of the failure of her department. "She is the fountainhead of prohibition enforcement in the Department of Justice. Does she mean, it is asked, that she has been hamstrung and that she will be hamstrung in the future unless Secretary Hoover is given the reins of government?" wrote the *Washington Post*. The paper suggested that Democrats might want to haul Mabel in front of Congress to get her to explain herself, adding, however, that "she is a very forceful person and might perhaps tell of the handicaps prohibition enforcement encounters in certain communities," an admission that could embarrass some officials.

Though publicly he supported Prohibition, privately Hoover admitted to his aide Bradley Nash that his position on the Eighteenth Amendment had everything to do with politics and nothing to do with his personal beliefs. "I promised all the women's organizations in the United States that I wouldn't move against Prohibition," he told Nash, adding, "Anything west of the Mississippi will vote dry anyway, and I have to think of both of those aspects."

Ella believed Hoover was "peculiarly fitted for the Presidency" because his brain was "free of the fumes of alcohol." She would have been appalled to know that every evening Hoover stopped on his way home from the Commerce Department to have cocktails at the Belgian Embassy, a cherished treat that he looked forward to as "the pause between the errors and trials of the day and hopes of the night," his biographer noted. After Hoover's announcement, Ella had visited him in his office and assured him that if he spoke out forcefully for the Eighteenth Amendment, she could promise him the votes of southern women, who historically had voted Democratic. How she would accomplish this, she didn't say, but she was determined that New York Governor Al Smith, the Democrats' presumptive nominee and a committed Wet, would never be president.

At stake was not only the presidency, but also a host of slots for Congress and state office. At the regional meeting of the WCTU in Kansas City in February, Ella had issued a blacklist of Wet Democratic office seekers with Al Smith at the top. Then in May, a few weeks before the presidential conventions, she spoke to three gatherings of church leaders: the Southern Baptist Women's Missionary Society at Chattanooga, the Methodist Episcopal General Conference at Kansas City, and the General Assembly of the Presbyterian Church in Tulsa. Without mentioning Smith by name, she hammered home the importance of electing candidates who vigorously supported Prohibition, which women had fought so fiercely to see passed.

While Ella remained deluded that the campaign was "a clear-cut Wet-Dry contest," Pauline understood that it's nearly impossible in any presidential election to persuade voters that a single issue is key. She had no respect for people like Ella with "one plank minds." They didn't understand the nuances of voters' motivations, that women (and men) had many reasons to oppose Smith besides his stance on Prohibition: his lack of education; his identification with urban, immigrant Catholics; his ignorance of the problems of rural farmers; his inexperience in foreign affairs; his association with the corruption of Tammany Hall; and his repeal, as New York governor, of the state's Mullan-Gage Act. Enacted in 1921, Mullan-Gage made it a crime to carry liquor without a permit, rendering hip flasks, that ubiquitous accessory of Jazz Age tipplers, as illegal as handguns. The law was hailed by Ella, the WCTU, and the hard right Christians of New York, while its revocation, Daniel Okrent noted, made Smith "the worst hated man in America," in the "heaven-rattling" words of evangelical broadcaster Reverend Bob Jones. At least in some quarters.

Initially, Pauline had not supported Hoover, as she preferred Coolidge and hoped until the last minute he would change his mind and seek reelection. Like her friend Ruth McCormick, however, she was in "politics like a man," and that meant playing the men's game, supporting the front-runner once it was clear he would likely be the candidate no matter her personal feelings. She would do what she could to get him elected, and she agreed to serve as director of the Women's Republican Campaign in the East. The party relied on her organizing skills and connections to get out the vote, but the men had frozen her out of a more substantive role. Hoover would not seek her advice, as Coolidge had in 1924, and no members of the US Congress would ask her to serve on their campaign committees. This was because of a bombshell she dropped just a few days before the convention.

In an article in the June 13, 1928, issue of *Outlook*, Pauline announced that she now considered Prohibition a failure and a menace, writing, "I was one of the women who favored Prohibition when I heard it discussed in the abstract, but I am now convinced it has proved a failure. It is true we no longer see the corner saloon; but in many cases has it not merely moved to the back of the store or up or down one flight under the name of a 'speak-easy'?" Indirectly attacking Ella Boole, Pauline noted that the WCTU "gets tremendous publicity, claiming to speak for the women of America." Not true, Pauline insisted. In a statement that anticipated the grassroots movement she would start the following year, Pauline pointed out that the number of women Drys "is greatly diminishing, and, in my opinion, as soon as the women opposed to Prohibition organize and become articulate, they will be able to do more toward bringing about a change in the conditions which exist today than any organization composed solely of men."

What Pauline didn't mention in the article was her elder son's alcohol use, though she was well aware of the campus drinking that had exacerbated Morton Smith's problem when he was a student at Yale. "It is true that in our universities, groups can no longer go together to a rathskeller and drink their beer genially and in the open. Is it not true that they are making their own gin and drinking it furtively in their own rooms? Indeed, the authorities of certain colleges have instituted the practice of searching the students' rooms without their consent and during their absence," and often discovering stashes of liquor. Many women like her had favored Prohibition because they thought it would completely eliminate the temptation to drink to excess from their children's lives, she wrote, "only to find their offspring growing up with a total lack of respect for the Constitution and the law generally."

Pauline noted that drinking had also greatly increased among teenage girls who sometimes were hired by Prohibition agents as bait to catch bootleggers and speakeasy operators. She pasted in her scrapbook a story about nineteen-year-old Eleanor Jackson, who ended up in the alcoholic ward of a hospital after a night of hard drinking in Buffalo, New York, clubs with a local Prohibition agent, Ralph Dell, who'd paid her to help him gather evidence. Dell, who'd been drinking heavily himself, crashed his car while taking Eleanor home, and the girl was found by a passing police car staggering along a dark road with blood streaming from cuts on her face. (The clipping didn't say what became of Dell.) The policeman charged Eleanor with public intoxication, and she was sent to the hospital to dry out. It wasn't the first time she'd partied with Dell on official business. Eleanor later told authorities that seven arrests had resulted from her nights out with Dell eating, drinking, and dancing in Buffalo speaks and that she'd earned $70 for her efforts, presumably money provided by the government.

Pauline supported Hoover she said because he stood for "Republican principles, Republican accomplishments and traditions." She believed he would make good on his promise that, if elected, he would order a commission to study Prohibition, and if the commission's report showed the failure of the Eighteenth Amendment, he would advocate a change in the law.

◇

TEN

KANSAS CITY

IF ALL THE REPUBLICAN MEN in America were suddenly to drop dead, the 1928 Republican Convention in Kansas City, Missouri, "undoubtedly would continue just the same," because women would step in to fill their shoes, the *Kansas City Star* predicted. Thousands of women had descended on the city, and they were no longer content with mere honorary vice chairmanships on trivial committees, which they'd been stuck with at the presidential convention in Cleveland four years earlier. They were demanding a substantive role. "Try and think of some bit of convention business in which women are not closely and actively concerned. It can't be done," asserted the *Star*. "Try and find a conference, a candidate's headquarters or a sub-committee meeting at which women are not present and vocal. Equally impossible."

The overall impression at the convention was that women were a political force. In the milling crowds thronging the city's hotel lobbies and convention hall, there seemed to be as many women as men. Every woman's club and organization in Kansas City held receptions, teas, dinners, and open houses for their visiting Republican sisters. The candidates' headquarters and hotels kept lounge rooms for women open at all hours and stocked with refreshments. Radios and loudspeakers at the convention hall and the hotel lobbies kept women in constant touch with the proceedings.

Despite the *Star*'s hopeful words and the nods to women at the convention, it was all window dressing. The men who controlled politics weren't about to give women any real power. To start, men controlled the composition of the state delegations, and only 68 women delegates had been chosen in 1928, compared with 124 in 1924, a backsliding that reflected the lack of real progress for women in the political sphere. Sexism wasn't just a problem in the Republican Party, as Eleanor Roosevelt, who worked in the Democrats' Women's Division, noted in 1928. "Beneath the veneer of courtesy . . . there is a widespread male hostility—age-old perhaps—against sharing with [women] any actual control," she wrote. Women "are refused serious consideration by the men leaders . . . what they want, what they have to say, is regarded as of little weight. In fact, they have no actual influence or say at all in the consequential councils of their parties." Roosevelt continued:

> When meetings are to be held at which momentous matters are to be decided, the women members often are not asked. When they are notified of important meetings where important matters are to be ratified, they generally find all these things have been planned and prepared without consultation with them in secret confabs of the men beforehand. If they have objections to proposed policies or candidates, they are adroitly overruled. They are not allowed to run for office to any appreciable extent, and if they propose candidates of their own sex, reasons are usually found for their elimination.

Roosevelt pointed out that by 1928, two women had been elected governors (in Texas and Wyoming). During the Seventieth Congress (1927–29), there were five women in the US House of Representatives, and many more in state legislatures. "Infinitely more examples come to mind," Roosevelt wrote, "of women who were either denied a nomination or who were offered it only when inevitable defeat stared the party leaders in the face." The suffragists who'd fought for the vote were getting older and dropping out of the fight for political power. What was needed was a new generation of women who would become expert in how the intricate machinery of politics worked. "They must learn to talk the language of men. They must not only master the phraseology, but also understand the machinery which men have built up through years of practical experience. Against the men bosses there must be women bosses who can talk as equals with the backing of a coherent organization of women voters behind them," Roosevelt wrote.

She advised women to play the game the way men do, which often meant grandstanding, bending the truth, echoing party positions they didn't necessarily believe in, supporting candidates even if one's heart wasn't in it, and using other specious means to justify their ends. That's exactly what Ella Boole, Mabel Walker Willebrandt, and Pauline Sabin did. All three were natural leaders who closely observed how male politicians plotted their winning strategies. None of them felt strongly about Hoover; still, they expected to benefit from his election. That he would end up disappointing them would be no surprise. Politicians, after all, are in the business of disappointing. It's almost part of their job description.

PAULINE ARRIVED IN KANSAS CITY a few days before the convention opened. No sooner had she checked into her suite at the Hotel Muehlebach, the most luxurious hotel in town, than she began firing off telegrams and working the phones to secure commitments for Hoover from a group of unclaimed delegates. Though women had not voted in large numbers in the 1924 election, Pauline predicted they would swarm the polls in 1928. She based her prediction on the large numbers of women volunteering for Hoover and those who had also donated money to his campaign.

Still, many Republicans distrusted Hoover's loyalty to GOP policies and opposed his candidacy. Leading the anti-Hooverites was

Ruth Hanna McCormick, who was running for Congress from Illinois. Ruth supported the former Illinois Governor Frank Lowden, whose support was so thin that a correspondent for the *New York World* cracked, "The widow McCormick is supposed to be the brains of the movement against Hoover. They are calling her Joan of Arc, but that is all wrong because Joan of Arc had a white horse and Mrs. McCormick hasn't even got a dark one."

The Stop Hoover campaign at the convention, though, threatened to derail the commerce secretary's candidacy. So did his poor public speaking. Hoover was terrible on the podium and stump. In every primary where he had challenged a favorite son, he'd lost, defeated by Frank Lowden in Illinois, Senator Jim Watson in Indiana, Senator Guy D. Goff in West Virginia, and Senator George Norris in Nebraska, who was supported for the presidency by a group of farm bloc legislators. At the convention, Lowden, Watson, and Senator Charles Curtis of Kansas, the Senate Majority leader, joined together to halt Hoover's victory on the first ballot. A Draft Coolidge faction also threatened to disrupt a Hoover nomination.

But at the Republican National Committee hearing to decide the fate of sixty contested delegates, the Hoover forces prevailed. The *Kansas City Star* attributed the Hoover sweep "to feminine maneuvers." Most of them belonged to Mabel. The *New York Times* declared her the feminine star of the convention. "In the eyes of the party leaders, whenever her name is mentioned, there is a dazed, far-away look not unlike that of a well-known bootlegger who beholding for the first time the woman responsible for his conviction and incarceration . . . exclaimed incredulously, 'What, that peach of a girl?'" the paper wrote.

Time called her "the most conspicuous woman in Kansas City after the Convention began," describing her in the "girlie-girlie" society speak she loathed: "Young-looking, shapely, smartly dressed, full of vitality." The magazine noted that her husband, "much older than herself, is an invalid." Mabel did nothing to correct such statements. Her divorce had not yet become public knowledge, and an old, sickly husband was a good excuse for why she didn't have a man by her side in Kansas City. She did, however, have her parents.

Mabel arrived in town with Myrtle and David Walker and took rooms for the three of them at the Aladdin Hotel. Her parents had been gone from their home in Temple, California, for nearly two months, with most of that time spent in Washington with Mabel. She'd recently moved to a large two-story clapboard house at 3303 Eighteenth Street NW with her roommates Annabel Matthews and Louise Stanley, who drove the Walkers around Washington to see the marble monuments in Mabel's spanking-new Ford. During their visit, the Walkers helped care for Dorothy and enjoyed evenings out at the theater with tickets procured by Mabel and day trips to Mount Vernon and Annapolis. David Walker planted flowers around the house, which sat next to the home of the very Wet Maryland Democrat Senator Millard E. Tydings.

Mabel had vigorously committed herself to Hoover in a series of high-profile speeches before the convention. Speaking at a dinner at the Business Women's Republican Club at the City Club of Kansas City, Mabel said, "Only as women earn their place in a party can they expect to give real service in government; only as they learn tolerance and accept disappointments and their victories with good sportsmanship can they expect to win political achievements on even terms with the men." Republican leaders took note. Because they believed they could count on Mabel's unfailing devotion to the GOP and her expected influence on the women's vote, the men awarded her an extraordinary plum—the chairmanship of the important Committee on Credentials, which was responsible for investigating disputed delegates and their claims. Mabel became the first woman to ever head a committee at a Republican convention.

She proved herself an exceptionally effective politician, though "nobody looking at Mrs. Willebrandt was prepared for anything of the kind," noted the *New York Times*. "She is young. She is pretty. She looks at you disarmingly with wide, earnest, trustful brown eyes behind which functions one of the keenest legal minds in the United

States." She had the ambition to match. Mabel enjoyed influencing events and demonstrating her power to important people. Before the convention, Mabel and her friend Ida Koverman, a Republican from California who'd worked as the executive secretary of Coolidge's presidential campaign in 1924, schemed (successfully) to get Louis B. Mayer elected as a delegate to the convention. Though he lived in Santa Monica, Mayer represented Culver City, home of his film company MGM.

Mabel had presided at the Hoover mass meeting at the Ararat Temple on June 9 and three days later turned a luncheon of the Women's National Committee for Law Enforcement "into a rousing Hoover meeting" within ten minutes of starting her speech. The next day she ran a grueling twelve-hour session of the Credentials Committee that went on until three in the morning. She examined the protests of the contested delegates and found in favor of Hoover's supporters, thus securing the commerce secretary's nomination. The tiny back room where the committee met was jammed to a standstill with onlookers and reporters. One recorded the historic moment Mabel called the group to order. She did so, "calmly, undisturbed by the heat," with "the excess of manhood and the questioning political glances" trained on her, the *Washington Evening Star* noted.

After the meeting, Mabel spent several hours writing her report of the Credentials Committee findings. Then, she gulped a cup of coffee, changed clothes, and hurried to the convention floor. As she arrived, police at the door were turning back a crowd shouting, "We Don't Want Hoover," their raucous voices rising above the band playing "America." Mabel paid them no mind. She had stopped them; Hoover had won. Then, she made her way to the flag-draped dais and took her place. "Her appearance on the stand gave a touch of novelty, which the seemingly tired delegates relished," reported the Associated Press. When it was her turn at the podium, Mabel spoke with ease into the microphone, as the crowd gazed in wonder to see a woman on a national political stage.

She looked "as fresh as a daisy" in a black crepe de chine dress with a white collar and cuffs, a small diamond bar brooch on her chest, and a red-white-and-blue delegate badge pinned to her right shoulder. The only clue to her endless workload were the bruise-like purple circles under her eyes. Mabel's low, rich voice amplified with immense speakers, seemed to reach every corner of the hall. The conventioneers remained remarkably quiet and attentive as she spoke. Time reported that "she got tangled up on some state names but finished with plenty of stingo." When she announced the committee approval of the Hoover delegation from Texas, a shout of "Atta boy" resounded from a far end of the gallery, near where the Walkers sat, looking on proudly. Mabel's mother shook a rattle so exuberantly that it broke in two, so she switched to waving her Hoover flag. A reporter who interviewed Myrtle Walker, found it "easy to trace the energy of the assistant attorney general to the ruddy-faced little woman who was a country school teacher in Western Kansas before she became a farmer's wife." In a journal David Walker kept of the Walkers' 1928 travels, he described Mabel's ten-minute speech as a "marvel for clearness, logic, enunciation and articulation." He noted that when she finished speaking, the crowd roared to its feet clapping and cheering.

Later, Mabel changed into a long evening gown with orchids pinned to the shoulder strap. When Hoover was nominated on the first ballot, she "jubilated" near the platform, jumping up from her seat, grabbing a flag, and leading a cheering group of Hoover supporters on a victory jaunt through the aisles. Mabel, with Koverman's help, had plotted to have Louis B. Mayer among those who seconded the candidate's nomination. But the MGM chief had been tarnished by publicity linking him to the purchase of stock in a fraudulent petroleum company, and the Republican men refused to allow it.

Twenty-five minutes later, Mabel had resumed her seat near Mayer in the California section, where she "initiated a great business of backslapping, hand clasping and general whoopee." For once, she'd allowed herself to relax and loosen up. As the *Washington Evening Star* reported, "Even the large, perfect waves of her simply dressed hair became a bit disarranged." Delegates, officials and politicians mobbed Mabel with congratulations. A few whispered that if Hoover became president, he'd surely appoint Mabel attorney general, which would make her the first woman ever to hold a cabinet post. Mabel thought that would be even better than being a judge.

ELEVEN

HOOVER FOR PRESIDENT

A S EXPECTED, THIRTEEN DAYS LATER at the Democratic National Convention in Houston, Al Smith became his party's candidate for president. Now, Ella Boole swung into action. The 1928 election was the first time in the WCTU's fifty-four-year history that the organization actively campaigned for or against a presidential candidate. Ella went overboard, with the national headquarters and state chapters working "at high speed," as she put it, even before the presidential campaign committees had opened offices. She later claimed she never wrote a letter "ordering our women to support Hoover." But this was clearly her effort to revise history. Everything the WCTU did from June through voting day in November strove to put Hoover in the White House. Many WCTU chapters essentially became campaign offices for Hoover, organizing rallies and clinics to instruct women in ballot marking, sponsoring speakers to attack Smith, and setting up Hoover booths at state and county fairs. Some local chapters also asked their members to contribute at least one dollar directly to Hoover's campaign. WCTU chapters in every state of the nation published a monthly newsletter, which, as Ella put it, "burned and blazed with enthusiasm for the cause, carried ammunition to use against the enemy and gave information to offset the vicious Wet propaganda."

Of course, the WCTU had its own Dry propaganda. In South Dakota, the group put up roadside billboards reading: "The presidential highway must be a dry way." Other state chapters sent women house to house to canvass potential voters and make sure every eligible Dry was registered. Nearly nine thousand WCTU members were tasked with monitoring newspaper sentiment on the election in their towns and reporting back to the national office. Where Wet views were strong, they bombarded the local newspapers with letters to the editor promoting the Dry cause.

The national WCTU publishing office in Evanston, Illinois, printed an avalanche of anti-Smith literature, some of it directed at children in the hopes that they would shame their parents into voting Dry. They also distributed more than two million posters with Hoover's image and ten million copies of a leaflet cataloging Al Smith's Wet record. The printers at the WCTU publishing house in Evanston churned all day and night to print the one-page document. One day the rubber rollers on the overworked presses melted from excessive heat and stopped cold. They were soon repaired, however, and the manic printing resumed. The leaflet, which one Smith supporter called an example of "the sinister lobbying of the Church crowd," listed thirteen of Smith's anti-Prohibition votes, including his vote in 1908 as a New York assemblyman to permit saloons near churches and schools. The leaflet also dredged up a remark Smith had made five years earlier, saying he would be glad to modify the Prohibition law to allow for low alcohol beer to be sold "if that would get us anywhere near the time when we can put a foot on the brass rail and blow off the froth." The problem was Smith had made the remark facetiously in answer to a reporter's question and said emphatically that he did not favor the return of the saloon, "which is and ought to be a defunct institution in this country." When called out for spreading misinformation (and, apparently, taking the quote out of context to smear Smith), Ella gave as an excuse that she was in Europe drumming up support for temperance when the leaflet was printed and didn't know anything about it.

It wasn't the WCTU's only misstep.

Some of its members were appalled at the organization's involvement in partisan politics, and Wet-leaning newspapers across the nation gleefully reported stories about Ella's troops who refused to support Hoover. The negative publicity exploded in Idabel, Oklahoma—one of the driest states in the nation—in September 1928, when the WCTU sent an organizer to this overwhelmingly Democratic town to set up a new local chapter. It looked suspiciously like an attempt to recruit votes for Hoover. After all, Ella had promised Hoover in her private meeting with him before his nomination that she could deliver the votes of southern women. But her move in Idabel backfired spectacularly. The local WCTU organizer, Annie B. Hagler, enlisted sixty-two women in the McCurtain County WCTU and immediately deluged them with Hoover campaign literature. The next day, however, twenty-two of these women met at the office of a local county judge and passed a set of resolutions endorsing Smith for president. Despite Smith's avowed Wetness, the Idabel women said they were confident he would enforce the Prohibition laws if elected and "bitterly" denounced the Republican Party for its "failure to suppress the traffic in intoxicating liquor."

Soon afterward, Ella herself arrived in Oklahoma to attend a temperance conference in Enid. People told her that local Democrats had "played a trick" on Annie Hagler by giving a dollar to the women who agreed to go to her WCTU chapter meeting and sign up. "As soon as these temporary white ribboners"—many of whom, Ella charged in her 1929 book, *Give Prohibition Its Chance*, were the wives of Democratic Party officials and workers—had joined, "they repaired quickly, even before a single meeting had been held, to the office of a local politician and adopted resolutions favouring Governor Smith." Ella insisted, "Of course this was done for the benefit of the newspapers . . . the local Idabel paper used its largest and blackest type" to report the incident. "It was seized upon with glee all over the county, where the story was sent through a local representative of a national press association," Ella noted.

It's impossible to know if the Idabel women had indeed been

bribed. What is certain is that the WCTU's scheming in Oklahoma bumped up against the deep racism of the South. In Idabel, the story about the local chapter endorsing Smith appeared on the front page of the *McCurtain Gazette* next to a letter to the editor from a woman who claimed to have switched her allegiance from Hoover to Smith after a trip to Washington during which she discovered that in Commerce Secretary Hoover's office White girls were compelled to work at desks next to Black men and to use the restrooms with Black girls.

Ella bristled at the notion that the WCTU had forgotten its true purpose by embroiling itself in politics. Universal temperance remained the group's chief goal and *that*, Ella firmly believed, depended on Smith's defeat. To ensure Hoover's election, she also relied on the WCTU's Black leaders, who believed, as she did, that total abstinence from alcohol was an essential element of rightful living that would mitigate racial injustice. What's more, for Black voters not to support Hoover, she believed, was tantamount to race betrayal.

Black women and men yearned for a strong federal government that would hew closely to its constitutional obligations. They worried that any modification of the Eighteenth Amendment, not to mention its outright repeal, threatened the continuation of the so-called Reconstruction amendments that were passed in the wake of the Civil War: the Thirteenth Amendment abolishing slavery, the Fourteenth Amendment defining American citizenship as a protected federal right, and the Fifteenth Amendment enfranchising Black men. The *Philadelphia Tribune* quoted a Black dentist, Dr. V. Pinnock Bailey, who, though he was a Wet in principle, would never support repeal of the Eighteenth Amendment because, he reasoned, echoing the sentiments of many Black people, "If you once repeal any feature of the Constitution of the United States, you open the gates for other similar repeals." Black people's fears were reinforced by White Dry leaders such as Bishop James Cannon, who tried to intimidate Black voters in Indiana by outrageously warning them that overturning the Eighteenth Amendment would lead to the return of slavery.

Some of the Black WCTU leaders were also activists in the

Colored Women's Department of the Republican National Committee and the independent National League of Republican Colored
Women (NLRCW), formed in 1924. The women in these organizations were well positioned to canvass legions of Black voters, yet their
efforts were undercut by White Republican organizers who wanted
to deny them full participation. Mary Cordelia Booze—the daughter of a formerly enslaved couple who with her family owned a plantation in the all-Black town of Mound Bayou, Mississippi—was the
first African American woman to sit on the Republican National
Committee and was a regular victim of what the Black newspapers
called "Jane Crow," that is, discrimination toward Black women. (The
Booze moniker likely was a source of vexation for her, especially given
her Dry views, which were also predominant in Mound Bayou.) At a
July 1928 meeting of the Republican committeewomen at a hotel in
Washington, DC, Mary Booze was barred from having lunch with the
group, though she was allowed to pose with White members for photographs. Pauline Sabin was in attendance but is not on the record
making any statements about this shameful episode.

Mary Booze herself, perhaps not wanting to alienate the White
women in power, claimed that she missed the lunch because of a previous engagement. Her explanation fooled no one. To the reporters,
Black and White, writing about the incident, it was another example
of racism in the Republican Party, which was most obvious and egre-
gious in Booze's native South. In an August 4 letter signed by every
member of the NLRCW, including Booze, the organization appealed
directly to Mabel Walker Willebrandt. "Is there a definite movement on the part of the National Republican Committee function-
ing through your office to rid the Republican Party of Negro leadership in the South? We find it difficult, in the face of this question
to offset the insidious propaganda which is being broadcast most
effectively by the Democratic Party, whose Presidential candidate
has been nationally known for his singularly fair attitude in dealing with our group." The Republican Party, of course, did not function through Mabel's office. The NLRCW women probably thought

Mabel had more power to influence RNC policy than she actually did. If she responded to their letter, her reply is lost.

More troubling still was the Republicans' appeal to White supremacists, including the Ku Klux Klan. In her book *The Second Coming of the KKK*, scholar Linda Gordon describes a Klan resurgence in the 1920s, which was fed by a politics of resentment driven by a backlash of White, rural, and small-town Americans against a changing nation. The KKK, which had formed in the wake of the Civil War to fight the rights of freed slaves, spread its hatred to include immigrants, urban elites, Jews, and Catholics, all of whom they feared took jobs away from native-born Protestants and were in thrall to saloon culture and political machines. There's no evidence that Ella cultivated White supremacists in her zeal to draw southern votes to Hoover. But many Black women who worried that a vote for Hoover would be tantamount to a vote for the Klan turned to the Democratic Party and Smith. As the civil rights activist Nannie Helen Burroughs explained, "black voters want to be sure they are voting against the klan, and they know the klan is against Smith. They are not for Smith, but against the klan."

Of course, the Democratic Party had shown itself as indifferent to racism as the Republican Party and equally out of touch with the needs of the Black community. The convention that nominated Smith had met in Houston, the site of a recent lynching. Seeking a diversion one afternoon, a group of delegates visited the site and gawked at a fragment of noose left behind by the White mob, an act of insensitivity that appalled a writer for the *Houston Informer*, a local Black newspaper. No Black delegates attended the convention; Black spectators were segregated in a cagelike area set off by wire fencing. What's more, as an appeal to White voters in the solidly Democratic South, Smith had named as his running mate the senior senator from Arkansas, Joseph Taylor Robinson. Still, as Samuel O'Dell noted in the journal *Phylon*, some Black voters supported Smith because they "perceived him as a member of another persecuted minority" whose election would be a great blow to bigotry.

Tellingly, in 1928 the Black press overwhelmingly defected from the party of Lincoln to support Smith. At least eighteen of the nation's most influential Black newspapers endorsed the New York governor, including the *Chicago Defender* and the *Baltimore Afro-American*. But this support was tempered with an insistence that White candidates pay attention to the concerns of Black people. "Now the Race is tired of this studied indifference to its problems and its needs. It is tired of letting its strong voting power be used as the cat's paw to draw out of the political fire the chestnuts for every cause that can employ a few silver-tongued orators. We have decided to assert our own cause and to insist upon its recognition and we have decided that we'll block consideration of every other cause, so far as our strength permits us until our own cause gets a hearing," wrote an editorialist for the *Chicago Defender*. "We have resolved that no repeal of the Prohibition amendment will go through if we can help it, until some action is taken on the disgraceful, flagrant violation of the Civil Rights amendments," the editorial continued. "The United States government is spending thousands and even millions of dollars in an elaborate enforcement machinery to carry out the 18th amendment, but the three Civil War amendments are openly flouted throughout the South and frequently in the North, and not a penny is spent to enforce them."

And yet, some Black people wanted Prohibition repealed because they believed it was hurting their communities most of all. Stories in the Black press highlighted how "the Negro is the greatest sufferer from the evils of dry legislation," as reported in the *Afro-American News*. A Black Philadelphia lawyer who studied lists of trial cases in the Philadelphia courts found that "the criminal statistics of the Negro" had substantially increased under Prohibition and that forty out of every one hundred prisoners were charged with offenses that would not have been crimes before the Eighteenth Amendment. Most of the prisoners are of "the poor, underprivileged class who are caught with a half-pint in the kitchen closet," he wrote, while prosperous White people routinely got away with violating the law.

In Chicago and other cities, too, discrimination against Black people was unbound. In her study of the politics of crime control in twentieth-century Chicago, the scholar Nora Krinitsky found that an official campaign against racially integrated speaks in the 1920s escalated into harassment of interracial couples and increased police violence on the city's largely Black South Side.

TWELVE

◇

HOOVER WINS

IN 1928, MABEL WALKER WILLEBRANDT'S fierce ambition to become either the first female attorney general or the first woman federal judge depended on the election of Hoover. She campaigned tirelessly for him, but her zeal to see Hoover as president led to several lapses of judgment that ended her government career.

It started when she ordered a series of raids on Manhattan speakeasies on June 28, the night Al Smith was nominated for president at the Democratic convention in Houston. Throughout her tenure as assistant attorney general, Mabel had counted on the US Attorney for the Southern District of New York, Emory Buckner, to manage the city's speaks, and Buckner had successfully shut many of them down—at least temporarily—by relying on the legal doctrine of civil forfeiture. He would give money from his own pocket to lawyers on his staff and send them forth to buy drinks at the speaks. Afterward, the lawyers would appear before a judge, swear they'd bought liquor at the Colony Restaurant, say, or the Club Deauville—two speaks Buckner shut down by this method—and the judge would issue an injunction ordering the establishments closed. Soon afterward, court officers would clamp padlocks on the clubs' doors, shuttering them for at least six months. The closures became so common that impresario Billy Rose produced a Broadway revue for which he also wrote the songs, titled *Padlocks of 1927*," which starred Texas Guinan riding around the stage on a white horse. But in 1927 Buckner had resigned and was succeeded as US Attorney by Charles Tuttle. Had Buckner still been in office, however, Mabel probably would not have trusted him to deal with New York's speaks in 1928. Now, a presidential election was at stake, not to mention her own career. To maximize publicity and to send the public and politicians a message, she took charge of closing down the biggest, most high-profile Manhattan clubs. Her chief target was the Queen of the Night herself, Texas Guinan.

Mabel instructed federal undercover agent James L. White to "get Guinan," a job he found so delectable that he kept returning to her club, the Salon Royale, many more times than duty required, sometimes with his wife and another federal agent in tow. On his first night at the club, White, dressed in a black tuxedo, ordered a bottle of champagne for $25, which a waiter poured into a glass pitcher before delivering to White's table. White chatted up Tex and confided that he hailed from Denver. When he returned a few nights later, she greeted him with "Hello, Denver! I knew you would come back to see me!" White asked Tex to join him for a drink, but she refused. "Well, everybody knows, I've never had a drink in my life," she later explained.

Near 3 a.m. on June 28, a few hours after New York Governor Al Smith accepted the Democratic nomination for president and minutes before the last call at Manhattan's speaks, a swarm of undercover agents, including James L. White, rose from the tables where they'd been drinking up and down the roaring Forties and Fifties of Manhattan's Wet Zone. "Folks, we are enforcement agents. This place is now in the hands of the federal government. All guests must leave at once," the undercover agents announced, adding, "Please pay your checks before you go."

Mabel had been planning the operation for six months under the deepest secrecy. Ignoring local officials, whom she blamed for rampant violations of the Volstead Act in New York, she had brought in men from her own intelligence team and partnered them with handpicked agents, such as White, from Denver, Fort Worth, and Kansas City, chosen for their discretion, trustworthiness, good looks, and ability to pose variously as aristocrats, cattlemen, retired military colonels, and heirs of industrial kings. Few of them had a clear idea what they were preparing for, only that it was something big. Night after night, from January to June, they dressed in evening clothes and went out on the town, posing as sophisticated big spenders. Collectively, they ran up a tab of $75,000, authorized by Mabel and paid by the government, in hotel bills and restaurant and bar tabs, often with glamorous women in tow, all to make their carousing seem more authentic. To guard against any last-minute leaks on the day of the raids, Mabel locked White and her other agents inside New York's Prohibition headquarters at One Park Avenue and cut the phone lines. She didn't reveal their assignment until moments before they went out that night.

When it was over, "Mabel's Moppers," as one newspaper dubbed the agents, had shut down a dozen or so speaks (the exact number is in dispute) and had arrested 104 employees, from hat-check girls and musicians, to waiters and club owners. The raids were marked by unusual thoroughness, with the agents spending hours searching for hidden caches of liquor, counting chairs and tables, and interrogating patrons, some of whom had hastily stashed bottles of liquor in their pockets. Within hours, padlocks had snapped shut over the bars of nightclub entrances up and down Broadway, turning the Great White Way into a necklace of rusty bolts.

Among the most notorious offenders arrested that night was Nils T. Granlund, an entertainment producer and radio announcer who was part owner of the Frivolity Club. But the agents didn't get the prime catch, Texas Guinan, who had either been warned that "something was up" and stayed home, or had overslept and failed to make it to the club by 3 a.m., as she claimed to her manager. In any case, she was nowhere to be seen when the agents raided the Salon Royale. Tex, however, regretted missing the excitement. She decided she'd lost an excellent publicity opportunity. Wrapped in a fur stole despite the summer warmth, she marched downtown to the police station where the arrested speakeasy employees had been taken. There she met Helen Morgan, an alcoholic torch singer and former Ziegfield star who ran a popular speak called the Summer Home. Morgan apparently had had the same idea as Tex, as she, too, had evaded arrest by slipping out the back door when the raiders arrived at her club.

Mabel may have been Tex's archenemy, as the papers noted, but Tex told reporters she admired the assistant attorney general for her ingenuity and determination in planning the successful raids. "She's a great woman. I'm proud of her. I'd like to know her. She's got more spunk than a dozen men," Tex said. The story went out from a syndicated news service and made headlines around the nation, since the "whole continent dangles from the New York telegraph wires," as the *New Yorker* put it. Actually, Tex hated and resented Mabel, whom she referred to privately as "the old school marm," though Tex was older than Mabel by five years. She told her manager that Mabel was out to persecute her personally. "If Willebrandt can make a bust out of me, she will make a monument for herself," she said. Her manager agreed because "to demolish Guinan meant to demolish all other night clubs and their entertainers as Texas represented the key pin of them all," he wrote.

Mabel succeeded only in temporarily driving Tex out of town. Meantime, a storm of vitriol rained on the assistant attorney general for timing the raids to coincide with Smith's nomination, as if to highlight the lawlessness that prevailed under his governance of New York. "An eighth-grade school child" could discern Mabel's political scheming, charged Mary T. Norton, a Democratic congresswoman from New Jersey. Mabel infuriated New York's Southern District prosecutor Charles Tuttle by going over his head in ordering the raids, and then, at every step of the operation, using her own people, loyalists she could trust, to carry out her orders. Even the search warrants on which the agents proceeded were signed by one of her Washington assistants and presented to a federal judge instead of a US commissioner, a state official, as was the usual procedure.

To counter further criticism that Mabel's "dragnet" had caught mostly small fish and to bolster the evidence against the club operators, Mabel issued 125 subpoenas to prominent citizens whose names had been found on nightclub mailing lists and patron ledgers, including, it was reported, a former New York mayor and Evelyn Nesbit, whose millionaire husband Harry K. Thaw had murdered the society architect Stanford White in a jealous rage over Nesbit's affections in 1906. A rumor flew around town that Mabel had a reserve list of five thousand nightclub patrons and possible witnesses, who again included some of New York's most illustrious citizens.

On August 20, a mob swarmed the fourth floor of the federal building at Foley Square to answer Mabel's subpoenas. A front-page story in the *Washington Post* called the scene a "gaudy Roman holiday" of wealthy Broadway-ites, among them Wall Street bankers, lawyers, a prominent interior decorator, and "society folks." They waited to testify before the grand jury with bookkeepers, police inspectors, and "two colored women." After a day of this chaos, the exasperated Tuttle called a halt to the proceedings, which he described as "a fishing expedition." He'd been upstate at Chautauqua delivering a speech when Mabel ordered the subpoenas and claimed he had been totally unaware of her plans. Enraged, Mabel wired her boss, Attorney General John G. Sargent, who had succeeded Harlan Stone in 1925, that Tuttle knew perfectly well about the subpoenas, as she had personally informed him. It was yet another example of the sexism she'd observed throughout her career—a man accusing a woman of unprofessional deviousness with no evidence—and she seethed at Tuttle's "indefensible" attack on her and his "cheap newspaper grandstanding play." Mabel followed the wire to Sargent with a searing telegram to Tuttle chastising him for not honoring her request to say nothing publicly, adding that his behavior had done "untold damage" to the government's chance to enlarge her cases against the speaks. Witnesses had cooperated before his outburst, she charged, but since then, their willingness to talk had evaporated.

Tuttle had no intention of allowing Mabel to expand the cases by piling on more defendants. He abhorred the hauling of large numbers of nightclub patrons before the grand jury and subjecting them to "pitiless publicity," when it was sufficient for the purposes of gathering evidence to interview ten or so in the privacy of the prosecutor's office. Soon afterward, the grand jury proceedings were halted altogether, but the criticism of Mabel did not let up, continuing through the summer. At the end of August, when the US attorney in Minneapolis began padlocking private homes where residents had allegedly been selling liquor, another press furor ensued. Mabel denied that she had ordered this latest blast of padlocking without the due process of affidavit and search warrant. "I am trying to enforce the law," she told reporters. "It is my sworn duty, but I am proceeding toward that duty under the law and the interpretation of the law as rendered by the courts." It's hard not to see the comment as disingenuous, for in that summer of 1928, when she felt the brass ring within her grasp, fierce ambition played into all of Mabel's professional actions. She was driven by the hope that in a few short months Hoover would be elected and she would be attorney general.

In July, Mabel traveled to Biloxi, Mississippi, to obtain an indictment on graft charges against Perry W. Howard, a prominent Black attorney and Republican committeeman, and seven of his associates. It's unclear if Mabel had angled for this assignment or if Hoover had asked her to do it, but it had nothing to do with her duties enforcing Prohibition and everything to do with getting Hoover elected. The candidate was avid to rid the solidly Democratic South of Black Republican leadership in the hope of attracting more southern White voters to the GOP. Mabel was only too willing to help, as the Black press noted. "Mrs. Mabel Walker Willebrandt has suspended operations looking after bootleggers in the North, East and West and is now engaged in gunning for progressive Negroes in the South," wrote the *Richmond Planet* on July 28, adding presciently, "It will not be long before she will find out to her sorrow that she was never trained for that kind of business."

Mabel's prosecution of Howard, who lived in Washington, pitted the city's most powerful woman against its most prominent African American man. In 1921, President Harding had appointed Howard, the light-skinned, blue-eyed son of a formerly enslaved couple, as special assistant to the attorney general, making him the highest-paid Black employee in the US government. At the time, Democrats dominated his home state. Mississippi's small Republican Party consisted mostly of a tiny Black electorate controlled by Howard and his associates. As the only southern state where GOP politics were not ruled by White politicians, Mississippi stayed firmly Republican by doling out jobs and favors. "In a political order inflexibly governed by the principles of white supremacy, black disenfranchisement, and one-party rule, a nearly all-black Republican organization could find no meaningful role in the conduct of local and state affairs," wrote historian Neil R. McMillen. "The only avenue of expression open to Mississippi's black citizens was to be found in Republican factionalism. They jockeyed for the perquisites of party office. They fought for the prestige of being party functionaries, convention delegates, and patronage dispensers."

Howard and his cronies had some influence in state and local elections, but they also played a role in the nomination of Republican presidential candidates, thanks to an irregular candidate-selection process that gave southern delegates disproportionate representation, a system that, McMillen noted, "invited corruption." As a member of Howard's machine explained, "During the presidential campaigns, our committee performs its only cause for being. . . . We proselytize these few score Negroes to vote . . . and, after pocketing the handouts from the party slush fund—and this is the only real purpose of our organization—we put our committee back in moth balls to await another presidential election."

Allegations that Howard's machine functionaries accepted bribes in exchange for federal jobs had swirled through Washington for years. In the July 1928 indictment, Mabel charged that a post office employee had paid Howard $1,500 in exchange for the position of deputy federal marshal in Mississippi's judicial Southern District.

Howard had long been a figure of controversy in the Black community, regarded by many as an Uncle Tom, "a staying-in with the white folks" Black man and not a true race leader. He was seen as an opportunist who campaigned for Republican candidates among northern Blacks, but did nothing to expand and mobilize the Black electorate in his home state. The Black activist and future Nobel laureate Ralph Bunche called him "a better lily-white than a white Mississippian could be." Howard opposed the almost all-Black pullman porters union, viewing it as a communist front controlled by Moscow. Astoundingly, he also joined southern White politicians in 1922 in opposing an anti-lynching bill.

Though only a small percentage of eligible African Americans in Mississippi succeeded in voting, Hoover thought that if he could purge the state of Black GOP leadership, he would attract more White voters. While abhorring Howard's "Uncle Tomism," Black intellectuals, writers, and activists nevertheless rallied to his defense against Mabel's indictment. Prominent Black leaders such as NAACP founder and *Crisis* editor W. E. B. Du Bois and scholar and writer Kelly Miller, as well as ministers of the African Methodist Episcopal Church, charged that Howard had been singled out for prosecution because of his skin color. They claimed Howard was no guiltier than legions of corrupt White politicians. For example, Mabel's mentor and former boss, Harry Daugherty, had faced charges similar to those against Howard, and Mabel had vigorously defended him.

Black Republicans were especially infuriated that Hoover had used them at the Kansas City convention to win the nomination and then schemed to purge them from the party to win support from White southerners in the general election. That Hoover was using a woman to do it struck them as particularly cynical and conniving. Calling Mabel a "modern day Portia," Kelly Miller excoriated her introduction of "sex psychology" into the case against Howard, for "a White woman prosecuting a Negro man in Mississippi" would practically guarantee a conviction.

White Democrats in Mississippi wanted to keep Howard in

control of the state Republicans, and to this end they contributed to his defense. Amazingly, at the end of Howard's trial, before the all-White jury deliberated, the grand dragon of the Mississippi Ku Klux Klan himself marched into the courtroom, seated himself near the jury box, and proceeded to stare intently into the eyes of each juror, a gesture that was interpreted as his support for Howard. In the end, the jury "honored Jim Crow more than the rule of law," by finding Howard not guilty. Mabel tried him a second time; again he was acquitted. She considered trying him a third time but decided against it. By then, her reputation among southern Black people had been severely damaged. "If someone in authority will put a padlock on Mrs. Mabel Walker Willebrandt's tongue and a chain on her foolish legal blunders, the chances of landing the Honorable Herbert Hoover in the White House of the nation will be materially increased," wrote the *Richmond Planet*. "This lady is ostentatiously in love with herself and the office she holds. . . . The wise thing for her to do in the interest of the brilliant nominee and the Republican Party is to 'go way back and sit down.'"

That was the last thing Mabel would do.

THOUGH MABEL'S PROSECUTION of Howard most likely had been Hoover's idea, the candidate worried that her aggressive zeal not only in the Mississippian's case, but also in going after the New York speaks on the night of Smith's nomination, was doing his campaign more harm than good. He summoned her to a meeting at his campaign headquarters with H. Edmund Machold, the Republican state chair of New York, and William H. Hill, chair of the New York Hoover campaign committee. Mabel denied to reporters that Hoover had reprimanded her or ordered her to stop her Dry crusade in New York, but she offered no explanation for the purpose of the meeting.

Around this time, the Democratic chair John Raskob charged that Mabel was planning an attack on more New York speaks on the night of Smith's acceptance speech in Albany by sending a hundred agents to conduct raids. At a breakfast meeting at the Hoovers'

Washington home, Mabel told the candidate she planned no such thing, and according to Lou Hoover's secretary, the candidate told her "not to worry" about it.

BY SEPTEMBER, THE SMITH and Hoover campaigns were in full swing. Though the official planks of both parties supported enforcement of the Volstead Act, everyone knew Smith opposed Prohibition. Nevertheless, he assured voters that if elected, he'd uphold the law, though he favored giving control to the states to determine whether some alcoholic content could be allowed in beverages such as beer. In a radio debate with Eleanor Roosevelt, Mabel called out Smith as a committed Wet whose public statements "clash with the spirit of his party's pledge." She warned voters that if elected, Smith would use the powers of his office to chip at way at Prohibition as much as he could.

For his part, Hoover insisted he would keep his promise to the WCTU and every other women's organization in America that he would never move against Prohibition. He needed Mabel to reinforce this message with voters. A year earlier, Mabel had told her parents, "I owe nothing to Hoover, and I do not have personal respect for him enough to do any campaigning." Now, however, she saw how useful a President Hoover could be to her career. But after the debacle of the Howard prosecutions and the sharp criticism of the New York raids, she was still reluctant to campaign for him. Also, she didn't see how she could take on more work, as she already put in eighteen-hour days. Still, she wanted to be the nation's first woman attorney general more than she desired sleep, so she agreed to campaign.

She was in Topeka, Kansas, in August to witness Charles Curtis's formal acceptance as Hoover's running mate. Curtis, a Kansas attorney who was one-quarter Native American, had spent part of his childhood on a Kaw Nation reservation with his maternal grandparents, living in a tepee and speaking Kanza, the indigenous language. The so-called notification exercise took place on the red-white-and-blue bunting-draped steps of the State House, not far from where

Curtis had been born sixty-eight years earlier in a log cabin. About "30,000 people were there," Mabel reported to her parents, adding that if they happened to be at the movies when a newsreel of the event was shown, "you may see me. I sat just behind Curtis before his speech and was behind him as he spoke. His speech was ringing and clear." Her own speeches on Hoover's behalf were less successful. On the stump, she often appeared belligerent, as she castigated Smith for flouting federal law in failing to enforce Prohibition, for cooperating with the underworld in not shuttering the speaks, and, in general, for thumbing his nose at the Constitution.

In the campaign playbook Hoover had laid out for his staff, the candidate had essentially said to talk Dry in Dry communities and Wet in in Wet ones; in other words, straddle the fence and try to please everyone. This Mabel could not do. Audiences did not respond well to her militant Dry message, but what alternative did she have? Prohibition enforcement was her job! She wrote to her parents of her "discouragement which I must not voice over this whole Republican set up."

When the campaign ordered her to Ohio in September, she demurred, writing Hoover's campaign chair Hubert Work, "I seem to be a sort of storm center. In the minds of many I guess I personify 'Prohibition.' Apparently, there is much difference of view as to campaign tactics on Prohibition—and as a consequence a diversity of views on whether I harm or help." She had been assigned to give three speeches in September in the Midwest and even more in October in New Jersey, Massachusetts, and New York. "It is too hard work," she complained to Work, "and I'm too tired and obliged to work too hard to keep my official duties performed when I absent myself for speech-making to go to sure states or to little women's luncheon meetings. . . . Consequently, I am . . . notifying you that I am withdrawing from any participation in the campaign. Please wire Congressman [Walter J.] Newton [head of the national committee's speakers bureau] that my name is to be withdrawn from speakers' lists. You can merely say that press of official duties makes it impossible for me to accept any speaking engagements whatsoever."

But the Republican Party would not let Mabel off the hook. They needed her celebrity, her youth, her energy, and her status as the most famous woman in the US government to present their case to voters, especially to bring women to the polls to cast ballots for Hoover. Once in front of an audience, Mabel couldn't be anything less than forceful and persuasive. She could play the political game as hard and connivingly as any man, which is probably why the RNC sent her to Springfield, Ohio, in September to rally a large gathering of Methodist ministers. Her speech was a resounding attack on Smith's Tammany connections and New York's lawlessness under his governorship. Tammany "had reared him, gave him his power, Tammany's desires were his convictions," she said. Hoover, in contrast, answered only to his God. "There are 2,000 pastors here. You have in your churches more than 600,000 members of the Methodist churches in Ohio alone. That is enough to swing the election. The 600,000 have friends in other states. Write to them."

Never once in the speech did Mabel mention Smith's religion. Indeed, one of Hoover's rules for his campaign staff was to never bring up the candidate's Catholic faith. What's more, the speech had been approved ahead of time by the RNC's Catholic general counsel, James F. Burke. Mabel was not anti-Catholic. Toward the end of her life, she would join the Catholic Church herself. But as Daniel Okrent wrote in *Last Call*, words like "Tammany," "underworld," and "lawlessness" were powerful triggers, and "the nature of the audience," not to mention "the attempt to mobilize the gathered Methodists and turn them into an active-duty army for Hoover provoked from Smith a response that placed the religious issue at center stage, no doubt satisfying the drys' most cynical operatives." Smith countered with a speech in Oklahoma City that assailed the Ku Klux Klan (which had burned a cross in the nearby countryside the day of his arrival), the Republican Party in general, and Mabel Willebrandt in particular, for turning his faith into a political issue. Their conduct, said Smith, was a treasonable attack on American liberty itself. Hoover refused to comment on Mabel's speech to the Methodist ministers, but privately he denounced Smith's remarks as "barbaric."

News of Mabel's speech and Smith's response made headlines across the nation and brought a storm of vitriol on Mabel. "Mrs. Willebrandt Runs Amuck," blazed a typical headline. An editorial in the *New York Times* urged Hoover to pull her off the campaign trail. She was a blight on the Justice Department, *New York Evening World* editor Oswald Garrison Villard charged, while the *New York Daily News* bemoaned that "no one in authority puts the brakes on her ninety-seven horsepower tongue." Plenty of Republicans wanted her muzzled. "Attorney General Sargent's office was deluged with wires and letters to call her home," Dorothy Brown wrote. The New Jersey Democratic Senator Edward I. Edwards derided her Springfield speech as "a disgrace" to the Justice Department. But the most humiliating blows came from women, who in the previous seven years of Mabel's tenure in Washington had celebrated, even idolized her, as a shining role model. The Women's Committee for the Repeal of the Eighteenth Amendment demanded that she not be allowed to campaign. In St. Paul, Minnesota, the Business and Professional Women's Association rescinded its invitation to her to speak.

Still, the Republicans insisted Mabel continue campaigning, so she traveled back to Ohio, to the city of Lorain, on September 23 to give a speech to another group of Methodists. Her intent this time was to answer Smith's charge and, if possible, to defuse the religious issue. In her talk, she stressed the fifty-year battle of the Methodists for Prohibition, a struggle that "never asked a man's church or his party if his acts and utterances were against liquor." She claimed that Smith was hiding behind his church, "afraid to come out and face the record that he has made as a champion of the liquor traffic."

In a speech two days later to a group of Presbyterians in Warren, Ohio, Mabel focused on Smith's Wet record and Tammany connections and avoided the topic of religion. A smattering of positive coverage of this talk was undercut by news reports that the Republican National Committee had repudiated her comments to the Methodists in Springfield. A furious Mabel asked Hubert Work to issue a strong statement supporting her. Instead, Work lied to the press that he had not even read all of Mabel's speeches, that none of them had been approved by the RNC, and that, essentially, she was acting as a "free-lance" campaigner A confidential letter Work wrote to Mabel, however, revealed that the RNC had in fact planned her political speaking tours, that Republican operatives had carefully studied her speeches before she delivered them, and that she had occasionally modified a speech according to suggestions made by Republican officials.

On September 27, Mabel fired off an angry letter to Work with a copy to Hoover, charging that the "lack of backing from his office" had exacerbated the religious intolerance charge against her. Mabel was embarrassed, humiliated, and heartbroken over the negative publicity. Work knew perfectly well that she had "not made a single speech that wasn't arranged through his office, quoting from telegrams sent by the RNC giving her various speaking assignments." She also reminded Work that when she had tried to quit the campaign in early September, he had insisted she continue.

Mabel especially worried that the negative publicity would affect the opinion of old friends in California, that they'd think her years in Washington had changed her and made her power-mad. "Surely you and Sarah do not believe these things of me!" she wailed to her old friend Frank Doherty in Los Angeles. While admitting, "I do enjoy a real, clean fight, political, legal or otherwise, but most of us have a vulnerable spot where we can really be hurt, and the charge of religious intolerance found mine."

Mabel became a scapegoat for those who believed women didn't belong in public life. The scandal that overtook her was inevitable; she had to be punished for wanting and seeking power. Mabel was typical of women in politics, California Senator Hiram Johnson complained to the Republican operative Harold Ickes; Though "she has performed the duties of her office with fair success, she is a devotee of power and worships" at the altar of "the prevailing dynasty." What he really didn't like about her was that she refused to act like one of the boys. Mabel "never sympathized with the easy give and take of politics," as practiced by the men, the *New Yorker* noted. She even "cultivates a certain pride in the aversion that most politicians have for entering her office."

As the public attacks against Mabel continued, they became uglier and more personal. Reporters dug up details of her divorce, which had gone under the radar four years earlier, discovering that Arthur had sued to end the marriage, citing Mabel's disregard for "the solemnity" of her vows that had led her "wilfully and without cause" to desert her husband. One enterprising journalist tracked down Arthur, who still worked as a schoolteacher, at the home in Huntington Park, California, he shared with his mother. Mabel's ex declined to comment except to say that he wanted "to remain as divorced" from her public life as he was from her personally.

A reporter for the *Los Angeles Evening Post-Record* drove out to Temple, California, to photograph and interview Mabel's parents at their ranch. Arthur Willebrandt "is a very fine man," Myrtle Walker said. The couple "just couldn't get along together. Mabel wanted a career—she has always been ambitious—and Mr. Willebrandt wanted a home-loving wife. That's all. Mabel wanted to keep on climbing toward the top while he just wanted her to stay home." The story appeared under the headline "Mrs. Willebrandt Was Divorced as Poor Housewife," under a picture of the Walkers sitting on their living room couch gazing lovingly at a large formal portrait of Mabel held by Myrtle. After the article appeared, the couple got a letter threatening to bomb their house if Mabel didn't stop campaigning. Hate mail also poured into Mabel's office. One New York businessman wrote, "To judge from the story of your life as given in the press, you seem to be one of those women with a heart like a stock ticker that does not beat over anything except money and publicity. When you found your husband could not give you enough of these you deserted him. As to Methodism, it may be as good a vehicle as any to land some people in Heaven, but I have grave doubts that it will ever get you there."

The press assault on her personal life was "just too much" on top of all the other negative publicity she'd received that fall. The day the news of her divorce broke in the press, Mabel collapsed in tears at her desk. Her friend Grace B. Knoeller, a Treasury Department lawyer who worked as a classification officer in the Prohibition Department, hurried Mabel outside to Grace's car and drove her through the streets of Washington, as Mabel sobbed uncontrollably. It was a rare moment of release. Mabel had to pull herself together; she had too much work to do, including several cases to argue before the Supreme Court. What's more, the scandal over her speeches in Ohio had not exempted her from further campaigning. The RNC sent her to Kentucky, South Dakota, Minnesota, and Los Angeles. This time, though, as Dorothy Brown noted, "She showed the texts of her speeches to [her boss] Attorney General Sargent, conferred with Hoover before leaving, and secured an Associated Press release that she was speaking under the direction of the RNC."

RNC CHAIR HUBERT WORK had incensed Pauline Sabin almost as much as he'd enraged Mabel. Work had excluded Pauline and other women from the GOP advisory panel that would orchestrate Hoover's campaign, a decision Pauline called "a very grave mistake. . . . If women are to share responsibility for the success of this campaign, then they should also share in its direction and confidences." Ever the loyal Republican, however, she determined to do whatever she could to elect Hoover. After all, she thrived on organizing and enjoyed nothing more than a rousing political fight.

Her chief challenge in the months leading up to November was mobilizing the women's vote in New York, Al Smith's and her own home state. In July, she met with a group of Republican women leaders who came up with a plan to blitz female voters with packets of postcards asking each woman to recruit another woman to Hoover's side. Pauline also was one of the Women's National Republican Club's "flying squadron" of fifty speakers who fanned out over the state to talk to women in their homes. She organized teas and luncheons and, in September, hosted a two-day conference for a hundred

Republican women at Bayberry Land that included swimming parties on her private beach, a private movie screening at a local theater, and a trip by bus to Montauk Point for a seaside clambake. At
the last minute, the clambake was rained out, but Pauline had made
her point to the male Republican leaders, whose smokers and stag
parties were entrenched political entertainments. "We women are
beginning to enjoy our politics, too," she noted astringently.

Political observers expected a big turnout of women voters.
"This year the President of the United States will probably be chosen by a woman," predicted journalist Anne O'Hare McCormick in
the *New York Times Magazine*. Prohibition and religion, the central issues of the campaign, were seen as special concerns of women.
After all, women were the leaders of the temperance movement, the
moral protectors of home and family, and the keepers of religious
traditions. Urban, immigrant, Catholic women and southern Black
women presumably would vote for Smith, while White, native-born
Protestant women would cast their ballots for Hoover and keeping
America Dry.

In the end, Hoover won in a landslide. He took the Electoral College by 444 votes to 87 in an astonishing 70 percent voter turnout.
Ella Boole saw it as a resounding win for Prohibition and gave credit
to God and women. At a WCTU praise meeting at King's Chapel in
Boston the following week, women from across the nation voiced
their heartfelt thanks for the great victory "which He alone could
have brought about," noted Ella, adding, "it came in answer to united
prayer." Women's turnout did indeed jump 8 percent in 1928 over the
1924 presidential election, but so did men's, as J. Kevin Corder and
Christina Wolbrecht noted in their study of women's voting patterns,
*Counting Women's Ballots: Female Voters from Suffrage Through
the New Deal*. "Contrary to expectations, women were not uniquely
mobilized in 1928. Rather in terms of percentage point increases in
turnout, both men and women were mobilized . . . largely in the same
way and to the same extent."

What's more, Hoover's landslide was hardly the endorsement of

Prohibition that it seemed. Anti-Catholic prejudice no doubt contributed a larger role to Smith's defeat than his stance on the Eighteenth Amendment. The near decade of Republican prosperity, however, probably played the biggest role in cinching a Democratic defeat. That prosperity would soon collapse and with it the great "noble experiment" that Hoover described in his acceptance speech for the presidential nomination, which he himself, like so many Americans, no longer believed in at all.

THIRTEEN

◇

PAULINE'S REVOLT

I T WAS EARLY EVENING in mid-November 1928 with the moonlight bright over the East River. Barges rolled slowly along on rip-
pling black water, as chunky Checker cabs and sleek cars jammed
the street outside One Sutton Place South, the Sabins' Manhattan
home. Inside, women in silk gowns and men in black tie chatted in
the art-filled salon, while a band played the latest jazz. Pauline and
Charlie Sabin were hosting a party for New York Republicans to celebrate the election earlier that month of President Herbert Hoover.
Pauline had worked diligently to raise funds for his campaign, and
she made sure everything was perfect for the party. The mirrors and
silver glistened, and fresh flowers filled vases on every polished surface. Dressed in floor-length blue velvet by Worth, her red-gold hair
marcelled and strings of pearls around her slender neck, Pauline
floated through the crowd of congressmen, senators, clubwomen,
and donors, smiling radiantly and greeting everyone by name.

Though Prohibition was in its eighth year, the liquor and wine
flowed. Before the law had gone into effect, Charlie Sabin had stock-
piled a stash of bottles in New York and in a secret room behind a
door of false books in the library of the couple's Long Island estate.
Hoover had ridden to the White House on a platform that promised
strict enforcement of the Volstead Act, but Pauline knew he privately

opposed Prohibition. She also knew he had to be careful what he said publicly during the campaign. Now that he'd been resoundingly elected, she believed he would do something about the wicked Eighteenth Amendment.

Pauline had less faith in the Republicans at her party who voted Dry but were getting roaring drunk on her liquor, grabbing glasses of champagne off waiters' trays and downing them in two gulps. That November—a year before the Wall Street crash—they were riding high, having their sidecars and drinking them, too. The nation had elected the most parched Congress in American history with 80 Drys to 16 Wets in the Senate and 329 Drys to 190 Wets in the House. Though the evening was a big success, Pauline was still fuming about the drunken politicians when she slipped into bed next to Charlie at 3 a.m. Their hypocrisy disgusted her. "I can't stand anything so double-faced," she said.

NEARLY FOUR MONTHS LATER, at 5:15 on the evening of March 3, Pauline left New York's Penn Station in a special train car that had been chartered by the RNC to carry prominent Republican women to Washington for Hoover's inauguration. The newly elected congresswoman Ruth Pratt, the first female representative from New York, joined Pauline in the plush-seated car. Like Pauline, Pratt was a post-suffrage powerhouse who combined a love of politics with fierce righteousness. "It's a great satisfaction for me to wade in and fight, fight, fight for better housing conditions, for the abolishing of some of the tenements that are unfit for animals," Pratt, who served as a two-term New York City alderman before running for Congress, once said in explaining why she'd entered public life.

The next day, Pauline and Pratt took their seats on the East Portico of the Capitol. Mabel Willebrandt and Ella Boole also were in the stands, huddled under the black domes of umbrellas as a soft rain fell. President-elect Hoover stepped to the platform with President Coolidge, followed by the cabinet and Supreme Court Chief Justice William Howard Taft. Anticipating the start of the ceremony, the crowd stopped cheering, but only dead silence followed. Lou Hoover and Grace Coolidge were missing. They had gone to the Capitol Building and lost track of time as they wandered the galleries sharing thoughts of what it meant to be First Lady. Only when they heard the faint strains of "Hail to the Chief" wafting from the Marine Band shell at the White House—a signal that the proceedings were about to begin without them—did they remember where they were supposed to be. They hurried back and were present in time to witness Hoover's oath of office.

Hoover had promised during the campaign to examine Prohibition once he became president. But he owed his election to the Drys, so he did what politicians regularly do and sidestepped the subject. In his inaugural speech, he talked in generalities about the danger of disregarding the law and lambasted states that did not take their responsibility for law enforcement seriously. "The worst evil of disregard for some law," the new president proclaimed, "is that it destroys respect for all law." Then he announced his intention to address this terrible problem: He would form a blue-ribbon commission to study the problem of American justice. Former attorney general George W. Wickersham would head it.

Ella smiled and nodded. She had heard what she wanted to hear. "In less than ten minutes from the time he had taken the oath of office the whole world knew that prohibition was safe in his hands," she wrote in *Give Prohibition Its Chance*. As a gesture of Hoover's Dry support, the *Union Signal* reported, several hundred glasses for wine, cognac, cordial, and other liquors, which graced the tables at state dinners and receptions during many past administrations, were now removed from the White House china cabinets by the new president's domestic staff, packed up, and carted off to an obscure government storage facility.

Pauline was shocked that Hoover said nothing about the problem of Prohibition itself, about the crime engendered by bootlegging, the lives lost in gangland battles over the illegal liquor trade, the surge of drunk driving, the poisonous booze flooding the market, the proliferation of speakeasies, and the glorification of alcohol that had led to spikes in binge drinking. Nor did he mention the lack of funding that crippled attempts to enforce the Volstead Act.

Four days later, on March 8, Pauline resigned from the Republican National Committee, a defection that made news not only in the *New York Times*, but also in newspapers from Chicago and Washington, to Atlanta and Los Angeles. She gave no reason other than that she had served for six years as the only woman member of the RNC from New York, and she believed the time had come for another woman to assume her place. In speeches during the campaign, Pauline had taken a strong stand against bigotry, and some papers speculated that one reason for her resignation was her disappointment that Hoover had failed to show his support for religious tolerance by appointing a Roman Catholic to a high cabinet post. But in fact, she had resigned in disgust. She saw that Hoover would practice politics as usual, that his indebtedness to the Drys would override any obligation he might have felt to take a firm stand on Prohibition. "I had thought during the campaign that by his promise of an investigating commission Mr. Hoover meant one to concentrate on the results of the Prohibition Law alone," she later said. "I had worked for him on that belief. When I heard his Inaugural Address I realized the Commission was to investigate our whole Federal system of jurisprudence. I made up my mind I was fooled."

She was sick of the strictures of party politics that were controlled by men, sick of the hypocrites in government who drank to excess while taking as gospel the WCTU's insistence that American women unfailingly supported Prohibition. For a woman of Pauline's background and position to leave the Republican Party was a radical act and a wrenching break with her past. The GOP had been the party of her father and grandfather. It was the party of Lincoln, the abolitionists, and the suffragists, founded in 1854 when fifty-four Americans, including three women, started a political organization to oppose the Kansas-Nebraska Act, which threatened to expand slavery into new territories.

The women's rights movement that had begun at Seneca Falls in 1848 had been closely associated with the GOP and its battle to end slavery and to win votes for Black men and all women, Black and White. Long before women won the right to vote, they worked hard for the Republican Party, making speeches and writing and distributing campaign literature that opposed the Democratic Party, which stood for southern Whites, bigotry, and the Ku Klux Klan. But the 1928 election and Al Smith's candidacy had set in motion a major realignment of America's political parties. There was no accurate polling in the 1920s, but this much was known: For the first time in the nation's history, Democrats carried America's ten largest cities. In 1928, Smith had won almost twice as many votes as Democratic presidential candidates had in 1920 and 1924. "Catholics flocked to Smith, of course, but so had other wets who finally had a candidate willing to fly their banner," wrote Daniel Okrent. "By openly waving the wet flag, a man who had emerged from the nation's most notorious machine had initiated the radical reinvention of his soon-to-be-dominant party."

After the 1928 election, Pauline became close to Al Smith and his family, an intimacy that would extend through the generations. Her granddaughters would be friendly with Smith's grandchildren; a great-granddaughter of Pauline's would date a great-grandson of Al Smith's. Initially, Pauline and Smith had bonded over a shared determination to see Prohibition end. As they got to know each other, they discovered they enjoyed each other's company. Pauline's friendship with Smith compensated for some of the Republican associates who dropped her when she left the GOP.

Her break with the Republican Party also took a toll on her health. She came down with a ferocious flu and high fever, though she had recovered enough by April 3 to show up at the Hotel Roosevelt for a luncheon in her honor given by a group of Republican women who, though Pauline had left the party, wanted to honor her years of service to the GOP. Looking pale, but fetching in a knit suit and cloche hat, she announced that going forward she would devote herself to overturning Prohibition because, as she explained, it conflicts with my views of the proper functions of the Federal Government and because in operation it has led to more violation of and contempt for law, both by private individuals and public officials, and to more hypocrisy than anything else in our national life. I feel it has created the greatest organized criminal class that ever existed in this or any other country, and, above all, because the motive which caused its enactment is a motive which I abhor, and of which Prohibition itself is but one manifestation.

To tell citizens what they must or must not do in their strictly personal conduct . . . is a function which government should not attempt. It is the age-old effort of the fanatic which has been behind every invasion of personal liberty in the past. No right-thinking man or woman wants the return of the legalized saloon, but worse than the saloon would be to permanently enthrone hypocrisy as the dominant force in our country."

The next day, letters and donations, ranging from nickels wrapped in tissue paper to large bills, began pouring into Pauline's mailboxes in the city and country from women who urged her to start a Repeal organization. "There was a large group ready to be organized, wanting to be organized," Pauline recalled later, adding somewhat grandiosely, "the road before me was so plainly indicated I could not turn back from it." She "talked things over with some women I knew, and I wrote some letters and sent some telegrams," she recalled, and she invited a group to a meeting at her Manhattan apartment. The sixteen women who met at One Sutton Place on a sunny April afternoon formed a force field of indigo in Pauline's peach-walled salon. They were among the bluest of America's blue bloods, with names like Sloane, Pratt, Mather, Stuyvesant, and Van Rensselaer. They lived in Park Avenue palaces, summered in grand mansions in Newport and Southampton, threw lavish parties, and sat on charity boards for hospitals and museums. "She got them excited and fired up for the first time in their lives about something outside their narrow, privileged world," said her granddaughter Mrs. Pauline Sabin Smith Willis.

Two blue bloods who didn't join were Pauline's girlhood friends, the contrarian Alice Longworth, who loathed women's organizations and avoided joining them, and Eleanor Roosevelt. Eleanor declined, she told Anne Hinkley, one of Pauline's lieutenants who'd urged Roosevelt to join, "because as you know I am a 'dry.'" Also, she disapproved of what she construed was Pauline's aim in making it "easy for all of us to have anything we might want," at least in the way of liquor. Roosevelt did not object to the limited sale and drinking of light wines and beer, and thought "the states should be given the power to pass what laws they deemed necessary, though I would always be amongst the group of people who tried to make the states as dry as possible where any kind of intoxicating liquor was concerned."

Though in 1929 nearly 93 percent of adult American women married, two celibates were among Pauline's first recruits: Sarah Schuyler Butler, the young activist daughter of Nicholas Murray Butler, the president of Columbia University (though Butler would marry four years later), and Maude K. Wetmore, a middle-aged political organizer and historic preservationist. Over coffee and sweets, Pauline revealed her plan to start a national women's organization to work toward overturning the Eighteenth Amendment and asked for help from the women gathered in her living room. No doubt that meant hefty donations of cash, as Pauline's publicity plans were ambitious, and the organization, which she called the Women's Organization for National Prohibition Reform, would not require dues. Immediately, Pauline assembled a staff and went to work sending out membership forms to women's groups throughout the nation. The forms read:

> Because I believe that national prohibition has incited crime and increased lawlessness, hypocrisy, and corruption;
>
> Because I believe that the cause of real temperance has been retarded and that sumptuary laws have no place in the Federal Constitution;
>
> I propose to work for some change in the law which will bring about a sane solution of the problem, and therefore, enroll as a member of the Women's Organization for National Prohibition Reform.

At two subsequent meetings, plans were refined. Pauline rented an office at 21 East Fortieth Street and secured a commitment from the editor of *Outlook* to publish articles about the group. Its unfortunately clunky moniker nevertheless avoided the word "repeal," which Pauline was afraid might scare off some women. She also believed that "reform" was a more valuable word as it highlighted her organization's emphasis on bettering social conditions. The press mostly referred to the group by its acronym WONPR.

Before Pauline, no one had been able to exploit America's immense discontent with Prohibition and organize an effective Repeal movement. Throughout the Jazz Age, the largest group opposing the Eighteenth Amendment had been the Association Against the Prohibition Amendment (AAPA), an elitist cabal of wealthy White men who were America's financial and business leaders. Until 1932, the AAPA confined its membership to men who made large donations to the organization. The group's leadership knew they weren't reaching "the common people," though "multitudes of them want to be reached," James Wadsworth pointed out. Still, to avoid "some undesirables" infecting the AAPA, he added, it was best to keep it exclusive. As a result, it was hopelessly ineffective.

Though Pauline belonged to the same world of wealth and social position—her husband, after all, was the titular treasurer of the AAPA and many of WONPR's earliest members were the wives of AAPA men—she worked to build an inclusive, nonpartisan, grassroots movement and disarm critics who claimed that WONPR was just a bunch of "damned millionaires" who cared only about lowering their taxes and being left alone to drink cocktails in their mansions.

But perhaps the most important element of Pauline's success was her unfailing belief that Repeal actually *could* be accomplished. Few, if any, of the male leaders of Dry groups had such faith. Even Captain William H. Stayton, the US Navy lawyer who founded the AAPA, accused his organization of being defeatist. "They were against Prohibition, but believed that it was unbeatable," Stayton told H. L. Mencken. "They would say, 'Oh, you can never repeal the Eighteenth Amendment. Thirteen small states will stand out against you and where will you be?'" Slayton acknowledged to Mencken that Pauline and her followers "knew better."

Working people and the poor would benefit the most from Repeal, Pauline argued. They were the ones most often sickened and killed from poisonous bootleg, the ones most likely to be arrested, fined, or jailed for violating the Volstead Act. She called Prohibition "the greatest piece of class legislation ever enacted in this country," and soon after starting WONPR she embarked on an aggressive campaign to enroll women from all walks of life. By 1932, 15 percent of WONPR's members were industrial workers, 19 percent were office workers, 37 percent were housewives, 15 percent were business and professional women, and 1 percent were artists, authors, and actresses. The members also included astrologists, aviatrixes, detectives, missionaries, and police officers. Pauline understood the significance of an organization that included women from so many varied professions, and she enlisted Grace Cogswell Root, the daughter-in-law of Elihu Root, Theodore Roosevelt's secretary of state and a former US senator from New York, to write WONPR's history and preserve its legacy.

Despite her illustrious pedigree, Pauline "was not a snob," said Mrs. Willis. "She could talk to anyone." And she never wasted an opportunity to highlight WONPR's goal to be inclusive. When a wealthy Philadelphia socialite, Mrs. George Strawbridge, publicly asked Main Line hostesses to ban cocktails at their parties to set an example for ordinary Americans, Pauline shot back, "I am amazed that Mrs. Strawbridge's grasp of the fundamentals of Prohibition is so slight that she believes this problem, which touches every household in America, can be solved by the agreement of a comparatively few people of social prominence to discontinue serving cocktails at social functions. I am afraid Mrs. Strawbridge overestimates the influence of so-called society upon the great masses of American people."

She chose as her righthand woman, however, her fellow aristocrat Ione Page Nicoll, with whom Pauline became very close. Ione was the mother of two sons and two daughters ranging in age from sixteen to three (at the time WONPR started) with her husband Courtlandt Nicoll, a lawyer and onetime state senator, who traced his roots in New York to 1664 and the state's first governor, Sir Richard Nicolls (the family later dropped the "s.")

Ione, which means "violet" in Greek, was known for her classic beauty and vivid coloring. When she made her debut in 1907, the *New York Times* called her "one of the most beautiful girls in society. Her hair is very dark and her eyes are so dark a blue as to often be taken for black. Her skin is a clear marble white, but with much color in the cheeks." Twenty-five years later, as she entered middle age, the *New York Daily News* was still calling Ione one of America's "prettiest spellbinders."

She also had an intellectual side nourished by studying Greek, religious history, the Bible, and the US Constitution, but her passion, like Pauline's, was politics. A shared experience of tragedy also drew them together. In March 1920, a few months before Pauline lost her baby, Ione's beloved younger sister Lily was killed in a horseback riding accident, leaving behind a husband and two small children. Ione was devastated, but threw herself into a full schedule of activities to distract herself from grief. Dressed in all black, as required of a society woman in mourning, she presided as president of the Woman's National Republican Club (the same post Pauline had once held) and served as campaign secretary for financier Ogden L. Mills in his successful bid for a seat in the US House for the Seventeenth District in New York.

Ione didn't hesitate when Pauline asked her to be her deputy and chair of WONPR's New York branch. It became "the most interesting thing I've ever done," recalled Ione, who immediately resigned from the Woman's National Republican Club to show her commitment to WONPR's nonpartisan agenda. The job combined "everything" she loved—the intellectual, the political, the moral, "one's knowledge of people."

When Pauline wasn't available, she relied on Ione, who was a gifted speaker with "a concise quality of mind," as Grace Root noted,

Ione Nicoll, Pauline Sabin's WONPR deputy, whom the *New York Times* called "one of the prettiest spellbinders" in New York society. Courtesy of Katrina Wagner, granddaughter of Ione Nicoll.

to deliver WONPR's message in town halls and at rallies, and to talk to the press. Unlike Pauline—for whom "it was her way or not at all," Mrs. Willis said—Ione had a flexible personality. She provided "a restraining hand" on Pauline's dictatorial tendencies. "There was never a problem that they did not meet and work out side by side," wrote Root.

Throughout the summer of 1929, Ione and Pauline worked in two small rooms in the WONPR office on East Fortieth Street, later moving to larger quarters at 485 Madison Avenue. Pauline's independently wealthy friends signed on to help, all toiling without pay, as no one except a small clerical staff received a salary. Two volunteer publicists scoured newspapers from around the nation and clipped every mention of Prohibition and Repeal, which they added to the towers of newsprint on their desks. They also produced a mountain of gear emblazoned with Repeal slogans: motor plates, scarves, neckties, cigarettes, matches, and playing cards, which they sold from a shop in their headquarters and at a special concession booth set up at Bergdorf Goodman. One visitor to WONPR headquarters found the intense, urgent atmosphere reminiscent of "the old suffrage days," with women hard at work at desks, chairs strewn about, and the door open to encourage passersby to enter and learn about their crusade.

It took Pauline a remarkably short amount of time to get WONPR up and running. Following the basic business plan of the Red Cross, but sharpening it to perfection, Pauline identified and sought out the top women leaders in every state, who formed local chapters. In less than two months, she had set up a national advisory council of 121 women representatives in twenty-six states, a speaker's bureau to train women to speak at meetings and hearings and to lobby politicians, and a group of recruiters to sign up troops across the nation. Among WONPR's most famous recruits was celebrity author Emily Post, whose smash 1922 guide to manners, *Etiquette in Society, in Business, in Politics and at Home*, ignored Prohibition while bossily instructing hostesses on the correct questions to pose before filling a dinner guest's goblet with wine: "Cider, Sir?" "Champagne?" Or "Do you care for a whiskey and soda?" Another early WONPR member, Georgia Madden, wrote stirring articles and books about social justice under the pen name George Madden Martin. She had been one of the first women writers to protest against the Dry lobby as early as 1901 when the canteens at army posts were abolished. A Democrat from Kentucky, Madden also opposed racial oppression and had a leadership role in the Association of Southern Women for the Prevention of Lynching.

These popular women of achievement gave WONPR an aura of relevance and helped attract members. Writers were particularly prized by Pauline for their communication skills. After Adria Locke Langley—a single mother from Schuyler, New York—published an article in her local newspaper about the work women were doing to combat corruption among politicians, one of Pauline's associates contacted her. Langley immediately signed on and became one of WONPR's most active organizers. A powerhouse of enterprise and energy, Langley supported herself and her daughter with a series of odd jobs, including as a traveling saleswoman, a riveter, a social worker, a teacher, and a freelance journalist, and coined the phrase "cocoanut congressmen" to refer to hypocritical politicians who were "dry on the outside, but wet on the inside." After World War II, Langley would publish a best-selling novel based on the life of Louisiana politician Huey Long, *A Lion in the Streets*. As Langley explained, "the story shows how dictators rise on the feelings of the common people and fall when the honesty inherent in democracy catches up with them." A *New York Post* article gave Langley credit for personally signing up 200,000 new WONPR members, an unverifiable, no doubt wildly exaggerated number. Still, Langley did show uncommon zeal in recruiting and often found herself in perilous situations. While canvassing in Cooperstown, New York, where Dry sentiments were high, an angry citizen shot at her car as she drove away, smashing the windshield. Later, the local police handcuffed her and locked her in jail on the trumped-up charge that she was spreading communist propaganda.

Pioneering investigative journalist Ida Tarbell, the most famous female "muckraker" of the day, also supported WONPR, though she is not mentioned in Grace Root's history of the organization. Pauline might have wanted to distance herself from Tarbell, whose widely read 1929 pamphlet *Is Prohibition Forcing Civil War?* suggested that the divisiveness set off by Prohibition could plunge the nation in another war between the states. Tarbell warned of extremists on both sides "who were like dangerous animals running loose in the country, the type of disagreeing fanatics who harden one another's heads and heat one another's tempers until restraint is out of the question. Get enough of them and you have a war. That is what happened in 1861." Tarbell's solution in the interest of "temperance, order, and peace" was a modification of the law, "one giving us, let us say, light wines and beers, but forbidding hard liquor."

For Pauline, however, the only answer was complete and total Repeal.

She kept close tabs on the activities of the state chapters, and whenever a new one formed, she or Ione would travel to speak at the opening meeting. In some chapters, two WONPR leaders would be chosen—one Democrat and one Republican to recruit women from both parties. In other places, special organizations were established for particular ethnic groups, including Greeks, Russians, Rumanians, Ukrainians, and Poles. In Arizona, WONPR sponsored radio talks in both English and Spanish. In Delaware, a large number of women were recruited through a shop that was open daily for one month that served as a center of information and education and provided talks by prominent citizens. New York and Missouri held free classes in public speaking to train members to give Repeal talks. In Rhode Island, which showed a 200 percent increase in membership in one year (from 1930 to 1931), Pauline's troops cultivated new members by recruiting the managers in establishments that employed large numbers of women, including hotels, private clubs, factories, cleaning and dyeing works, and department stores. The Tennessee WONPR chapter maintained a weekly Repeal column in six newspapers and even helped start a Wet paper in Nashville.

Pauline also enlisted Black women to canvass in their communities and organize separate Black WONPR chapters. The record of WONPR membership and activities among Black women is sparse. The Delaware branch, one of the few states for which even sketchy information is known, claimed support from "the better class of colored people," who were also "church leaders." The Black clergy still supported Prohibition, as did many Black intellectuals. But some Black female activists rejected the clergy's stance on Prohibition and supported Repeal. Pauline A. Young and her aunt Alice Dunbar Nelson were perhaps typical of the fiercely independent Black women who joined WONPR. Young and Nelson were two of the most prominent Black women in Delaware. Young had been born in Medford, Massachusetts, but moved with her mother, two sisters, and brother to Wilmington, Delaware, after her father, a successful caterer, died when she was two. The family lived with her maternal grandmother, a formerly enslaved seamstress, and her widowed Aunt Alice, a poet, journalist, and activist who was between marriages at the time. "I had three mothers, all widows," Young later recalled in an oral history. Her mother and aunt taught at the all-Black Howard K–12 school that Young attended with her siblings and children who'd been bused in from locales as far away as Dover, Pennsylvania. "It was forced busing," Young said, one of the myriad Jim Crow injustices that constricted Black lives. "About the only public places in town open to us were the library and railway station," she recalled. From a young age, Young was "race conscious and militant about it."

Young's aunt had connections among the nation's Black elites and Black dignitaries, such as W. E. B. Du Bois and activist leader and writer James Weldon Johnson, who were barred from the local hotels, stayed at her home whenever they were in town. These men reinforced the sense of courage her family had inspired in her to stand up for her rights. When she'd wandered into St. Andrew's Church as a child and was told to move from the sanctuary to the gallery, the only place Black people were allowed, she went home and never returned. Soon afterward, at age twelve, she attended her first NAACP meeting and worked beside her aunt to register Black people to vote. Later, in Newport News, Virginia, where she briefly taught school, she protested at a Ku Klux Klan parade on Main Street, and once was thrown off a city bus for refusing to give up her seat to a White man. Denied admission to the University of Delaware because of her race, Young commuted every day to the University of Pennsylvania, where she was the only Black student in the School of Education. "I was running for trains all the time, on the [Wilmington] end and the Philadelphia end," she recalled. She returned to Wilmington to teach at Howard and, after earning a degree in library science, organized and ran the school's library for twenty years.

IT'S IMPOSSIBLE TO KNOW how many Black women joined WONPR, as the organization's national membership records have not survived. Pauline never commented on the number of minority women among her troops, but one thing was clear—she had amassed a large army from across the country and every sector of society. Pauline's powerful message drew women from all ethnicities, classes, political parties, and regions of the nation. Women suffragists who'd broken windows and gone to jail to fight for their right to vote and anti-suffragists who'd opposed the Nineteenth Amendment because they were frightened of change, including James Wadsworth's wife, Alice; women who'd driven ambulances on the European front during the Great War, and housewives who'd stayed home to raise children; rural farm women, factory workers, urban immigrants, shopgirls, students. "The women I represent come from every walk of life. They are home women, professional women, business women . . . women engaged in the arts, teachers, social workers . . . waitresses, hairdressers, clerks, women engaged in industry," Pauline said in a speech in Chicago. "There is I think no occupation to which women are admitted in this country that is not included in our membership." In the twelve years since suffrage, she added, "Our political affiliations [have been] as diverse as our vocations. We have been Democrats, Republicans and Socialists, but for the purpose of this crusade we are none of those things. We are repealists!"

Pauline was known for her quick mind and instinct to go for the jugular, and also her ability to do several things at once, to confer with a visiting WONPR state chair from California, say, while perusing a letter from a senator and telephoning a newspaper editor in

Chicago. She knew how government worked and had connections that reached to the Oval Office. More than anything she loved the game of politics. She hurried through the corridors of Congress, high heels clicking on marble floors, and sat in senators' offices, a slender rose of a woman in a tweed suit by Worth and a cap of strawberry-blonde curls, impressing everyone with her elegance, her wit, and her devastating intelligence. "Like a flash," she would grasp the political significance of every move made by the Wets and every trap laid by the Drys, Grace Root noted.

Repeal, Pauline insisted, was the most important issue to face the nation since the Civil War, the key to improved life for all Americans. Repeal meant the end to gangsters, youth-corrupting, crime-breeding speakeasies, poisonous illegal liquor, and incompetent Prohibition agents, who were hardly untouchable. It meant the return of licensed bars forbidden to minors, well-paying jobs in the beer and liquor industry, and millions of dollars in renewed liquor taxes to fund crucial civic institutions, from schools and fire departments to highways and libraries.

Pauline wrote articles and gave speeches from train platforms, in church basements, in town halls, and in university auditoriums. Once, she visited thirty-two cities in two weeks, Despite the grueling schedule, she felt exhilarated by public speaking. "I am human enough to frankly admit it is sort of fun when people clap when you start and don't hiss before you finish," she wrote in her diary with characteristic understatement. She loved helping shy people overcome their fears of public speaking and gave trembling women stepping to the podium for the first time her favorite trick for feeling confident in front of a crowd: imagine that everyone in the audience is naked. She felt certain this technique would work to relax even the most skittish college girl, office worker, or housewife. "Honestly, didn't you enjoy it when you got going?" Pauline often would say to women after their talks.

She also warned them not to talk over the heads of their audiences, perhaps imparting the advice Teddy Roosevelt once gave her father, "Never forget that 70% of every audience has the mentality of a child." WONPR volunteers trained and coached by Pauline gave speeches before labor unions for waitresses and laundry workers and, in California, the Native Daughters of the Golden West. They spoke before the National Association of Women Painters and Sculptors, the Women's Medical Association, the Nurses' Association, the League of Catholic Women, and Gold Star mothers. They also canvassed door to door in cities, villages, and towns. They set up booths at horse shows, flower shows, and county fairs, often opposite WCTU booths. In Kentucky, one volunteer reported that the WCTU had very little success wooing people away from the WONPR booth because "our women were more amiable and laughed with the crowd instead of preaching to them." Whenever permission to open a booth was denied to WONPR by Dry fair organizers, the women just moved to the lobbies of nearby hotels.

The bolder WONPR members crashed WCTU meetings wearing white buttons emblazoned with "Repeal" in bold black in the same place over their hearts where WCTU members pinned their white ribbons. Ella accused them of trying to steal her women. In October 1929, the WCTU claimed a membership of "nearly 600,000," but the truth was that defections from the organization were happening in response to a national anti-Prohibition trend. To compensate for their loss of members, rumor had it, the WCTU was padding its rolls by conscripting elementary schoolchildren. The WCTU's thinning ranks were especially severe in the South. The Georgia-based head of the WCTU's evangelical department concluded in 1929 that the organization had paid a heavy price in southern states for its support of Hoover and the Republican Party in the 1928 election. Some branches had lost from two to sixty-five members, while others had been totally wiped out.

But the worst blow to WCTU finances, as to those of the nation, came on "Black Thursday," October 24, when a tsunami of selling orders bombarded the New York Stock Exchange and hurled the Dow Jones Industrial Average into free fall. Though the WCTU did

Four Sabines in 1931, part of "the most vigorous element"
of American womanhood who were making their suffrage
count. Library of Congress, Prints & Photographs Division,
photograph by Harris & Ewing, LC-DIG-hec-36339.

not have money in the stock market, the crash and ensuing Depression, the "whole economic mess," as *Vanity Fair* put it, "cut into the funds of the Goodly. The country churches no longer plunk their pennies at the pleading of Mrs. Ella Boole." No one any longer believed "that Prohibition is the secret of our Prosperity when they see that we still have Prohibition," although "Prosperity" had been "mislaid."

Meantime, WONPR seemed unfazed by the crash. The *Union Signal* frequently questioned the source of the organization's funding, especially as it appeared to thrive as the rest of the nation fell to pieces. Jesse W. Nicholson, chair of the National Women's Democratic Law Enforcement League, insisted that WONPR could not be run on donations from ordinary citizens, as Pauline claimed, that it was the wealthy husbands of a handful of society women who paid the organization's bills. "I know there are not enough women throughout the nation who want booze returned who are willing to finance so huge an undertaking," especially during a Depression, she wrote. There's little doubt that WONPR's wealthy members and their husbands were its chief backers. These one percenters had managed to hold on to their fortunes through shrewd investments and serendipitous timing. Consequently, WONPR never had trouble paying for its publicity juggernaut: the slick brochures, which they distributed outside schools, factories, department stores, beauty parlors, train stations, country clubs, and hospitals; the planes that buzzed farms and villages, dropping Repeal brochures; and the shiny roadsters fixed with loudspeakers that swept down Main Streets across America through which they blared Repeal bulletins. During elections, Pauline also hired skywriting planes to trail her message to VOTE REPEAL high above the earth, as if God himself was a Wet.

Pauline also used radio extensively and aggressively. In the boom twenties, the growth of a new consumer economy and mass credit had led to a buying frenzy of radios, and by the end of the decade, twelve million American families owned the boxy consoles that cost between $35 and $200 each. The price plummeted during the Depression to about $10, and many people—even those living on the edge of poverty who'd given up their vacuum cleaners, dining room sets, and cars—held on to their radios. Gathering around the wireless in the evening to listen to the news, music, or a scripted drama crackling through a mesh speaker became a daily ritual for many Americans. Pauline exploited this habit, airing four-minute radio spots twice a day in some locales, using female speakers in the morning to target women and male speakers in the evening to target men.

To get the facts regarding conditions under Prohibition, WONPR organized and funded several major studies. One study canvassed the opinions of workingmen's wives across the nation to discover if the Eighteenth Amendment had had a positive effect on their lives. In most communities, there were many more speakeasies than there had ever been saloons and thus more opportunity for their husbands to drink and become inebriated. Another study surveyed high school teachers and university presidents on the drinking habits of students, confirming Pauline's conviction "that young America is drinking far more than ever before," Pauline noted.

Years later, when a young PhD candidate in history sought to explain how WONPR paid for all this, Pauline refused to show him the group's financial records. "It's none of your business, and anyway, it's of no interest to the public," she told him tartly.

FOURTEEN

THE FAMOUS AND THE FALLEN

A LMOST OVERNIGHT, PAULINE SABIN became as much of an It Girl as the Hollywood star Clara Bow, whose strange magnetism drew both men and women. Every speech and interview Pauline gave, every parade and protest she organized, every debate she engaged in was covered widely in the press. Movietone cameras whirred and caught her lilting voice. Her hair gleamed and her eyes glowed, giving her words an irresistible allure. In quoting one of Pauline's attacks on Prohibition, the *Chicago Tribune* explained, "These vehement words were spoken not by the old fashion type of platform termagant, but by a lady sitting in her beautifully appointed drawing room—rare books, good pictures and rich tapestries all around her. They were spoken by a woman who might with clear conscience be playing around at Miami Beach or on the Riviera, instead of directing 15 secretaries, planning nation-wide campaigns, answering bundles of letters and speaking twice a week at public meetings."

Pauline's beauty, charisma, and stylishness, especially when contrasted in photographs and newsreels to dowdy, elderly Ella Boole, gave her movement a decided edge that was reinforced by laudatory coverage in the women's magazines *Vogue*, *Harper's Bazaar*, *McCall's*, and *Ladies' Home Journal*. These publications, which had

huge readerships, portrayed Pauline's followers as beguiling, youth-
ful, and smart, and helped make support for Repeal a key element
of identity for a woman who wanted to appear modern and au cou-
rant. Pauline played the glamour card whenever she could, posing
in a couture evening gown for *Vogue* and sending her prettiest lieutenants to vamp the driest politicians. The press dubbed these fetching women "the Sabines." "Young, pretty and intelligent, they do not
want anything selfish," wrote *Vanity Fair*. Nor "are they trying to
take the joy out of anybody's life. . . . They merely want Congress to
correct a nauseating abuse of political authority and they have done
more in two years to make Repeal possible than the men of America
have done in a decade." Supporting Repeal became as fashionable as
hot jazz, bobbed hair, Ford Roadsters, and the Charleston. But much
more than trendiness was at play here. Pauline made Prohibition *the*
women's issue of the late 1920s. The Sabines were part of the most
"vigorous element" of American women "who had learned to reason
for themselves and had thus taken the first step in making their suffrage mean true government," Grace Root wrote. The press covered
the Sabines obsessively. More than five hundred newspapers across
America wrote about the group's launch in May 1929, and from there
the attention escalated.

Ella read the stories about Pauline and her new organization in
the New York papers and scoffed. She wouldn't waver in her conviction that "women will not desert *their* issue." Prohibition was essential to her own identity as a reformer and as a woman who was morally superior to men. In spite of the evidence screaming around her,
she clung to the idea that most American women felt the same way.
To believe otherwise would mean she'd lost faith that women spoke
as one voice on the era's definitive moral issue. At the same time,
Ella feared the defection of her sisters to Pauline's side. What was
at stake was much more than the return of the liquor trade and the
saloon. She believed Repeal threatened the very status of women
in the public sphere—most importantly, the political power they'd
been building since suffrage. What Ella dreaded above all, as the

A group of Sabines and their male supporters in August 1932 toward
the end of a nationwide bus tour in search of alcoholics who'd been
reformed by Prohibition. Courtesy of the Hagley Museum and Library.

historian Catherine Gilbert Murdock put it, was "permanent masculine hegemony."

Before Pauline's group emerged, Ella had not worried too much
about the various women's anti-Prohibition organizations that had
previously risen and faded. Among the most significant had been the
Molly Pitcher Club, a New York–based auxiliary of the AAPA. Named
after the Revolutionary War heroine who carried water to men on
the battlefield, the club never attracted a large membership, owing
at least in part to the abrasive personality and extreme libertarian-
ism of its leader, M. Louise Gross. She had grown up in a working-
class family in White Plains, New York, and attended Fordham Law
School. After working as a clerk in a White Plains law firm, Gross
became secretary to New York City Tammany Hall district leader

Thomas F. Foley, a close associate of New York Governor Al Smith. Gross boasted to reporters that she violated the Eighteenth Amendment whenever she got the chance, adding that she also had no objection to the use of opium, though whether she indulged herself, she didn't say. As head of the Molly Pitcher Club, she had led a contingent of 120 women to Albany in 1923 to urge Smith to repeal the Mullan-Gage Act, the state Prohibition enforcement measure, which he eventually did. After this, the group petered out, but it was resurrected a couple of years later as the Women's Committee for the Modification of the Volstead Act, and then renamed the Women's Committee for the Repeal of the Eighteenth Amendment. At the same time, as Catherine Gilbert Murdock noted in *Domesticating Drink*, Gross ran another women's Repeal group, the Women's Moderation Union (WMU), whose very immoderate slogan "Repeal or Rebellion" seemed intended to offend nearly everyone.

As head of the WMU, Gross asked Pauline in March 1929 to serve on one of the organization's committees, and Pauline declined. Not satisfied, Gross wrote to Pierre S. du Pont, head of the Association Against the Prohibition Amendment, asking him to prevail on Pauline's husband Charlie, the AAPA's titular treasurer, to convince Pauline to join the WMU. Gross told du Pont she was even willing to give up the leadership if only Pauline would come on board. But du Pont refused to intervene. Pauline's snub enraged Gross. "She will do our Cause more harm than good if she doesn't come in with us for a while, at least," Gross wrote her secretary, Mrs. David Holmes Morton. "I cannot imagine a woman politician playing such stupid politics, she ought to [know] better than to try and disrupt existing organizations and make trouble, that isn't the way to win a Cause, and she's not going to get very far with such tactics." Gross instructed Mrs. Morton not to "mention anything about Mrs. Sabin or her organization as we don't want to give her any extra publicity or be drawn into any controversy with her."

Of course, it was Pauline, not Gross, who knew how to play smart politics and win a *cause*. She understood, as Kenneth D. Rose wrote, "that the power of a political organization is dependent both upon its ability to articulate the beliefs and concerns of a wide cross section of the population and upon a complementary vagueness as to specifics. Sabin was able to retain a large constituency by stressing ideas that were common to all." In her myriad speeches, Pauline emphasized that the most serious threat to women, children, and the family was not liquor; it was Prohibition, thus turning Ella's "home protection" arguments on their head. Pauline often spoke about "true temperance" based on each individual's decision not to drink to excess, as opposed to temperance forced on people by the "fanatic" who has "been behind every invasion of personal liberty in America's past." Pauline believed that "whether my boys drank or not was my responsibility" and should not be turned over to the government.

She also emphasized that Prohibition was the foe of *true* temperance because it resulted in the breakdown of society to the point of national crisis. As Ione Nicoll noted, "Not since the Civil War have the American people been faced by so great a problem." Crime had become so rampant throughout the nation, as Ida Tarbell wrote, there were weeks when the day's news read like reports from a war zone.

"I know of nothing since the days of the campaign for women's suffrage to equal the campaign which women are now conducting for repeal of the Eighteenth Amendment," Pauline told the *New York Times*. "It is a crusade and it can only be explained by the fact that women throughout the country feel that their children and their homes are endangered by the evils of Prohibition." Pauline knew that anything certain and unbending can be subverted and broken. A chief vulnerability of the Drys lay in the rigidity of the movement's leaders, particularly Ella. Especially damaging to Ella's position was the Protestant religiosity of her message. She hadn't deviated from the nineteenth-century evangelical rhetoric employed by the WCTU president Frances Willard, a language of piety that was at sharp odds with Jazz Age values. WONPR charged that WCTU women were puppets of the evangelical churches. As evidence, one WCTU defector to Pauline's troops claimed that women in Harrington, Delaware, were "blindly swayed" by whatever the two Methodist ministers in the county told them to do. Other Delaware WONPR members claimed that in some rural areas of the state, Methodist church groups threatened to boycott Wet storekeepers and business owners.

MABEL WALKER WILLEBRANDT also found herself at odds with the cultural climate of the 1920s, which was growing increasingly anti-Prohibition by the day. She couldn't wait to be released from her duties trying to enforce a law most adults loathed, but her future remained uncertain. "Probably the most interesting single appointive problem with which Mr. Hoover will have to deal is presented by that sugary and soulful lady Mrs. Walker Willebrandt," wrote columnist Frank Kent in the *Baltimore Sun*. Easing Mabel's anxiety over whether the president would give her a plum job in his administration was the knowledge that she still had many friends and supporters in Washington. A reminder of this came early in February, when she attended the last dinner of the subcabinet members of Coolidge's administration, which included twenty-seven male undersecretaries and assistants—and Mabel. The men paid her "the loveliest tributes," she told her parents. At the end of the evening, a man from the Treasury who oversaw department budgets, drove her home and sat for a while with her by the fire in her living room. He promised to "get back not only the rest of my raises [and] all the new appointments I needed (from some devious swiping from another appropriation)." It's unknown if he was successful.

Adding to Mabel's troubles was her fraught personal life, which continued to cause her deep pain. In December, she had taken Dorothy to California to spend Christmas with her parents, whom she relied on to help mold Dorothy's character, "as I am with her so little except on these trips," she lamented. After the New Year, she returned to Washington alone, leaving the little girl in the care of the Walkers. "Won't you try to get Dorothy to stand on two feet straightly and be simple and direct?" she implored her parents. "Talk to her as you would to a grown up. Please write to me your estimate of her mental life . . . and what you think she needs and what promising features appear which I should foster. It will help me so much if you would both do that. . . . I'm not with her enough . . . to get what's going on in the development of her little consciousness."

During the previous year, Mabel had tried to arrange things to give Dorothy a more normal family life. That included adopting another child to provide Dorothy with a sibling and once again reconsidering marriage to Fred Horowitz, though she had firmly turned him down in 1925. The child who came into her home in the fall of 1928 was a boy she wanted to name after Fred. She loved Fred's Hebrew moniker, Efraim (which she misspelled as "Frayim"), and planned to give it to "their" son. Though the circumstances are murky and only alluded to in a letter to her parents, Mabel apparently realized quickly that she couldn't cope with a second child and soon gave up the boy, who was called "John" when he came to live with her. "It's taken every ounce I had to keep 'chin up' during the day this year—at night even during the campaigns last summer," she confessed to her parents. "Not since November all I could do was to crumple at the day[']s end and grieve for little John—I think he was intended for me. In view of the internal wreck I was, giving him up was all I could do for his sake, but his loss is grievous and continuously and just symbolizes the whole devastating year."

While on the West Coast with Dorothy during the Christmas holiday, she had spent time with Fred, who had begun to see another woman, Luella Rykoff. Still, the Walkers had not abandoned hope that Mabel and Fred would marry. They constantly talked up Fred and suggested that his attentions to Luella were due to Mabel's earlier rejection of him. In a letter to his daughter, David Walker bemoaned Mabel's treatment of her old friend. "Do you realize how many times you have slighted or even snubbed his attentions?" he asked her. Fred regularly made the long trek to and from Los Angeles to see Mabel in Washington and sometimes to transport Dorothy to the West Coast to visit her grandparents. "In the press of business or your habitual mad rush from one angle to another you may not have realized your apparent indifference or slight" of him during the times "when he had come all the way to Washington" to be with her.

Myrtle also complained that some of Mabel's California friends, including Winnie Ellis, had urged Fred to marry Luella, since, unlike Mabel, she was Jewish. Another friend, a woman identified in letters only as "Vic," continually harped to Fred that it "would be unwise for a Jew to marry one not a Jew," Myrtle told her daughter. Myrtle added that Vic "thinks you'd be more than foolish" to marry Fred "because of the religious difference." But to Myrtle all that counted was Fred's devotion. "Mabel, if you could see his face light up as I have when he is near you, you could not doubt his love. He has never loved anyone but you and is a marvel to me for his constancy all these years. Don't let anything Winnie says influence you and pay no attention to Vic."

Myrtle suggested that Mabel could erase the traumas of her Washington years, including the bad press she received during the recent presidential campaign, by marrying Fred and taking his name. As "Mrs. Horowitz" she could shed all associations with "Mrs. Willebrandt," who by 1929, because of her controversial behavior during the 1928 presidential campaign, had become "the most notorious woman in America," in the words of syndicated columnist Frank Kent. Fred traveled to Washington in March to be Mabel's date at Hoover's inauguration. Unbeknownst to Mabel, his brief betrothal to Luella Rykoff had been announced in the *Los Angeles Times* three months earlier on November 11. It appeared in small type, buried on a long gray page with myriad other engagement, wedding, and birth announcements and had gone unnoticed by Mabel's family and friends. The engagement was short-lived, however; Luella broke it off when a friend introduced her to Samuel H. Maslon, a Harvard-educated former clerk of US Supreme Court Justice Louis Brandeis and the founding partner of a large Minneapolis law firm. Luella married Maslon on February 11, 1929. Fred had not bothered to tell Mabel any of this before he traveled to Washington.

Perhaps he wanted to spare Mabel unnecessary anguish. Perhaps because the engagement was so brief, he didn't think it counted. But when Mabel found out, she felt profoundly betrayed. She never again considered marriage to Fred. As she explained to her father, "Papa dear, you may say that I have treated Fred unfairly and I know it's true in a thousand ways, . . . [but] how can he, to me, withhold the truth? Last fall I wired him over and over about John and about naming him for Fred—'John Frayim'—and Fred answered all these wires—he knew what they meant—he signed himself 'lovingly' and never gave me an inkling of his infatuation for and being constantly with the girl he was about to marry. How could he withhold the information from me?" It seemed not to have occurred to Mabel that Fred might finally have grown tired of waiting for her to make up her mind.

MABEL KNEW THAT ALTHOUGH the forces of the Drys, including Ella Boole and the WCTU, backed her for Hoover's attorney general, she was a long shot for the job after her missteps in the recent presidential campaign. Hoover had asked her for her opinion of several candidates he was considering and Mabel outlined the characteristics she thought Hoover should look for in the nation's top lawyer. They were mostly qualities she herself abundantly possessed: The attorney general must be a "doer who could inspire faith, an executive with the ability to put morale into indifferent men." He or she must also be politically astute, experienced in political tactics, and be ready to "wrestle with political influence" in the DOJ and the US attorneys' offices throughout the nation. She also advised Hoover not to select an attorney general of "powerful personal ambitions." A "lesser legal light of unquestioned and unselfish loyalty" would be much safer. Perhaps that was a reference to her own extreme loyalty to Hoover in the campaign that got him elected, though her own "powerful personal ambition" had led her to overreach in ways that were now embarrassing to the new president.

Whatever hopes Mabel had that she'd become America's first female attorney general were crushed when she answered the phone at home on the evening of February 22 and immediately recognized the voice of the president-elect on the other end. "Anyone on the line?" he asked in his typically curt diction.

"It's clear," said Mabel.

Hoover apologized for calling instead of inviting Mabel to his home, but said he thought an in-person meeting might lead to gossip about the reason they were conferring. Then he dropped a bombshell. "I just wanted to tell you that the new attorney general is a friend of yours."

Mabel's heart sank. She didn't get the job. Hoover's choice was Solicitor General William D. Mitchell, whom she had sparred with occasionally on government policies and was hardly a friend. "A Democrat, neither Wet nor Dry, he was supported by Chief Justice Taft and Senator Borah," as Dorothy Brown wrote. "Dean Roscoe Pound of Harvard called him the best fitted candidate to be appointed to the post in thirty years. Clearly, Hoover had opted to remove the prohibition controversy from the Justice Department with this above-reproach appointment." Hoover assured Mabel that he and Mitchell wanted her to stay on "at least for a while. It will be best for you. You deserve the recognition it will mean and the work deserves it and needs you." Mabel tried to keep her voice level to hide her anger and hurt. She'd "stay a while," she said calmly. After the phone call, she vented her roiling emotions in a letter to her parents. "It goes to prove the thing I have feared, and my instinct has told me long ago— that fundamentally he doesn't feel on a level with women nor deal with them as men. The real truth is that he needs to have me stay for a while, but instead of saying so frankly he put it that *I* needed it—as tho he were doing me a great favor."

Mabel knew there was no point in getting "in such a furor of mind" over the rejection, but she couldn't imagine how she would get through the next few months. She felt defeated and in despair. To make matters worse, she immediately angered her new boss—who held the job *she* should have had—when the *Chicago Tribune* broke a story that Mabel had planted spies in federal prisons to get evidence on bootlegging operations. Mabel hadn't bothered to tell Mitchell about the spies, perhaps getting a petty satisfaction in ignoring his authority. As soon as he found out, however, Mitchell ordered all undercover agents to exit the nation's penitentiaries. Meanwhile, other public officials roundly condemned the practice, generating more negative publicity for Mabel. "Any plan which draws the courts, or the officers of the courts, into a scheme for issuing fake or fraudulent processes or commitments, is essentially vicious," said Senator William Borah of Idaho, echoing the sentiments of many of his colleagues in Congress. But that wasn't the end of it. The *Philadelphia Sunday Transcript* followed up with a story that Mabel had also overreached by employing female undercover agents in brothels and on the Montrealer, the train between Montreal and New York, to seize illegal liquor from citizens who were only drinking bootleg, not selling it.

Mitchell had further reason to be dissatisfied with his assistant attorney general that spring. In what should have been a prosecutorial triumph, Mabel also failed to put Texas Guinan behind bars.

FIFTEEN

TEX ON TRIAL

A T 9:30 IN THE MORNING on April 9, 1929, Texas Guinan's dark gray Excelsior slowed to a crawl as it approached a raucous crowd gathered outside Manhattan's federal courthouse at 40 Foley Square, where her trial on public nuisance charges was about to start in room 331. Tex's fans had been waiting for hours in the balmy blue morning for a glimpse of the notorious hostess, whose latest film, *Queen of the Nightclubs*, was playing in a movie palace uptown. After the Salon Royale was padlocked the previous June, Tex had traveled to Hollywood to film the talkie, her first. The *New York Times* critic had tepidly praised the movie as "a somewhat entertaining thriller" with a murder, "which *must* happen in every night club on the screen." Tex's trial promised to be more exciting.

The reliably conservative jurist Edwin S. Thomas, whom Mabel had imported "from the serenity of Connecticut," as Tex's manager put it, to replace a Wet Tammany judge, had not yet appeared on the bench, when Tex entered the courtroom dressed way past the nines in clouds of black satin and velvet, her cheeks heavily rouged, her eyes rimmed in kohl, and her piled-on diamond bracelets and rings causing "a temporary eclipse of the sun," one reporter joked. "All rise!" shouted a wag in the far reaches of the gallery. The mostly male spectators jumped up clapping, as Tex, grinning broadly, pushed through the gate past the balding, tight-lipped prosecutor Norman J. Morrison, to join her lawyer Maxwell E. Lopin at the defense table. Tex had hired the young, inexperienced Lopin, a friend of her longtime attorney, after being turned down by Clarence Darrow and every other trial lawyer she'd approached about representing her. No one wanted the impossible task of defending Tex, because "the world knew she was guilty," wrote Louise Berliner, Tex's biographer and Lopin's granddaughter.

Win or lose, Lopin was eager to be associated with a high-profile client like Tex, who had no trouble manipulating Lopin. She ended up running the trial "pretty much as she pleased," Berliner noted. That meant turning it into a vaudeville show. Tex carried a lavender chiffon "snicker cloth" and held it ostentatiously to her face when federal agent John J. Mitchell testified that he patronized the Salon Royale twice because he "had to," but kept going back because he "wanted to." After seeing the floor show a couple of times, another agent, James L. White, said it became monotonous. He described witnessing a man who'd gotten "very, very drunk" carried out of the Salon Royale by two bouncers, as Tex, accompanied by the orchestra, sang, "Out the window you must go, you must go, you must go." Quipped Texas, according to White, "He is from Chicago. That is what he gets for bringing his own." The undercover agent testified that he also sometimes brought liquor with him to the club and when that ran out, he'd order more. He purchased champagne and whiskey on many nights, he said, paying $25 for a quart of champagne and $5 for a half pint of whiskey, which were delivered to his table in water pitchers. White, who posed as a businessman from Denver, said he liked Texas "very, very much" and admitted that he had once asked her to go out with him and his wife "to paint the town red." Tex testified that White had sent her orchids and other flowers five or six times. She also said he asked her once if he could take one of her girls out to other nightclubs.

At the lunch recess, White approached Tex as she sat on a bench in the corridor with her lawyer and spoke to her in a friendly tone.

"Tex Sends Her 'Love' to Mabel" in this Winsor McCay cartoon
that appeared in the *New York American* during Tex's 1929 trial.
The San Francisco Academy of Comic Art Collection, The Ohio
State University Billy Ireland Cartoon Library & Museum.

"I'm afraid you think me rather ungentlemanly, and in the patois of
your friends, may be calling me a 'rat,' but—"

Tex cut him off. "Oh no," she said, smiling viciously. "You are only
a little mouse studying to be a rat."

After lunch, a parade of witnesses testified that they were served
wine and champagne at the club. Still, Tex insisted on the witness
stand she didn't know anything about it. She told the truth, however,
about never touching the stuff herself. She also emphasized that she
didn't own the club, though, according to a Salon Royale accountant,
she received 50 percent of the profits, giving her a handsome income
from $6,000 to $12,000 a month. She was merely a hostess, albeit
an extremely well-paid one, who had broken no law.

The prosecutor questioned Tex about why nine of her waiters
had pled guilty if there was no liquor at the Salon Royale. Later, Tex

deadpanned to reporters, "Those people are all Greeks. They don't know what guilty means." Laughter often erupted among the spectators during Tex's testimony, causing a scowling Judge Thomas to pound his gavel. "This is not a show, but a trial!" he shouted. The reporters and spectators, though, treated it as entertainment, and they gave Tex raves for her "performance" on the stand. "I can't help admiring a person with such pleasant self-assurance," one woman said as she left the courtroom.

After two days of testimony, the jury deliberated for just fifty-five minutes and acquitted Tex on all charges. When the verdict was announced, the courtroom burst into loud whoops and cheers. A couple of Tex's supporters hoisted her onto their shoulders and carried her into the elevator and up two floors to the pressroom, where she posed for photographers and chatted with reporters, to whom she'd given colorful quotes throughout the trial. "Me a nuisance?" she'd said earlier in reference to one of the charges against her. "Mabel Walker Willebrandt is my idea of a large nuisance. My God! I'm just an entertainer. If things have got to pass where entertainers are nuisances, then why doesn't Mrs. Willebrandt close up Will Rogers and Eddie Cantor and a few more who are trying to brighten life up with jokes and smiles?"

Outside, Tex's fans had jammed the street in front of the courthouse. News of the verdict had rippled through the crowd, and when Tex appeared in the doorway beaming, more cheering rang out. As she made her way down the courthouse steps, she stopped from time to time to press her thumb into a little pad of ink she carried in her purse, then blotted her print on the photographs thrust toward her.

Judge Thomas had instructed the jury to return a guilty verdict if they found that Texas knew liquor was served at the Salon Royale. The very idea that a speakeasy hostess would be oblivious to the booze sloshing around her was ridiculous, of course, and the evidence against her was overwhelming. Still, the jury had ignored the judge, demonstrating its contempt for Prohibition. "The case became a sort of insurance policy for . . . victims of dry agents' zeal," John S.

Stein, Tex's manager and publicist, and Grace Hayward, an actress and playwright, wrote in an unpublished biography of Tex. "How any jury can have the [nerve] to convict a penny-ante bootlegger after Miss Guinan's acquittal, I can't see."

That evening her supporters feted Tex at a "Victory Ball" at her latest speak, Club Intime on West Fifty-Fourth Street in the heart of the Wet Way. The club sat in the basement of the twelve-story Harding Hotel, a mobster hive owned by Owney Madden. The actress Mae West, Madden's lover, lived upstairs, as did a gaggle of showgirls, boxers, playwrights, and gangsters, including Jack "Legs" Diamond, who kept a stash of guns in his room that he rented out from time to time to Madden's thugs. At Tex's party, confetti and paper streamers swirled through the air, raining down on the politicians, businessmen, actors, socialites, flappers, and pressmen who'd crowded the club to celebrate Tex's acquittal. Movie cameras set up against the back wall whirred and flashbulbs popped. When Tex arrived at midnight, the orchestra swung into "The Prisoner's Song," a 1924 hit that included the lyric "I'll be carried to the new jail tomorrow leaving my poor darling all alone." Revelers swarmed Tex, pulling off red sequins from her scarlet tulle and satin gown to keep as mementos.

Mabel had wanted to make an example of Tex, but the effort had backfired. The *Brooklyn Daily Eagle* blamed the prosecutor Morrison for allowing Tex to talk at length during cross-examination. He should have known that "if Miss Guinan is permitted to dominate the situation, she dominates it." Now, perched on an upright piano that had been wheeled into the middle of the tiny dance floor, Tex read telegrams from supporters, including one from Fiorello La Guardia, the Democratic congressman from New York. "Congratulations," the future mayor of the city messaged. "We all give the little girl a great big hand."

Tex's problems with the law, however, had not ended. The day after her victory party at Club Intime, New York Police Commissioner Grover Whalen told a gathering of the Church Laymen's Committee of the Greater New York Federation of Churches that Tex's trial was one of the most "disgusting pieces of publicity" he had ever seen and her acquittal an "affront to law and order." "You and I both know that Miss Guinan was guilty of the charges made against her," he added. Whalen also accused Tex of contributing to the moral degradation of the young girls in her employ, implying that she hired them out as prostitutes, which Tex insisted she never did.

Soon afterward, Whalen's men raided Club Intime. Tex, who might have been tipped off to the raid, had stayed home that night. The detectives arrested her manager for operating a cabaret without a license and, after discovering liquor on the premises, hauled two of the speak's waiters to the police station. They also slapped Club Intime with violations for dispensing food in unsanitary conditions and ignoring fire safety regulations, before evicting the speak from the hotel and posting a policeman at the door.

One day in late April, Tex showed up on West Fifty-Fourth Street to find the sidewalk in front of the Harding Hotel piled with draperies, chairs, tables, and a piano. Several employees were sitting on costume trunks nearby. To avoid further "persecution" from Whalen, Tex decided to forgo opening another Manhattan speak and spent the summer presiding at a club on Long Island. On many afternoons, she could be found on the beach sunbathing in a red velvet swimsuit that she never dared get wet.

After Tex's acquittal, Leslie Salter, one of the government prosecutors, hurried to Washington to consult with Mabel on whether to go ahead with Helen Morgan's trial. The case against Morgan was weaker than the one against Tex. Helen did not preside as hostess at the club that employed her, which was called the Summer Home, though everyone referred to it as "Helen Morgan's Summer Home." Rather, she earned $750 a week to sing. Mabel decided to proceed with the case. The trial started on April 15, in the middle of Morgan's Broadway run, starring in *Showboat* as Julie LaVerne, a mixed-race entertainer who is passing as White. In court, Helen sat at the defense table in a simple black silk dress and black cloche hat with a silver fox scarf draped across her shoulders and her lovely, pale face scrubbed clean. Bottles seized during the Summer Home raid sat on the prosecutor's table, eight silent, slender-necked witnesses. Lon Tyson of Dallas, who had posed as a wealthy westerner during the speakeasy investigation, testified that he and other undercover agents "had schemed and plotted to trap Miss Morgan before they had ever entered her club."

Two agents testified that they bought whiskey, brandy, and champagne at the Summer Home, and when the club ran out of liquor, Morgan—who in sharp contrast to Tex was known to be a heavy drinker—sent a waiter to her house to fetch reinforcements. Tyson also said he brought his wife to the speak because, as he explained, "We had to have a lady with us when we went into high class night clubs." Though she wasn't an accredited agent, Mrs. Tyson received five dollars a day for making the rounds with her husband. One night, after the Summer Home closed, the couple took Morgan to another speak, the Furnace Club, to continue their drunken partying. Morgan, now completely soused, Tyson said, sat on the bar throwing dollar bills at the Black entertainers.

In the end, however, the all-male jury (it would be many years before women were allowed to sit on federal juries) acquitted Morgan, as they had Tex. Mabel made no public comment on the trials of either woman.

SIXTEEN

◇

PRIVATE PRACTICE

MYRTLE WALKER THOUGHT HOOVER would try to keep Mabel in her job to placate "the WCTU and the church crowd who do not realize how you lack authority to enforce Prohibition properly," she wrote her daughter. Mabel knew she would have little influence on the president when he refused her suggestion to move the Prohibition Bureau from the Department of Treasury to the Justice Department, which she and Attorney General Mitchell believed would significantly improve enforcement. For one thing, the granting of permits for legitimate industrial uses of alcohol had been severely corrupted due to the Treasury's close ties with the nation's distilleries. At the same time, the American Medical Association, which before Prohibition said alcohol had no therapeutic benefit, announced in 1922 that a large and varied number of diseases could be "helped" with liquor, from cancer and diabetes to snakebites and old age.

A lucrative offer to become Washington counsel for the Aviation Corporation and a contract to write a series of syndicated newspaper articles on her tenure as the Prohibition czarina, which would be a chance to tell her version of events, led Mabel to do what she knew she must. On May 26, she sent Hoover her letter of resignation and asked to be relieved of her duties by June 15.

Mabel Walker Willebrandt promoting air travel
with Amelia Earhart in 1930.

Ida Koverman, no doubt echoing the sentiments of many of
Mabel's friends, told the *Los Angeles Times* she was glad Mabel was
leaving government because she "would be crucified" if Prohibition
was overturned, and "no matter which way it goes," she would be
excoriated for all the failures of the Eighteenth Amendment. By this

time, Koverman was working as Louis B. Mayer's executive secretary and "damn near ran the studio," as MGM executive Robert Vogel put it. She read scripts (pushing the best ones to the top of the pile on Mayer's desk), scouted for stars, and cast some of the studio's preeminent movies.

Hoover responded to Mabel's resignation by expressing his "indebtedness" on behalf of himself and the entire nation for her "distinguished" public service in one of the most "difficult" jobs in government. He invited her to the White House for a farewell dinner. When she arrived, she passed the ladies' primping station that Mrs. Coolidge had installed at the end of the long corridor in the reception area. Arranged on a dressing table were a variety of nostrums, including powder, cotton balls, and hairpins for those old-fashioned women like Mabel who'd yet to bob their hair. When Mabel glanced in the large mirror above the dressing table, she saw a face etched with exhaustion and fine lines from her incessant smoking. She had just turned forty but looked older. The dark purple circles under her eyes had deepened, and her body had thickened.

She had done her best against terrible odds—at least she had that satisfaction. Hoover was effusive in his praise of her to her face and to the press, but she knew he was glad to be rid of her. What she didn't know was that he'd never appoint a woman to replace her, though Woodrow Wilson had named a woman as assistant US attorney general in the last year of his presidency, starting a tradition that Harding continued with Mabel. As Hoover wrote to one of his assistants soon after Mabel's resignation, "It is not proposed again to put a woman in the position of having to deal with criminal elements, their supporters and the wet press throughout the United States. A woman may be appointed in the Department of Justice but for an entirely different position."

The WCTU grieved the loss of "indispensable" Mabel, who was to them "the Joan of Arc" of Prohibition, the very "heart of the cause." Ella Boole warned her troops not to believe stories in the papers that Hoover had fired her. "It is not surprising that having served seven years in this very difficult position . . . having stood misrepresentation and abuse, she has felt that she has made her contribution and deserves a rest," she wrote in the *Union Signal*. The Wet press, however, was overjoyed to see Mabel go and wasted no opportunity to publish negative stories about her. When she was arrested for speeding down K Street in DC one winter night after she'd left office, reporters rushed to cover her appearance at traffic court a few days later. Mabel managed to elude the crowd of pressmen and photographers who'd gathered on the courthouse steps by slipping in through a side door and waiting in the judge's chambers until the proceeding began. After the judge fined her $10, she slipped back out the side door.

Mabel loved owning a car, that Jazz Age symbol of prosperity which few could afford. Like a character out of F. Scott Fitzgerald, she drove her black Ford sedan astonishingly fast. It gave her a rush of adrenaline and appealed to her adventuresome side. As counsel to the Aviation Corporation, she relished the chance to pioneer aeronautical law, but she also thrilled at the opportunity to meet the era's star aviators, including Charles Lindbergh, Jacqueline Cochran, and Amelia Earhart. Cochran became a close friend, and she worked with Earhart to promote commercial air travel for the Aeronautical Chamber of Commerce. Earhart complained that she was sometimes mistaken for Mabel, though aside from being about the same height and just two years apart in age, the two women did not resemble one another—physically, that is. They both, however, radiated an aura of exceptional strength and determination, and perhaps that's why people confused them.

Louis B. Mayer hired Mabel to counsel MGM, paying her a yearly retainer fee of about $75,000 for her advice on federal regulations, taxes, and other legal issues that might come up at the studio. She also represented his stable of stars including Jean Harlow, Clark Gable, Judy Garland, Jeanette MacDonald, Mickey Rooney, and Joan Crawford. At the same time, Mabel began advising California Fruit Trust Industries Ltd., an organization of grape growers who marketed a panoply of grape products from juice and jellies to candy and cooking sauces. They also made a grape concentrate called Vine-Glo, which when mixed with water and yeast fermented into table wine. It distressed Mabel that grape growers in her beloved California had suffered mightily from drought and low sales owing to Volstead, for which, ironically, she was partly responsible. In 1927, while still assistant attorney general, Mabel had assured a lobbyist representing California vineyards that the concentrate was legal. Two years later, as the group's attorney in a deepening Depression, she helped win Fruit Industries several million dollars in loans from the Federal Farm Board that enabled them to start a home wine-making operation. The Wets rejoiced at the news and started referring to Vine-Glo as "Willebrandt wine." Pauline Sabin noted wryly that Mabel, "once the Joan of Arc of the drys," was now "their Charlotte Corday," a reference to the young woman who stabbed to death Jean-Paul Marat during the French Revolution. *Noble Experiments*, a cocktail recipe book, featured "The Mabel Fruit Punch" made of rum, applejack, and concentrated grape juice, while a story circulating in the press referred to an unnamed California pharmacist who advertised his stock of the concentrate on the front page of his local newspaper as "Mabel's Grape Bricks" for $1.50 each.

Pauline wasn't the only one who accused Mabel of selling out to work for the enemy. It didn't help Mabel's reputation that the most vociferous opponents of Vine-Glo were the bootleggers who feared homemade wine would cut into their profits—a sign to the Drys that Mabel was in the liquor business. At the top of the list was Al Capone, whose attorneys met with a group of California grape growers to develop a rival to Vine-Glo. They also let it be known they would resist all competition. Donald Conn, a top Fruit Industries executive, took that as a threat and hired bodyguards to protect him from Capone's goons.

The *Union Signal* stayed silent on the controversy. Mabel met with Ella Boole to assure her that the stories attacking her for competing with gangsters were unfair and distorted, and she insisted she remained as committed to Prohibition as ever. A WCTU member named Elise Giles, however, wrote to Mabel that the president of the Southern California WCTU was "very disappointed" in the former assistant attorney general. "What a pity it is that a brilliant woman is willing to sell herself for a mass of pottage—to further the work of Satan—for gold." Mabel shared the letter with her father, who, furious at the "ignorant criticism and unjustifiable abuse" that had been heaped on his daughter since she left government, vented in a response to Giles. "Mrs. Willebrandt has not sold out," David Walker wrote. "She has suffered much for being faithful to her trust when it was her duty to prosecute violators of the law. She is now a private citizen and has a perfect right to accept any legitimate clientele within the law. Eight years of faithful service to the public should be sacrifice enough, out of the prime of her life to guarantee her integrity." After all, Mabel had done what men have often done upon leaving public office—leveraging their government experience and connections to earn money. "Like all other honest public officials," David Walker lamented, Mabel "was able to save but little while serving the public, and now she is wholly dependent on her practice for a livelihood and the support of her parents and adopted daughter."

Also, she had lost money investing in an ambitious California real estate project of Fred Horowitz's—the building of the Chateau Marmont, a swank apartment building on Sunset Boulevard that Fred had modeled on a chateau he'd seen in the French countryside on a European trip. The Chateau Marmont, reportedly the first earthquake-proof building in Los Angeles, featured rich wood paneling, elaborate wrought-iron trim work, and luxurious baths with tiles imported from Italy. Nearly all the forty-three apartments at the Chateau had been rented, but when the stock market crashed, the wealthy tenants, having lost their fortunes, fled in panic. Mabel had helped select the furniture and fabrics for the Chateau Marmont lobby. She'd also convinced her friends Laura Jane Emery and Winnie Ellis to invest with her in the elegant building. When they lost their money, they blamed Fred. No one, however, lost more money than Fred himself. To help him pay his bills, Mabel used her connections to get him a job as a special prosecutor in a series of Texas mail fraud cases for the DOJ. Eventually, Fred sold the building, which later became a hotel.

The real estate fiasco seems to have finally laid to rest any more talk about Mabel and Fred marrying. From this point forward, they would remain friends and, for several years, law partners with San Bernardino attorney P. N. McCloskey in the firm of Willebrandt, Horowitz and McCloskey. Mabel oversaw the firm's Washington office and sent Dorothy to a series of fashionable schools, including the Friends School, Sacred Heart School, and for high school, Madeira School in McLean, Virginia.

In the mid-1920s Carl Lomen, an entrepreneur who developed the Alaskan reindeer industry, pursued a romance with Mabel. She wasn't interested but introduced him to her friend and fellow lawyer Laura Volstead, daughter of Andrew Volstead, the Republican congressman from Minnesota who authored the Prohibition enforcement law. Mabel served as matron of honor at Laura and Carl's wedding (one of the few times she was photographed during these years wearing makeup in public); Dorothy was a flower girl.

After Carl, Mabel does not seem to have had any other suitors. Perhaps she never met anyone who attracted her as an equal partner or who could measure up to her beloved father. Observed her foster sister Maud Hubbard Brown, "I've never seen a man yet that was in your class. . . . I've wondered if you ever did meet one whose qualities you really admired—outside of your dad."

SEVENTEEN

◇

NOTORIOUS

W HILE MABEL AVOIDED romantic snares, Texas Guinan fell headlong into a series of amorous traps. In Chicago, where she had taken her showgirls in the fall of 1929 on a *Broadway Nights* tour sponsored by the theatrical producer Lee Shubert, she picked up an unsavory new lover named Harry O. Voiler. A married ticket broker several years younger than her forty-five years, Voiler had served time in prison for armed robbery. It may have been Voiler who persuaded Tex to violate her contract with Shubert by moonlighting at the Club Royale on Wabash Avenue downtown, though she doesn't seem to have suffered any consequences for it. Her *Broadway Nights* tour continued uninterrupted, moving on to Cleveland and Detroit for sold-out runs. On Tex's return to Chicago, Voiler arranged for her to hostess at the Green Mill, a club he sublet in the Uptown neighborhood on the city's Northside. Tex's family could not understand what she saw in Voiler, a sleazy thug who used her as a meal ticket and persuaded her to cover $27,000 in expenses at the Green Mill out of her own pocket, including the construction of a new dance floor.

Voiler dropped Tex in the middle of a vicious mob war. The Green Mill was in gangster George "Bugs" Moran's territory, but, apparently, it was owned by a group of Al Capone's men, including Jack

Tex and her showgirls in Chicago with drama critic Amy Leslie. DN-A-1981, Chicago Sun-Times/Chicago Daily News collection, Chicago History Museum.

"Machine Gun" McGurn, a particularly savage member of the Outfit, who'd changed his name from Gibaldi after emigrating from Sicily and who earned his nickname from his frequent use of a tommy gun to eliminate his rivals. McGurn also was quick to use knives. Two years earlier, after the singer Joe E. Lewis moved his act from the Green Mill to a new club owned by the Irish mob, McGurn cut off a portion of Lewis's tongue after slitting his throat. Amazingly, Lewis survived, though his voice was ruined.

McGurn was rumored to have planned and participated in Prohibition's most infamous episode of mob carnage—the St. Valentine's Day Massacre on February 14, 1929, when four of Capone's men murdered seven members of Moran's gang by lining them up and shooting them with machine guns in broad daylight in a Northside garage on Clark Street. McGurn was never brought to trial, however, due to his "baby blonde alibi." His girlfriend (and later wife) Louise Rolfe, an aspiring starlet, claimed she'd spent the entire day by McGurn's side.

Over the years, Tex had entertained Capone, McGurn, and other members of the Outfit when they were in New York on "business."

Mostly, that business was murder. To gain the advantage of surprise, New York mobsters often imported thugs from out of town to assassinate their rivals. The tabloids called this killer-for-hire enterprise "Murder, Inc." While partying at Tex's Manhattan clubs in their off-hours, the Chicago mobsters more or less behaved themselves by keeping their guns out of sight. On their home turf, though, they were more brazen and violent.

Chicago, in general, was rougher than New York—the violence more extreme and visible. At the Green Mill, several machine guns embedded in a wall of the mezzanine pointed toward the dance floor. The weapons were concealed behind a thick curtain, but Tex could never forget they were there. Though Voiler hired a bodyguard to escort Tex around town, she did not feel safe in the city. She later tried to make light of the danger in a syndicated newspaper column she wrote after retiring from nightclubs. "I heard of a fellow who was arrested in Chicago on the charge of vagrancy. He was carrying a machine gun, and it had no bullets," she joked. But the wisecrack hid the deep anxiety she'd felt at the time. When Lorraine Hayes, one of her "little children," as she called her showgirls, began an affair with Leon Sweitzer, a mobbed-up former policeman who held the lease on the Green Mill, Tex's unease grew. Lorraine, a comely, sloe-eyed blonde, started making "trouble," and Tex fired her at Voiler's insistence.

Perhaps Lorraine had something to do with the violence that erupted at the Green Mill on March 23 in the middle of a farewell party Tex had thrown for herself. It was six weeks before Voiler's lease on the club ran out, but Tex couldn't wait to get back to New York. At 4 a.m., while the revelers were still celebrating, shots rang out from the office upstairs where Sweitzer and Voiler were meeting. Apparently, Sweitzer demanded $2,000 from Voiler, the balance of his sublet. Perhaps they also argued over Lorraine's dismissal. Whatever the inciting incident, Voiler shot Sweitzer in the leg. Then, as Sweitzer attempted to flee, Voiler and his bodyguard, a thug named Arthur Reed who'd accompanied him to the club, continued to fire at Sweitzer, wounding him in the chest and arm. Minutes later, the shooters were arrested and taken to the nearest police station. Tex showed up soon after to bail them out, but the men were held on the grounds that Sweitzer might die of his wounds, in which case the charges against the men would be elevated from assault to murder. (As it turned out, Sweitzer recovered, and Voiler and Reed were eventually released.)

Soon after the shooting, Tex fled Caponeville, as the *New York Daily News* dubbed Chicago, on the eastbound Twentieth Century Limited, arriving in New York's Penn Station on March 30. A gaggle of reporters met her train, then followed her home to her Eighth Street apartment to interview her. As she unpacked in front of the reporters, her tiny Pekingese "Feets," named after mobster Hyman "Feets" Edson, ran about with a giant red pompom tied to his collar. Nestled in one of Tex's suitcases amid clouds of satin and chiffon were a solid-gold dresser set and a valuable mantel clock, which she proudly held up for photographers. She also shared with them a note from Al Capone that had accompanied the gifts: "For keeping your mouth shut."

Tex's bragging about her mobster pals and their expensive presents reflected their celebrity as glamorous outlaws, a perception largely created and bolstered by the tabloids. The press also nurtured the myth that these dangerous sociopaths murdered only each other, though eventually the public woke up to the truth. Tex herself, despite joking about her thuggish friends, had had her own rude awakening in Chicago. As the competition among the gangs had grown more intense and the violence had escalated, it was impossible for her to stay aloof. At the start of her career as a nightclub hostess, her criminal partners had been mostly silent; now they were shouting in her ears. Though the press had always covered her glowingly, she knew that could change in a moment. As she told her manager/publicist John Stein, "You are either notorious or a heroine and there's only one small jump between the two."

She yearned to stay on the heroine side of fame. Throughout the

Jazz Age, Tex was celebrated as a rebel who challenged the authority of a ridiculous law. Now, at the start of the thirties, she focused her outrage beyond Prohibition. On May 18, she joined a mass rally organized by the National Woman's Party to protest a recent New York State law that strictly limited overtime work for women in factories and mercantile establishments. Speaking to the crowd of three hundred women who had gathered at Town Hall, Tex argued that the so-called Mastick Law (after Republican state Senator Seabury C. Mastick, who had authored it) denied equal opportunity to women, as it prevented them, but not men, from working more than forty-eight hours a week.

Competition for jobs had grown increasingly fierce as the Depression progressed. Unemployment in 1930 registered at 8.7 percent. It would double in the next year and would triple in two years. Since employers wanted workers who were available for overtime, the law seemed designed to hurt women by keeping them out of jobs they vied for with men. As Tex noted, scrubwomen and nurses were exempt from the restrictive legislation, because "men do not want their jobs."

It's hard to see Tex as a great champion of women's rights. There's no evidence—except her own claims and those of her manager/publicist John Stein—that she protected her showgirls from sexual exploitation by New York's mobsters, madams, gangsters, and club customers. To her credit, though, she struggled to shield them from Mabel's Dry Snoopers and the vice squad, to keep them working and out of jail. She paid them decently—$35 a week, which was about half the average American salary, but they worked only a few hours every night.

At the end of September, Tex opened a new club, the Argonaut, at 151 West Fifty-Fourth Street—the same spot where she'd once presided over the 300 Club. As bandleader she hired the popular Jimmy Carr, boyfriend of the notorious madam Polly Adler, whose apartment-brothel sat a half block away. Adler frequented the Argonaut to see Carr, and when Tex began to suspect her of scouting for hookers among her showgirls, John Stein and Grace Hayward claimed she banned Adler from the club. "Who do you think you are, Queen Marie?" Adler told Tex, according to the authors. "The only difference between your place and mine is that you [have] an electric sign above your door."

"Yes, and the police let me keep mine lighted," Tex said sharply. Like many of the anecdotes in the Stein/Hayward manuscript, this one doesn't ring true. Adler and her posse of "prostipretties" had been regulars at Tex's clubs throughout the Jazz Age. They were part of the excitement and glamour of speakeasy culture and a logical place for Adler to prowl for lustful men with money to burn.

But the party was ending. Not only had the Depression and escalating gangland feuding dealt a blow to the ecosystem that kept the city's underworld humming, but a massive statewide investigation of corruption in New York City threatened to take it down completely. The chief investigator, the former New York State Court of Appeals Judge Samuel Seabury, oversaw the interrogation of more than two thousand witnesses and had evidence that forced Mayor Jimmy Walker from office and Polly Adler to leave town for six months. Frightened of being caught herself in Seabury's dragnet, Tex wanted to dissociate herself and her girls from Adler and her brothel as much as she could.

The Argonaut had not been open long, when, on October 8, an electrical fire started by a short circuit from a porter plugging in a vacuum cleaner broke out, causing $40,000 worth of damage. The mirrored walls, draperies, bandstand, musical instruments, and the piano on which Tex perched to banter with her customers were all destroyed. Nearly three weeks later, the club reopened, only to be raided. Police arrested the head waiter and an assistant manager and charged them with serving drink "set-ups" of cracked ice for patrons who'd brought in their own liquor. (Apparently, the police found no liquor on the premises.) Detectives also charged that an indecent dance had been staged at the club, most likely a "fan dance," an erotic tease in which a naked girl danced while manipulating two large feathered fans that gave just brief flashes of her body. The nuisance charge against the Argonaut employees eventually was dropped for insufficient evidence and the club remained open. But the atmosphere had shifted. People no longer had wads of money to spend on speaks. Tex was forced by the new normal of the Depression to slash her usual cover charge from seven dollars to three dollars and take a pay cut herself down to $750 a week.

The streets outside the speak had also become more dangerous, especially for extremely drunk citizens who were easy marks for unscrupulous taxi drivers and the many muggers who now prowled the Wet Way looking for victims. Adding to her troubles, Tex's raucous style of hostessing was going out of fashion, replaced by the sophisticated grande-dame mode of entertainers like Belle Livingstone, whose Fifty-Eighth Street County Club catered to a continental crowd of socialites, minor royalty, and ordinary folk who wanted to mingle with them. The club was tricked out to look like a European manor with marble floors, a brook stocked with goldfish, and lounges with Ping-Pong tables and backgammon games.

Tex's chief worry, though, was that she'd landed on the wrong side of perhaps the most vicious gangster of the Prohibition era—Dutch Schultz. Born Arthur Flegenheimer to German Jewish immigrants, he dropped out of school in the eighth grade to help support his mother and younger sister after his father abandoned the family. For a while, he worked at a neighborhood nightclub owned by a minor mobster and got his start in crime robbing crap games and burglarizing homes. After a stint in prison for burglary (his sentence was extended after he escaped and was recaptured), he worked for Schultz Trucking in the Bronx. Taking the company name as his own and borrowing the moniker "Dutch" from another thug, he quickly graduated to driving for Arnold Rothstein, the powerful Manhattan mobster who'd allegedly fixed the 1919 World Series, and committing robberies for other high-profile criminals like Legs Diamond and Lucky Luciano.

Schultz soon went out on his own and with his partner Joe Noe took control of the illegal booze market in the Bronx, forcing speak-easies along the Wet Way to buy their ether-spiked beer and muscling in on gangster Big Bill Dwyer's numbers and bootlegging rackets. The Dutchman, as Schultz was known on the street, aspired to the big-shot status of Owney Madden. He was "an arrogant egomaniac," in the words of bank robber Willie Sutton, and also a vicious sadist who once blinded a rival by rubbing a gauze cloth smeared with gonorrhea infection over his eyes as the man hung by his thumbs from a meat hook.

Tex knew the aspirational Schultz was trying out a new role as club owner. He'd recently bought the Chateau Madrid, and Tex feared that he wanted to muscle in on the Argonaut, too. She decided to leave New York and take her showgirls abroad to Paris. One afternoon, while rehearsing for her Parisian revue on the stage of the Savoy Theatre, Tex saw Dutch Schultz slip in and take a seat in the darkened orchestra section. At the break, he approached her and demanded a cut of her Paris gig's profits. The Dutchman had added theatrical producer to his résumé and was backing Fats Waller's musical revue *Hot Chocolates*. Tex refused. She'd stick with Owney Madden and the Combine, whom she believed could protect her. It would turn out to be a fatally naive belief.

What Tex didn't know was that where Mabel had failed to end her career using the law and the courts, Dutch Schultz would succeed with guns and violence.

EIGHTEEN

◇

BITTER SPIRITS

O N JANUARY 16, 1930, Ella Boole was the guest of honor and keynote speaker at a gathering of five hundred Drys at the Baptist Temple in Rochester, New York, to celebrate Prohibition's tenth anniversary. She looked older and more tired than she had a decade earlier at the conclave at the First Congregational Church in Washington, DC, marking the start of the Noble Experiment. She had believed then that her long battle against demon rum had been won; no one living would ever again see liquor sold legally in the United States. Now, that seemed far less certain. Though Ella would never admit it, everyone knew the Eighteenth Amendment had been a failure and that the majority of Americans favored its demise. In her speech, she ignored these facts and instead stressed the glorious end of the saloon. "Twenty-five million children have been born since the amendment went into effect: twenty-five million who will never see a saloon in this country."

Peppering her fifty-minute talk with the exaggerations and false information that would become known in a later era as "alternative" facts, Ella claimed that the WCTU had signed up way more new members than Pauline's group had recruited, that Prohibition enforcement had improved, and that alcoholism rates had fallen dramatically. At the end of the evening, which included more speeches and a musical performance, a vote was taken to send a telegram to President Hoover informing him of the WCTU's undying support for his firm backing of Volstead, and another telegram to Albany urging the state legislature to adopt a bill providing for New York State's cooperation in enforcing the law.

The next day Ella boarded a train headed west, arriving in Chicago in the middle of a snowstorm. At the WCTU headquarters in Evanston, she found the trees tinseled in white and flags in honor of Prohibition's anniversary hanging from the windows of the charming nine-room Gothic Revival house that had once been Frances Willard's home. She would be in town for a week of meetings to formulate WCTU policies for the upcoming year. Ella claimed to be buoyantly optimistic, again ignoring the facts and telling the press, "This year finds Congress and the people dryer than ever." In spite of the deepening Depression, she declared, "poverty is on the decrease."

Later, she joined a celebration at the Morrison Hotel downtown, where an immense tiered birthday cake with ten candles decorated the speakers' table. After slices were served to the four hundred white ribboners present, the women rose and sang out their anthem to the Eighteenth Amendment:

It's in the Constitution, and it's there, there to stay
Till the stars shall sink in silence
And the sun and moon decay.
Till the souls of men assemble on the final judgment day,
It's in the Constitution, and it's there, there to stay.

Not if Pauline Sabin could help it.

By this time, the press had seized on Ella and Pauline as symbols of the nation's Dry-Wet war and covered them as the commanding generals of opposing armies. Pauline herself encouraged the public perception of Ella as her archenemy. She frequently told reporters that it was hearing Ella boasting about her status as a representative of American women that pushed her to come out publicly

Ella Boole at Willard House in 1928. WCTU Archives, Evanston, IL.

against Prohibition. Pauline claimed she had had an epiphany while attending a congressional committee meeting in 1928, where Ella said, "I represent the women of America!" When she heard that, Pauline recalled, "I said to myself, 'well, lady, this is one woman you don't represent.' And with that I began to wonder whether in this broad country of ours there were a great many other women whom Mrs. Boole did not represent." Ella's testimony in the *Congressional*

Record, however, does not record her making this statement on that day. Perhaps Pauline heard her make it on the radio in a speech or in connection with another hearing. In any case, it certainly reflected Ella's sentiments, and it made a compelling origin story for WONPR.

Pauline relished going head-to-head with Ella in debates, and her passion to "rid this country of the domination of a well-organized, fanatical minority" infused her speeches. The WCTU claims that "ten years is not long enough to make this law effective," Pauline told an audience in Brooklyn. "I agree with them. And one hundred years will not be long enough to make the American people accept national prohibition for it is not in accord with America's philosophy of free will and tolerance to accept enforced abstinence. It is not the heritage of the American people to substitute a system of government spying for individual self-control."

Ella and her supporters reacted to Pauline's public appearances and the subsequent glowing publicity with bitter, envious hatred. Though the Sabines included women of all ages and from all walks of life, the WCTU singled out the young urban sophisticates among them for especially harsh criticism. The Sabines were accused of borrowing flirtation techniques from the movies, of studying flapper actresses like Colleen Moore and Clara Bow to "know just what finger to cock and at what angle while they are elegantly smoking cigarettes," an unwomanly habit that proved their impurity, according to the *Union Signal*.

The righteous ladies of the WCTU no doubt knew that smoking by women, long considered a sign of loose morals, was not just shedding its stigma, but becoming a symbol of emancipation. Cigarettes were now "torches of freedom," in the catchphrase popularized by public relations pioneer Edward Bernays. On the last day of March 1929, a few days before the first meeting of WONPR, Bernays enlisted a group of fashionable young women to march down Fifth Avenue during the popular Manhattan Easter Parade, ostentatiously puffing on cigarettes. Photos of the women parading and smoking appeared in newspapers across the country, and women in Detroit,

Boston, and San Francisco soon followed with similar demonstrations. "We hope that we accomplished what we set out to do—to kill a ridiculous taboo, symbolic of more important sex discrimination," wrote Nancy Hardin, one of the participants in the New York parade.

Ella's loathing of cigarettes, as out of step as it was with Jazz Age values, would turn out to be prescient. Smoking was, indeed, an "impure" habit, of which the health hazards were just starting to become known. Of the four chief characters in this book, Ella was the only one who never smoked and the only one who lived past seventy-four.

ON THE MORALITY OF SMOKING and drinking, the *Union Signal* was the least vituperative of the Dry papers. The *American Independent* in Kentucky reviled Pauline and her followers as a "drunken and immoral bunch of women, though rich as most of them are, they are no more than the scum of the earth, parading around in skirts, and possibly late at night flirting with other women's husbands at drunken and fashionable resorts." In a radio debate with a WONPR volunteer, Dr. D. Leigh Colvin—husband of Mamie Colvin, a close associate of Ella's—excoriated the Sabines for soliciting nickel donations from passersby on the street and "depriving the poor and unemployed of money." He denounced them as "Bacchanalian maidens parching for wine, wet women who, like the drunkards whom their program will produce, would take pennies off the eyes of the dead for the sake of legalizing booze."

In Dry Virginia, one WONPR worker reported that she received insulting anonymous letters, and in passing her on the street, some Dry women would step from the sidewalk and draw back their skirts. Other WONPR volunteers were chased by dogs and had the windows of their cars shot out. Hate mail regularly arrived at Pauline's homes. One letter from a woman in the Midwest denounced Pauline's work and concluded, "every evening I get down on my knees and pray to God to damn your soul." Even more alarming for Pauline, however, was awaking one morning at Bayberry Land to find a giant cross burning on her lawn.

But Pauline would not be intimidated. She loved nothing more than a good fight. She challenged Ella to a series of debates in New York in February 1931, which were held at women's organizations, including the Women's Republican Club, the Women's University Club, the American Women's Association, and the Smith College Club. Pauline arranged the venues and invited the audiences. Ella sent Mamie Colvin to speak, and "instead of a bona fide discussion," she charged, Mrs. Colvin "discovered that the meetings were packed with opponents of Prohibition who subjected Mrs. Colvin to considerable ill treatment," including heckling. As a result, Ella said, the WCTU would no longer participate in debates with Pauline's organization. Though she had "no doubt" the WCTU would be "charged with being afraid to appear in public," with the Sabines, she would not allow her women to be "victims of this kind of trick."

Jeanie Rumsey Sheppard, chair of the New York State branch of WONPR, denied that the Sabines had overrun the meetings, noting, "It would be difficult for any organization in New York State, which in 1926 declared itself against prohibition by a majority of 1,164,586, the largest ever recorded on any subject in the United States, to guarantee the Woman's Christian Temperance Union an entirely sympathetic audience. We were not aware of any rudeness or unusual expression of feeling at meetings addressed by Mrs. Colvin and our speakers."

ON FEBRUARY 12, 1930, THE JUDICIARY Committee of the House of Representatives opened its second hearing—the first in four years—on proposals to modify or outright repeal Prohibition. Two hundred spectators, mostly women, jammed the galleries and aisles. At precisely nine o'clock, the dripping Wet Republican representative from Pennsylvania, seventy-nine-year-old George S. Graham, chair of the Judiciary Committee, pounded his gavel and launched into a bristling attack on the Eighteenth Amendment and the Volstead Act, which, he thundered, "have been tested for ten years without satisfactory results. Enforcement has left a train of consequences most deplorable and depressing to every patriot."

Graham promised the Wets and Drys equal time, but he let the Wets kick off the long parade of witnesses. Pauline was among the first to speak. She came "to refute the contention that is often made by dry organizations that all the women of America favor national Prohibition," she said, her large emerald ring sparkling as she gestured with her left hand. She told of her contempt for "drinking dry" politicians and "the political cabal of the Anti-Saloon League." She bemoaned the "heart-burnings" of mothers whose children haunted the "co-educational speakeasy" that was "no improvement" over the saloons they'd replaced. Loud applause and cheering punctuated her remarks, and Grace Root overheard someone say, "We just came to see if this Mrs. Sabin could be as young and pretty as her pictures look."

The hearings continued for several weeks, and it wasn't until March 20 that Ella finally had her say. In a long, impassioned address to the committee, she sounded her great theme: the Eighteenth Amendment would stay in the Constitution because that was what women wanted. Without acknowledging the disasters wrought by Prohibition or the colossal failure to enforce it, she insisted that enforcement was *possible*, noting that the WCTU had added to its pledge requiring total abstinence from liquor a vow promising to also uphold Volstead. She took time to lambaste social drinkers, "the rich" and "the influential" who still believe in moderate drinking. She insisted that "every drunkard was at one time a moderate drinker who thought he could remain such." Therefore, she opposed any measure to allow beer and light wines, which in her view would only lead to hard drinking and the return of the evil saloon. No one applauded her remarks.

Ella blamed her cool reception at the hearings on the fact that the seats in the galleries were packed with Pauline's supporters. She said she heard a rumor that some of them were paid two dollars a day to attend. She also claimed that she and the other Drys had not been properly notified of the dates of the hearings, implying that this had been done deliberately to keep her people home. There was no evidence, however, for this claim, or for the rumor that the Sabines had been paid to jam the committee room. But Ella would not be discouraged. She relied on "Divine guidance" in all things and fervently believed that "He" would continue "to lead" and "help" her through all setbacks.

God could not save Ella, however, when she stepped into the lion's den at the Women's National Republican Club on April 8. The club had invited her and a WCTU colleague to give an analysis of ten years of Prohibition. The audience of New York sophisticates at 8 East Thirty-Seventh Street included Pauline, Ione Nicoll, and a gaggle of their supporters who were out for blood. Ella and Bertha Rembaugh, a trustee of the New York State Women's Committee for Law Enforcement, each spoke for thirty minutes. Ella used most of her time to outline the history and growth of the WCTU and to praise President Hoover for his support of the Eighteenth Amendment. She avoided any mention of the obvious failure to stop the liquor trade, saying success could be measured by "the disappearance of the saloon," and downplaying the existence of speakeasies as solely a New York problem. When she declared that fruit juices could be compounded into a better punch than any alcoholic beverage, the audience booed and hissed. The newspapers reported that Pauline and Ione, who were sitting at the back of the auditorium, led the heckling, which continued when Rembaugh followed Ella at the podium. Rembaugh insisted that Prohibition was succeeding with everyone but "the residents of Greenwich Village" and "the idle rich [who] are drinking themselves off the earth."

Then Ione rose to speak. "We are glad to hear from Mrs. Boole on the early history of the Woman's Christian Temperance Union and her recipes for punch made of fruit juices," she began, her voice oozing sarcasm. "But where was the discussion of the last ten years of Prohibition?" You call yourselves "the Woman's Christian Temperance Organization," she continued, but "where in the teachings of Christ do you find any objections to the use of intoxicating liquor?" Drawing on her deep knowledge of the Bible, Ione pointed to the

Gospel of St. Matthew, chapter XI, verse 19, which refers to Jesus as a "winebibber" "eating and drinking" like an ordinary man.

Then it was Pauline's turn. She noted that alcoholism and deaths from alcohol had increased dramatically during Prohibition. According to statistics she cited from the Metropolitan Life Insurance Company, there had been a 600 percent increase in alcohol-caused deaths among workingmen since 1920. Meanwhile, New York City's Bellevue Hospital had seen an increase of five thousand people brought to their alcoholic ward. "Are these the idle rich or from Greenwich Village?" she asked, her brown eyes sparking. As loud applause rang out, Ella's face reddened. But when a reporter asked her at the end of the meeting how she felt, she shrugged. "I'm used to it and half expected it," she said.

NINETEEN

THE SISTERHOOD OF REPEAL

W ONPR'S MASS RECRUITING EFFORTS led to membership cards pouring into the organization's national headquarters "in a veritable flood," Grace Root recalled. By the time of WONPR's first national conference in Cleveland in April 1930, the Sabines ranks had grown in less than a year to 100,000 women nationwide. Support for Repeal was bolstered by the worsening Depression and the promise that reopened breweries and distilleries would create jobs and bring in tax revenue. (After the stock market crash, federal revenue from the income tax had plummeted by 35 percent.) Meanwhile, the WCTU was losing members who couldn't afford the one-dollar yearly dues, and the bank that the once-flush Anti-Saloon League had relied on for credit had collapsed. The ASL couldn't pay its office rent or employee salaries and, like the WCTU, began to leach members.

Though Pauline Sabin had insisted that WONPR was nonpartisan, she drove herself and her troops deep into the 1930 congressional election, throwing the group's support behind Wet candidates, including Democrat James Hamilton Lewis, who was running for the Senate from Illinois, because he favored Repeal. In doing so, she pitted WONPR, a women's organization, against a Dry woman candidate who also happened to be her friend, Ruth McCormick,

Lewis's Republican challenger, whose association with the increasingly unpopular President Hoover and his disastrous handling of the Depression also lost McCormick votes. In the weeks leading up to the election, Pauline herself traveled to areas of the nation that were staunchly Dry, lending her glamour and celebrity to Wet candidates who faced tough races.

The election turned out to be a Democratic landslide—and a harbinger of the presidential election to come. Democrats won their largest majority in the history of congressional races, gaining eight seats in the Senate and fifty-three in the House, giving the new Congress thirty more Wets than Drys. One of them was James Hamilton Lewis, who beat McCormick by an overwhelming 64 percent of the vote.

BY THE TIME OF WONPR'S second annual conference in April 1931, membership had grown to 300,000. Pauline hired private train cars to transport delegates to Washington, DC, for the gathering. It was the height of cherry blossom season, and the trees lining the Tidal Basin reservoir frothed pink coronas. Around the Capitol, the parkways blazed with red and yellow tulips, and the White House lawns gleamed like green satin under cloudless blue skies. The Sabines looked as bright and cheerful as the weather. Wearing big white buttons emblazed with "REPEAL" in bold black, they filed into the Mayflower Hotel ballroom at 2 p.m. under a huge banner illustrating a young woman tearing in two a sign reading "PROHIBITION." Addresses by Pauline and Eleanor Robson Belmont—the stunning former stage star, social leader, and wife of millionaire August Belmont—followed.

Later that evening, tables were squeezed into the halls and on the balconies of the ballroom to accommodate eight hundred diners. After the dessert plates were cleared, the doors were opened to the public to hear speeches. Matthew Woll, vice president of the American Federation of Labor, described Prohibition as a "*dangerous* experiment" and said the members of his unions throughout the country would cooperate in the crusade against it. Esther L. Richards, a psychiatrist from Johns Hopkins University, analyzed the inevitable failure of Prohibition because of its conflict with the fundamental human instinct for pleasure.

The next morning, the delegates passed a resolution to send a petition affirming their desire for Repeal to the president and Congress. At the last minute, Hoover agreed to see the women. Perhaps the president "suddenly realized that there was meeting in Washington a body of women too important to be officially ignored," one reporter commented. Hoover had recently met with the WCTU and sent a formal message of blessing to the WCTU convention, so now "he has to at least even up the score a little bit." Several journalists, however, reported that the White House itself had instigated the meeting with WONPR. Hoover saw that Pauline, who had abandoned his party, was drawing fervent attention in the press, and in his weakened political state, he wanted to signal that he and the GOP still mattered.

At 12:30 p.m., five hundred WONPR delegates led by Pauline and Ione Nicoll took buses from the Mayflower Hotel to the White House. While the delegates waited on the lawn, Ione handed Hoover the resolution in the Oval Office. It declared that "the protest against the social and political iniquities of prohibition has gathered volume and intensity until the question is no longer 'Shall national prohibition endure?' but 'how shall we constitutionally rid ourselves of [it], as shown by eleven years of experiment to be unenforceable, to be the foe of temperance and the breeder of evils?'" The president replied, "I am very glad to have it." Hoover took time to shake hands with all five hundred Sabines as they filed into the Oval Office, then out through the French doors to the White House grounds.

Perhaps he was just being polite, as the resolution cited the squishiness of the recently released report of his Wickersham Commission, which Pauline had called a shadow-boxing exhibition, for not coming up with meaningful ideas for solving the Prohibition problem. Still, a slim majority of the eleven commissioners thought the law should be modified or ended. One commissioner, Tulane University law professor Monte M. Lemann, refused to sign the report at all, explaining that the only solution to the disaster of the Eighteenth Amendment was total Repeal.

DESPITE THE FINE WEATHER, Pauline caught a bad cold in Washington that developed into an ear infection, which spread to the mastoid bone behind her ear. With the introduction of antibiotics to treat ear infections after 1940, mastoid infections would become less common. Before then, however, mastoiditis posed a serious health threat, as the infection could spread to the brain and cause death. Pauline's illness became so severe that she underwent surgery on April 29 at Doctor's Hospital on East End Avenue in New York City, where years earlier her design firm Eighteenth Century Inc. had supervised the decoration of the lobbies and patients' rooms. The exact nature of the operation is unknown. What is certain is that Pauline's recovery was painful and slow, keeping her out of work for two months as she recuperated at Bayberry Land. In her absence, Maude Wetmore—an activist, amateur golfer, and daughter of a former governor of Rhode Island—served as WONPR's acting president, while Ione stepped in to fulfill Pauline's speaking engagements. Meanwhile, WONPR established a twelve-week crash course in public speaking at the Surrey Hotel on Manhattan's Upper East Side to train women to deliver a forceful Repeal message. Participants in the course were also required to attend lectures at WONPR's Anti-Prohibition Institute at the Hotel Commodore, where they learned the fundamental arguments for Repeal and were kept up-to-date on developments in the law.

Matthew Woll contributed $1,000 to WONPR toward joint meetings of the organization and members of labor unions. This "cooperation with labor should ensure many wives of laboring men joining the Woman's Organization and a large increase in its membership will certainly have a great effect upon our Congressmen and Senators," Woll wrote to Pierre S. du Pont. "I feel that [WONPR] is doing the most effective work for all of us. One reason for this is that the average Congressman is more afraid of one woman than he is of five men."

Pauline was determined to force every member of Congress to declare his (or her) stand on Prohibition and make clear that the Sabines would work against those who opposed Repeal or straddled the issue. "Our situation will remain the same until we purge our congress and state Legislatures of the type of man who votes dry and drinks wet. This condition is prevalent and alarming and it seems to me that an apathetic attitude toward this type of legislator may mean the destruction of the very foundation of our government," she warned. In the fall of 1931, WONPR sent the following letter to every US representative and senator with a self-addressed, stamped reply envelope:

> If elected, will you support a resolution for the straight repeal of the 18th amendment and the restoration to each state of its power to regulate the manufacture, sale and transportation of intoxicating beverages within its own limits? Such a Resolution to be submitted to Conventions in the several states for ratification or rejection.

Those politicians who ignored the letter were queried again, while those who refused to reply were rebuked by the WONPR chair in their state. "Is it really possible that you are unwilling to submit to your constituents the question of the repeal or retention of the Eighteenth Amendment?" read the form letter, which threatened the recalcitrant politician with retaliation in the form of negative newspaper articles about him (or her, as there were a handful of women in the House of Representatives at the time). "I am writing to ask for a definite reply before any publicity is given to these questionnaires."

In December 1931, Pauline announced the results: Of the 47.3 percent of politicians who replied, 59 percent favored the referendum, 19.5 percent were opposed, and 21.1 percent were uncommitted. Pauline displayed the response letters from the nation's congressional representatives and senators at WONPR headquarters for the press and the public to read, including this angry missive from Congressman Thomas Jefferson Busby, a Democrat from Mississippi, who wrote, "The Great Need as I see it is to Reform . . . the women . . . who are using every possible effort to defeat the Eighteenth Amendment. . . . I will appreciate it if you will quit sending me your circulars."

THAT SUMMER, WHILE PAULINE RECUPERATED in the peace and beauty of Bayberry Land, the gangster violence in New York escalated. On the evening of July 28, thugs leaning out the windows of a green sedan speeding up East 107th Street opened fire on a group of men standing outside an Italian social club. Several children playing on the stoop of an apartment house nearby were injured in the gunfire, and one five-year-old boy was killed. The "Harlem Baby Killing," as the tabloids dubbed the crime, jolted the nation, which had fooled itself that gangsters murdered only each other, a myth fostered by films and the popular press. Now the death of an innocent child made clear the terrible danger to ordinary citizens posed by underworld crime. Pauline predicted the carnage would only get "worse based on the record of the past ten years, the increasing lawlessness, and the effrontery of bootleg criminals."

It's hard to discern a specific turning point that tipped the scales inexorably toward Repeal, though it might have been a discovery in a junk shop in rural Kentucky by the secretary of WONPR's Louisville chapter, Gense J. Brashear. Idly flipping through an old scrapbook she'd purchased from the shopkeeper, Brashear came upon a letter that Jefferson Davis had written in June 1887 toward the end of his life announcing his unwavering opposition to Prohibition. (Davis's letter had been precipitated by a swirl of controversy surrounding a proposed amendment to the Texas Constitution outlawing liquor.) The banning of alcohol, wrote the former president of the Confederacy, still a god to many White southerners sixty years after the Civil War, "was a wooden horse" and an "enemy to state sovereignty. . . . To

destroy individual liberty and moral responsibility would be to erad-
icate one evil by the substitution of another."

In the process of authenticating the letter, a WONPR volunteer
turned up two others that expressed Davis's vehement opposition to
Prohibition. The discoveries made front-page news across the nation
and resulted in Pauline's organization finally breaking through the
wall of Dry prejudice in the South, which reflected the region's
hypocrisy and deep racism. As a columnist for the African American *Atlanta Daily World* wrote, "It seems a bit strange that while
the South furnished nearly all our lynchings and advocat[ed] at the
same time the total disenfranchisement of certain of its citizens, it
kept up a constant yell about Prohibition."

Pauline followed up the discovery of the Davis letter with a tri-
umphal speaking tour of South Carolina and Georgia, where she
captivated audiences with her "fine intelligence and breeding," the
Atlanta Constitution noted. The first stop was Charleston on February 29, where Pauline welcomed seventy-five members of WON-
PR's executive committee to The Oaks, the lavish plantation she and
Charlie had recently bought. Located about twenty miles from downtown, The Oaks sat at the end of a long road paved with white oyster
shells and lined with ancient trees that gave the property its name
and waved visitors up to a grand white stucco house. Once a vast rice
plantation, The Oaks had been home to a series of wealthy families
dating back to the seventeenth century. The rickety shacks that had
housed enslaved people had long ago been demolished. In the course
of a major renovation of the house, the Sabins also removed the two-
story Corinthian columns at the front portico, a cliché of antebellum
pretentiousness.

Pauline filled the house with priceless eighteenth-century
antiques and French impressionist art and planted lavish gardens.
Beyond, in the thick subtropical forests along the banks of Goose
Creek at the western end of The Oaks, bootleggers had set up moon-
shine distilleries. In the dead of night, cars regularly transported the
illegal booze out to trucks and boats destined for far-flung states. It's

unknown if Pauline learned of the rum-running in her backyard, or if the bootleggers had seen her announcement in the *Charleston News and Courier* on February 12 that she planned to "stage the largest anti-Prohibition demonstration ever held in South Carolina" and put the bootleggers out of business.

Charleston Mayor Burnet R. Maybank officially welcomed the Sabines to Charleston at a morning meeting at the Fort Sumter Hotel, where many of the women were staying. (Others found accommodations with friends who lived nearby.) A luncheon at The Oaks was followed by another meeting. The next day, Pauline was caught up in a whirlwind of teas, receptions, and garden tours designed to give as many people in the community as possible a chance to meet and be dazzled by her. Later, at 8:30 p.m., Senator Millard E. Tydings, a Democrat from Maryland and Mabel Willebrandt's next-door neighbor in Washington, gave the keynote at a rally attended by five hundred men and women at Hibernian Hall. The building— which resembled a Greek temple with a white stucco facade and six iconic columns under a classical pediment—had served in 1860 as headquarters for the faction of the Democratic Party that supported Stephen A. Douglas, a fervent states' rights advocate, for president against Abraham Lincoln. Tailoring his remarks for an audience still passionate about the supremacy of states' rights, Tydings said the debate over Repeal "is not a question of liquor or no liquor. It is a question of whether we want the state or the [federal] government to solve the problem of intemperance." Several times during his speech, a male voice in the rear of the crowd, shouted, "Speak out, brother, you're right!"

The following day, Pauline and her entourage traveled by train to Atlanta for another two-day round of dinners, rallies, luncheons, and speeches. Atlanta Mayor James Lee Key, a fierce Wet, welcomed the women to the city. The previous year, after Key had come out against Prohibition, a group of Drys pushed for a recall vote against him; it failed. Clark Howell, editor of the *Atlanta Constitution*, also vigorously supported Repeal. He gave the women extensive coverage in his newspaper, splashing reports of their events on the front page, running large photographs of them, and gushing over Pauline's "beauty," "subtle sense of humor," and "platform personality," that is, her vivaciousness and forcefulness as a speaker.

The four-day trip to Charleston and Atlanta was followed by WONPR's third national conference in Washington starting April 12, attended by more than a thousand delegates from around the nation. The *Union Signal* sniped that the delegates were all "socially prominent and wealthy" elitists who'd arrived in the city with their "secretaries, maids and chauffeurs," driving "costly limousines." Truth be told, the majority were ordinary, middle-class women, most of whom were wives and mothers. Some of them had out-of-work husbands or had lost jobs themselves as the nation sunk into the Depression, and they had arrived in Washington by coach-class train and bus. They posed for photographers on the east steps of the Capitol, a cloche-hatted army of Repeal warriors. Afterward, they filled the cavernous majority room of the Senate Office Building, where another round of Prohibition hearings was underway. Once again, Pauline was the star witness. "The Prohibition Amendment is poisoning our national life and it must be repealed!" she cried, as the Sabines, who overflowed the galleries and halls outside, cheered. Reporters noted that the women had taken up nearly every available seat and standing-room space; almost no men were present.

Pauline linked the kidnapping in March of the baby son of Charles and Anne Morrow Lindbergh, a heart-wrenching crime that had gripped the nation, to the culture of lawlessness that had thrived during Prohibition. And she excoriated those "temperance organizations," which, in their intransigent support of the Eighteenth Amendment, have become "the chief allies and friends of the outlaw classes. The time has come to end this unholy alliance!"

Later, the Sabines split up into delegations to call on Dry legislators. Many of them represented districts where the majority of citizens were Wet; nevertheless, these officials felt themselves in the clutch, as Pauline put it, "of an intolerant, fanatical, and oppressive

The Sisterhood of Repeal: Pauline Sabin surrounded by a sea of Sabines on the Capitol Steps in 1932. Courtesy of The Hagley Museum and Library.

minority," which they were too cowardly to oppose. Congressman Simeon D. Fess of Ohio, the chair of the Republican National Committee, was typical. A group of Sabines with photographers in tow called on him in his office, but he refused to pose for pictures with the women. "Absolutely not!" he huffed, before turning on his heel and slamming the door.

PAULINE DECLARED THE THIRD WEEK in May National Repeal Week, which she inaugurated with a radio address enjoining her followers to "wear the Wet label proudly, vote for Wet candidates and pile up Wet majorities." A publicity juggernaut followed with a relentless push for new members across the nation. In Missouri, 110 billboards greeted cars as they drove through the state, where ten

WONPR enrollment centers were opened. In downtown St. Louis, loudspeakers broadcast Repeal speeches from WONPR headquarters to the street outside. After the police issued the Sabines a warning following a complaint from the Anti-Saloon League that they were causing a nuisance, the women put up immense painted signs spelling out "Repeal" that sparked an even bigger stir. In Pennsylvania, buses fitted out with loudspeakers blaring a Repeal message toured the state's southeastern counties. Jacksonville, Florida, celebrated Repeal Week with a parade; a shop selling license plates, spare-tire covers, scarves, neckties, powder puffs, thimbles, and other gear; and a luncheon open to the public to which every candidate for state legislature was invited to speak. In North Carolina, the week was marked by a declaration for Repeal by a popular evangelist, and in Montana, a new WONPR unit was established, which immediately enrolled fifteen hundred members. Money boxes for donations

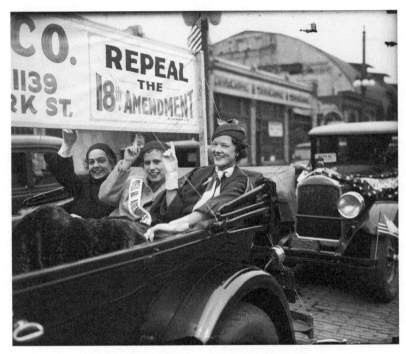

"The Wet Parade" in Chicago during National Repeal Week
in May 1932. © 1932 Chicago Tribune. All rights reserved.
Distributed by Tribune Content Agency, LLC.

were set up at restaurants, hotels, banks, and grocery stores. Fabric printed with "Repeal" was made into shirts for cowboys on ranches in the West and suit blouses for socialites in Manhattan.

Thousands of posters were distributed nationwide, depicting a mother in front of a ballot box with her two children beside her under a message in bold, black type: "Their Security Demands You Vote Repeal." The WCTU had always used images of maternity and family to promote *their* cause. Now WONPR in effect was saying, *We are the ones who have the best interests of women and children at heart.* Pauline vowed to plaster every fence post in America with the poster to make the nation Repeal conscious.

A huge mass meeting demanding a referendum on Repeal was held on May 25 in Atlanta in the city auditorium, where the entire balcony had been reserved for the city's "colored citizens." Pauline worried about whether she could attract southern Black people to her cause because the Black churches still overwhelmingly supported Prohibition, and Black ministers had great influence with their parishioners. A minister in Sumter, South Carolina, for example, had reportedly gathered thousands of abstinence pledges from Black adults on behalf of the African Methodist Episcopal Church.

It's unknown how many Black people showed up at the Atlanta Repeal event, though Pauline did make some inroads with both Black and White people in the South, including in the driest states of the nation, Alabama and Mississippi. She organized an Alabama WONPR chapter in June 1932, and within several months had enrolled three thousand members. A Mississippi chapter that had been formed a month later, in July, grew to five thousand members by the end of the year, a stunning achievement in the driest state of the nation, which had passed its own Prohibition law in 1908, and eleven years later had been the first state to ratify the Eighteenth Amendment.

TWENTY

◇

THE WOMEN'S WAR

"ONE NEED NOT BE a weather expert to tell which way the wind is blowing," Pauline Sabin said in 1931, long before Bob Dylan wrote the observation into a song. The nation was falling to pieces, and as the date of the presidential conventions approached in June, Americans sick of weak law enforcement, gangster violence, and deepening economic woes turned Wetward. That spring, WONPR's ranks surged to 1,009,252 members.

The Wet press, including the chain of influential papers owned by William Randolph Hearst, aided Pauline's cause by committing oceans of ink to exposing Dry corruption and promoting the Sabines. When the famously Dry John D. Rockefeller Jr.—who claimed that he, his father, and his grandfather had never taken a drop of intoxicating liquor—defected to Pauline's cause, it made headlines everywhere. "We are all delighted. He is our most powerful recruit yet," Pauline told reporters. "I can't invite him into our women's organization, but I certainly shall invite Mrs. Rockefeller." It's unknown if Abigail Rockefeller accepted Pauline's invitation. But had her mother-in-law been alive, she most certainly would never have joined a Repeal group. The young Laura Spellman, Rockefeller's mother, had been a passionate participant in the Woman's Crusade of the 1870s, kneeling on the sawdust floors of saloons in her native Ohio to protest the sale of liquor. Soon after Rockefeller's Big Switch, as the tabloids called his defection, tire king Harvey S. Firestone Sr. and Alfred P. Sloan Jr. of General Motors joined the Wet camp. There were cracks, too, in the clerical Dry wall. Explaining why the editors no longer supported the Eighteenth Amendment, the *Christian Leader*, the first religious newspaper to come out for Repeal, wrote, "We are in the worst political mess in our history. We must get out of it."

The courts also began to rebel against imposing sentences for minor violations of the Prohibition laws. A judge in Detroit refused to jail a woman convicted of brewing and selling beer to support her children, telling her, "The real tragedy of Prohibition is that it is making liars of us all. The fact that you violated it no longer means anything, especially in this city where the sentiment of the people is so strongly against it."

IN 1932, AMERICA WAS HEADED for a showdown on Prohibition, and the first clashes would be at the Republican National Convention in Chicago, where women would play a key role. With 93 women delegates and 297 alternates, there would be 33 more women confirming the GOP's choice of nominee than there had been in 1928.

Pauline arrived in Chicago on June 12 and was photographed in the lobby of the Congress Hotel, the GOP headquarters, standing on a chair hanging copies of the now-familiar Repeal poster depicting a mother voting with her young children by her side. Later, at the Blackstone Hotel, in her suite decorated in Louis V furniture, with pink peonies scattered about in large vases scenting the air, she sat for an interview with Maxine Davis, a United Press correspondent. Davis began her story, which ran the next day in papers across the nation, with the usual praise of Pauline's charm, wit, and looks, describing "her expressive eyes, the dimple in her left cheek," and "her slim figure" clad in printed blue silk, but Davis's tone was sharp. She mocked Pauline for her vanity and wealth, for "taking the time" from "her important work" to slip on her "heavy emerald and diamond bracelet, her five-carat emerald and diamond ring," and "to clasp on her pearls and snap on her button earrings," as if a woman who dressed expensively couldn't also be serious. And yet, Davis was insightful about Pauline's character, wondering if she ever admitted "to herself what she wants most. Perhaps it would be power. She has everything else."

Power was what Ella Boole wanted, too. At the World WCTU convention in Toronto the previous June, she had been elected president, making her goal now nothing short of a global liquor ban. It would be an immense task, since at the time Finland was the only country besides the United States that had Prohibition in place. Her immediate focus, however, was on keeping the Eighteenth Amendment strong in the United States, and to that end, she demanded the Republicans adopt a total Dry plank—that is, no modification whatsoever of the Prohibition laws.

While Pauline was hanging posters at the Congress Hotel, Ella arrived at the Third Presbyterian Church nearby for an alternative "Dry Loyalty" convention. Grimacing at a gaggle of boys lined up on the sidewalk in front of the church holding signs reading "We Want Beer," she made her way inside and settled in for a long session of prayers and speeches. When it was her turn at the podium, perhaps thinking of the annoying boys outside, she said she was not worried about the "wet propaganda which is seeking to sweep the Republican convention off its feet."

However, there was no shortage of Dry propaganda, too. Three days later, Ella watched Jane Addams, Chicago's most famous woman and a recent winner of the Nobel Prize, lead a parade of seven hundred autos down Madison Street. Standing in the open car, Addams waved to the crowd, a queen of peace and temperance whom Ella thrilled to have on her side. A bright ribbon of roadsters full of children holding aloft banners imploring "For Our Sake, Peace" trailed Addams's car.

The Repeal movement had become a women's movement, but Ella continued to delude herself that the feminine push to overturn the Eighteenth Amendment had somehow been fabricated by

Pauline in collusion with the press. "The Iron Chancellor of Prohibition," as the *New York Daily News* called Ella, complained that the papers gave Pauline and the Sabines too much publicity, most of it glowing, while rarely writing anything negative or unflattering about them. The *Union Signal* cited as an example a gathering of ten thousand Republicans at an anti-Prohibition rally at the Chicago Coliseum, where immense flags hung from the towering ceiling, which had been wrapped in four miles of red-white-and-blue bunting. Bands marched down the aisles playing "The Star-Spangled Banner" and other patriotic tunes, as delegates cheered and waved flags. The *Union Signal*, however, reported that the audio equipment malfunctioned so the audience couldn't hear the speeches, and by the time Pauline rose to speak, hordes of people had walked out. The mainstream press failed to mention either the audio malfunction or the mass walkout. The papers did, however, run large pictures of Pauline, looking lovely in a floaty white dress with a "pert and confident" hat perched at a slight angle on her strawberry-blonde curls. In one widely reprinted photo, she is sitting on the convention floor chatting with Chicago Mayor Anton Cermak, as Carnegie Tech president Samuel H. Church and Pierre du Pont gaze at her mooningly.

The *Union Signal* also claimed that the press failed to report the Wet hecklers who'd attempted to break up a Dry gathering at the Coliseum—which was four and a half miles from the Chicago Stadium, the scene of nominating at the convention—proving that "the opponents of Prohibition fear to have the truth told publicly." The hecklers were escorted from their seats, but they refused to leave, so they stood at the back by the doors listening to the proceedings. Ella and her troops pounded the point home in speeches and in the *Union Signal* that American women still supported Prohibition. "The women who are the mothers of the men who will guide this nation through storm and stress are standing as firmly for Prohibition as ever," Ella wrote in a special convention issue. Lucy W. Peabody, chair of the Women's National Committee for Law Enforcement and a close associate of Ella's (though she was a Boston blue blood, the type who usually gravitated to WONPR), expressed the view more militantly in a letter to President Hoover. "Show me a woman who wants to bring liquor back, and I'll show you a woman who is either abnormal or subnormal," she wrote. In Chicago, Ella ignored the large numbers of WONPR members, though they were a vivid, impossible-to-miss presence at the convention, as they marched en masse, wearing "REPEAL THE 18TH AMENDMENT" banners across their chests, from their headquarters at 75 East Monroe Street to the nearby Congress Hotel to attend daily meetings of the Resolutions Committee.

It's true that the convention press covered Pauline's activities more exhaustively than Ella's, though both women worked tirelessly for their side, attending meetings, rallies, and parades, and giving speeches and radio addresses. But neither Pauline nor Ella won in the end. Pauline's efforts to insert a Repeal plank into the GOP platform failed, as did Ella's push to force a plank that wholeheartedly supported Prohibition. Both women were outvoted by their male colleagues on the so-called strategy boards that worked out the party platforms. A furious Ella wanted to wire Hoover himself in protest— let the president decide his own platform—but again she was voted down, and no wire was sent.

As it turned out, a "gigantic straddle" was exactly what Hoover wanted, so as not to alienate voters on either side. The official Republican plank recommended neither Repeal nor a national referendum on the issue. But neither did it contain a statement fully supporting the Eighteenth Amendment. Ella threatened to bolt the GOP and form a Woman's Prohibition Party that would advance a woman to run on a Prohibition ticket against Hoover, though nothing came of it. When reporters asked her why she declined to officially endorse the president, she said sharply and disingenuously that the political work of the WCTU is confined "to issues rather than candidates."

Pauline was equally disappointed with the way things had turned out. The Republican plank was a complete flop that was written "to seem dry to the drys and wet to the wets," she told reporters, adding that "the days of pussy footing and evasion" were over. She directed the Sabines to bombard John J. Raskob, chair of the Democratic National Committee, with telegrams urging his party to adopt a Repeal plank at its upcoming convention.

In the end, the Democrats "went as wet as the seven seas," as Arthur Krock of the *New York Times* put it, adopting at their own convention in Chicago on June 30 a total Repeal plank. The once-Dry South and West, Krock noted, "deserted the amendment which they put in the Constitution in 1919 after fifty years of agitation." The Democratic South had been the deciding factor in enacting Prohibition, and in voting for its Repeal, "Democracy, like Saturn, was swallowing its own child," he added. Once again, the Chicago Stadium erupted in wild cheering, this time for the Democrats. The Sabines, those "silk stocking beauties," as one reporter called them, stood on their red seats, then swung into the impromptu parade that danced through the aisles, waving noisemakers and flags, finally posing in front of the speakers' platform to have their picture snapped as they held up a "VOTE REPEAL" banner. Pauline sat in her box high above the convention floor, beaming and accepting congratulations. "Well, *you* ought to be happy," Jouett Shouse, the new president of the Association Against the Prohibition Amendment (AAPA), told her, as he vigorously shook her hand. "Perfectly swell!" Pauline cried. "I am simply gibbering with excitement," she later confessed.

The next day, the convention nominated Franklin Delano Roosevelt for president. In his acceptance speech, the New York governor focused on the nation's dire economic state and pledged his aid "to the men and women forgotten in the political philosophy of the government of recent years." He promised to "restore America to its own people" and stated his firm commitment to the party's Repeal plank, declaring that "from this date on the eighteenth amendment is doomed."

At a meeting in early July, WONPR's executive committee, with Pauline at the head, voted to endorse FDR for president. A die-hard Republican faction of sixty-four women, mostly wealthy members of the Social Register, resigned in protest and issued a statement denouncing the WONPR committee's decision, which they complained turned a nonpartisan organization into a partisan one. The defectors issued a statement that they believed voters should exercise their own individual choice in voting and that in the middle of a Depression, it was unseemly to make "the sole test" of a candidate's "fitness" for the presidency, his attitude toward Prohibition. Pauline responded caustically. "I am very sorry that these ladies felt it necessary to publicly repudiate and admonish not only the national executive committee for keeping its word, but also the thousands of women who have untiringly and loyally given their time and strength for the last three years to endeavor to bring about a day of greater security for the workers, a day when criminals will lose control, a day of greater happiness for us all. I can find no comfort in this petition. But perhaps the Woman's Christian Temperance Union, the Anti-Saloon League, the Methodist Board of Prohibition, Temperance and Public Morals, and Bishop Cannon will."

Pauline charged that the defector's document had been written by President Hoover's Treasury Secretary Ogden L. Mills, who, when asked about it by reporters, shook his head. "Don't bring me into any women's quarrels," he fumed, displaying the reflexive sexism of the time. The kerfuffle showed, as Will Rogers quipped, "that politics is thicker than beer," and also what Sigmund Freud had identified in 1917 as the narcissism of minor difference: similar groups were the most likely to engage in feuds. Both factions of WONPR's executive committee were blue bloods who traveled in the same social circle as the Roosevelts and had strong opinions about them. As one Boston acquaintance of Roosevelt complained, FDR "is weaker than tissue paper. His wife has supplied all the backbone Frank ever had. He's two thirds for everything and wholly for nothing."

In the fall, Pauline's neighbors in Southampton also turned against her, when the local Hoover Club passed a resolution urging Republican women to refrain from joining WONPR during the presidential election. The defectors bolting, like Pauline's Southampton detractors, however, had little effect on WONPR's rank and file. "We have just begun to fight!" Pauline told reporter Maxine Davis. For Pauline and the Sabines, the fall lead-up to the election was a whirl-wind of radio addresses, rallies, parades, and speeches, including one before a crowd of forty thousand who had jammed Military Park in downtown Newark, New Jersey, demanding legal beer. Armies of Sabines carrying Repeal banners were photographed marching through cities and towns. Others stood in open cars blaring their message to "Vote FDR" through megaphones. When *Time* put Pauline on the cover in July, it signaled her status as a rare female political influencer, though in doubting her sway with "the populous class of rural women" who "suspect, envy and hate" society figures, the magazine failed to grasp the true extent of her power.

TWENTY-ONE

---◇---

SECOND ACTS

M ABEL WALKER WILLEBRANDT HAD APPEARED on *Time*'s cover a year earlier, on August 26, 1929, two months after her resignation as assistant US attorney general. In the story, she cited politics, including hypocritical politicians, as "the greatest handicap in the enforcement of Prohibition," a point she had emphasized in *The Inside of Prohibition*, her memoir about her time in government that had been published in January and released chapter by chapter in newspapers that summer. Mabel herself, however, had dropped out of the political game, though she reassured a crowd at a Republican rally in San Diego in October 1932 that she hadn't turned "wet or even damp." Despite Hoover's shabby treatment of her and his wishy-washy stance on Prohibition, she supported him for reelection, and she firmly believed that "the Eighteenth Amendment can be enforced, should be, and ultimately will be obeyed."

Those were her last public words on the issue. Mabel was enjoying great success in private practice, dividing her time between offices in Washington and Los Angeles. She became a pioneer in radio and aviation law, and as legal counsel for MGM, she represented some of Hollywood's most prominent figures. By this time, her friend Ida Koverman had joined Louis B. Mayer's staff, serving as a public relations expert, political adviser, and talent scout. Mabel worked with Koverman to ensure that Mayer had the ear of power-ful politicians in Washington, at a time when Hollywood was per-ceived as unwholesome and disreputable and was constantly threat-ened with censorship.

TEXAS GUINAN, MEANWHILE, WAS SINKING. In May 1931, Tex had closed her act at the Argonaut and booked her showgirls for a summer run in Paris at a nightclub in Montmartre. She had looked forward to a sojourn in the City of Light, where there were "no moral speed limits," no Prohibition, and plenty of live sex shows and nude reviews. She'd worked hard on the choreography of the show, which would have a Wild West theme, but she never got a chance to pre-sent it. When Tex and her group—which included singers, musi-cians, comedians, stagehands, a chauffeur, and several of the show-girls' mothers—arrived in Le Havre on the SS *Paris*, French officials refused to allow the Americans to disembark, citing their lack of proper visas. Tex believed the true reason was because the French government thought her a menace, a "sort of queen of the under-world" and a "female gangster and racketeer," as she noted in a *Too Hot for Paris* program quoted by Louise Berliner.

Within a week of arriving home, Tex came up with a new idea for a revue. She took her *Too Hot for Paris* show on the road, but it proved too scorching for mainstream America as well and closed after a month. The tour had been vexed from the start. In the Bronx, an explosive device left on window ledge of a roadside club where the group was performing exploded early one morning. Tex believed it had been planted by Dutch Schultz's men, and though no one was hurt, the violence deeply unnerved her. She started to think about getting out of show business entirely. Then Harry Voiler came back into her life and pressured her to go with him to Chicago to run a Capone-backed club called Planet Mars. When the *Too Hot* produc-ers threatened to sue her for breach of contract, Voiler's armed thugs paid them a visit, and afterward there was no more talk of lawsuits. But things hardly went well in Chicago. When Voiler went out of town, Tex took up with Capone hitman Sam "Golf Bag" Hunt (his nickname derived from his habit of carrying his semi-automatic gun in a golf bag). On his return, Voiler confronted the couple as they dined in Tex's hotel room. The relationship with Hunt broke up (he later married one of her showgirls), and soon after, Tex's stint at Planet Mars ended, too, when police raided the club on New Year's Eve, 1931.

Back in New York, Tex found herself unable to find a speakeasy that would take her on as a full-time hostess, though she managed to make guest appearances at various clubs around the Wet Way. She had returned from Chicago with a hot tip that assassins from Caponeland would soon arrive in New York to kill mob hitman Vince Coll, who was warring with Dutch Schultz. On the night of February 6, Tex was working at a Midtown club when she spotted her old friend Walter Winchell sitting at a table in a darkened corner observing and taking notes. Eager to prove that she still held power and influence in the murky demimonde where politics, journalism, show business, and crime intersected, she sidled up to Winchell and whispered in his ear. The next morning, Winchell's column in the *Daily Mirror* contained this item: "Local banditti have made one hotel a virtual arsenal and several hotspots are ditto because Master Coll is giving them the headache." A few hours later, Coll was machine-gunned down by a squad of Dutch Schultz's killers, as he made a call from a drugstore phone booth. The assassins weren't pleased that their plan had been revealed in the newspaper. Now Schultz was out for Winchell's blood, and the columnist reputedly paid $90,000 to call off the gangster's goons.

Tex feared that she'd be next and decided it was a great time to take a vacation abroad. She traveled to France, as she told reporters, to rest in beautiful surroundings, but also probably to prove to the world that the nation that had rejected her so icily the previous year now welcomed her warmly. In May, she was back in New York, to open a new club, La Casa, in Valley Stream on Long Island. She was unaware that Dutch Schultz owned the club, but found out when

Texas Guinan, Queen of the Night, at the height
of her fame in Jazz Age Manhattan.

she angered him by firing a showgirl who turned out to be his latest moll. From there she went to Montreal to hostess at the Frolics Club. Canada was out of Schultz's reach, but just to be on the safe side, she sent a driver in her bulletproof Rolls-Royce to follow her and chauffeur her around town.

The job in Montreal lasted through most of the winter, but by January 1933 Tex had returned to Chicago. There was nothing left for her in New York. No nightclubs wanted her and many of her friends had retired or were dead, including her old mentor, Larry Fay. Like many club owners, Fay had been forced to slash salaries at his latest club, Casa Blanca. One night he became the victim of his own modest gesture at unemployment relief when he was shot dead by the club's doorman, whose weekly salary Fay had cut from $100 to $60 so he could afford to hire another man. At least, that's how reporters covering the murder spun the story.

Tex's life was full of disappointment. She couldn't get anything to click. A return to Hollywood and acting in talkies seemed unlikely. She was getting older and was way past her prime as a leading lady. Still, she landed a role in *Broadway Thru a Keyhole*, a film based on Walter Winchell's best-selling book about a gangster who falls in love with a showgirl at one of Tex's clubs. Tex was deeply disappointed that her role, in which she played herself, was minor and fleeting.

She knew she didn't want to go back on the road. Her *Too Hot for Paris* tour had exhausted her; she quickly grew tired of traveling constantly on the "Whoopee Bus," which was crowded and seedy and anything but a fit setting for whoopee. She was playing to unglamorous crowds in unglamorous towns in obscure corners of the nation. In May, her spirits picked up when she secured a gig at the Chicago World's Fair. The cavernous pirate ship structure where she was booked to perform on the fairgrounds turned out to be too large a venue for her show's intimate style of entertainment. Still, Tex worked hard to accommodate her act to the huge space. But when officials changed the fair curfew to midnight, the hour Tex was typically just getting started, she decided to close the show.

Her best option now seemed a dramatic career change. She thought she might like to be a speaker and spiritual adviser in the mold of Aimee Semple McPherson, the Los Angeles celebrity evangelist. Tex had met McPherson in 1927, when the charismatic Californian stopped in New York on a twenty-two-city tour of revival meetings and faith-healing demonstrations, and visited the 300 Club. Like Tex, McPherson was essentially a performer. Her job was to entertain and make a lot of money doing it. She was famous for exciting audiences while speaking in tongues and "healing" the blind and the lame. After she "laid hands" on the afflicted, they could suddenly see and walk, tossing aside their crutches and rising from their wheelchairs to audience cheers.

At the time of her New York visit, McPherson had just suffered a blast of sensational publicity involving a bizarre incident during which she had disappeared for a month, sparking rumors, first, that she'd drowned in the ocean while visiting the beach and, later, that she'd been kidnapped. A ransom note delivered to her mother demanded $500,000. Police reported that another note surfaced threatening to sell her into "white slavery." Five weeks after she vanished, McPherson turned up in the Mexican town of Agua Prieta in Sonora with a story that she had been kidnapped by three Americans from whom she escaped by somehow sawing through the ropes they'd used to tie her up. The media regarded her story as a hoax. McPherson's married lover, an engineer at the Christian radio station owned by her church, also happened to disappear at the same time as McPherson, and at one point he was seen in a coastal town with an unidentified woman who suspiciously resembled the evangelist. The Los Angeles District Attorney called a grand jury to investigate, but eventually decided there wasn't enough evidence to indict McPherson on criminal charges.

None of this, though, dissuaded crowds from flocking to McPherson's cavernous Temple of the Foursquare Gospel church in the Echo Park section of Los Angeles. As with Tex, notoriety only seemed to fuel her fame. In McPherson, Tex saw a kindred spirit who pointed the way to capturing the public's attention outside traditional show business. As a start, she proposed that the two women hold a public debate on the meaning of happiness, but McPherson refused. No doubt she saw this as a publicity stunt to fuel Tex's ambitions, with no profit to herself. Around this time, Tex also tried to direct and star in a play, then a movie, based on McPherson's life, but nothing came of either.

To promote a new, wholesome image of herself, Tex claimed to be the mother of two adopted children, a boy who was seventeen in 1933 and lived with her sister in California while she was on the road, and a nine-year-old girl who lived next door to Tex in New York with the child's birth mother. Tex said she paid for both children's educations, music lessons for the little girl, and a motor boat for the boy, who aspired to be a film director. It's not known if there was any truth to the story, but Tex never said anything publicly about these children until her nightclub career fell apart.

In the fall of 1933, with no other prospects before her, Tex reluctantly went back on tour with her *Too Hot for Paris* ensemble, while still seeking opportunities to reinvent herself as an evangelist in Aimee's mold. When *Too Hot* stopped in Los Angeles, Tex showed up at the Foursquare Gospel church, where she kneeled in prayer and belted out hymns as photographers snapped her picture. Aimee was absent that Sunday, and the service was conducted by her co-pastor and rival, Rheba Crawford, a charismatic redhead who inspired the character of evangelist Sarah Brown in the Broadway musical *Guys and Dolls*. Next, Tex's agent searched for a church that would welcome her as a guest speaker, finding one in Tacoma, Washington, where Tex was booked for a show at the Music Box Theater. At the Church of the Healing Christ, pastor Dr. Henry Victor Morgan agreed to let Tex preach a sermon on "happiness." One Sunday with her latest manager and lover, Eddie Baker, and her press agent in tow, Tex arrived by taxi at the little stone church. Standing in a bright ray of sun from a nearby window and peering through black-rimmed glasses (which she tried to avoid wearing in public), she read from typewritten notes. "I have given my life in trying to make people happy," she said. "Perhaps some of you might not think it is a very good way, but I have made people laugh, and laughter is only a reflection of some form of happiness." She looked old and haggard. A few minutes into her remarks, Tex lost her thread and spoke haltingly and randomly about her showgirls who were back at their hotel sleeping, resting up for the evening's performance. "I have always been proud of my little girls and . . . and tried to protect them against the coarseness and the hard-boiled . . ." she stammered, then stopped abruptly and shuffled her notes. "I . . . I don't mean that." Tears of embarrassment and humiliation filled her eyes.

It was obvious to everyone that "La Guinan," the great Queen of the Night, was not herself.

TWENTY-TWO

———◇———

REPEAL

PAULINE SABIN AND THE SABINES kept up the pressure, holding rallies, blitzing towns and cities from coast-to-coast with Repeal literature, and canvassing voters door to door in an effort to oust local Dry candidates. In New Jersey, a Dry state senator in a Wet district who'd been in office for eighteen years and had a rock-ribbed political machine was defeated in the primary after WONPR decided to oppose him. Six weeks before the primaries, WONPR sent out three thousand cards to residents of the district explaining his connections to the Anti-Saloon League and knocking on voters' doors. He ended up being defeated by a hundred votes.

WONPR's publicity juggernaut continued through the general election, which resulted in FDR's landslide victory on November 8, 1932. Immediately, the new president embarked on an ambitious plan of programs to provide jobs and revive the moribund economy that became known as the New Deal. Pauline had held court on election night in a suite at the Biltmore Hotel in New York City, a few floors above the room where FDR and his entourage awaited the returns. All evening, she "drew a heavy" stream of "society" visitors, noted one reporter, "although it's only in recent years that the Democratic party has become fashionable." Pauline allowed herself a moment of self-satisfaction (a quality she despised in others and rarely indulged in herself). She couldn't help but think her "little organization" had played a role in pushing American politics in the right direction. The Sabines, however, were hardly "a little organization." They were an impassioned Sisterhood of Repeal, 1.3 million strong. Soon the nation would march in line behind them. Pauline felt optimistic about America's return to health and also about Repeal's prospects. The November election had ousted a slew of Dry politicians and gave Wets the majority in both the House and the Senate.

In February 1933, the Twenty-First Amendment to the US Constitution repealing the Eighteenth Amendment came up for debate in Congress. The proposed measure forbid the transportation of intoxicating liquor into states that chose to outlaw it and required a ratification process that would use special state conventions (rather than state legislatures) set up for this purpose. The Repeal resolution passed in the Senate by a vote of 63 to 23 and, four days later, in the House by a vote of 289 to 121. Speaking for Pauline and WONPR, Ione Nicoll told the press the Sabines were cautiously optimistic. "I am glad that the United States at last has acceded to the demands of the people and has taken the first step toward ridding the country of the evils of national Prohibition," she said.

But Pauline knew the battle was far from won; thirty-six of the nation's forty-eight states still had to ratify the amendment before it became law. She pushed forward, traveling constantly to press her cause. Pauline made it WONPR's mission to educate the public on the mechanics of the special conventions and warned her supporters against complacency at a luncheon in May at the Commodore Hotel in Manhattan. Ratification was hardly "a walk-over," she noted. According to a feature of the US Constitution, a Dry state like Idaho with just 459,000 citizens had as much weight as a Wet state like New York with three times as many people. It was entirely possible that even if a majority of voters wanted Repeal, it wouldn't happen. A great deal of work still needed to be done to ensure a large turnout in each state to elect convention delegates. "We repealists now face perhaps the hardest engagement of our fight," Pauline said. "We have shown that Repeal is the will of the people. But enacting that will into law means overcoming one obstacle after another; means tedious labor and ever-lasting vigilance."

In a color-coded map of varying shades of gray to black distributed to each guest at the Commodore luncheon, she classified twenty states as "safely wet"; six as "good prospects for ratification; eleven hopeful; eight doubtful and three dry." She assured her supporters this classification does not mean "we have decided that ratification is impossible" in any one state, only "the degree of effort" required to bring about success. One problem was that in three of the states Pauline considered hopeful, the legislatures had adjourned for the current term, and two were not due to return for another nine months, until January 1934. Valuable momentum might be lost and Prohibitionists could gain a foothold, unless special elections were held in those states.

ELLA BOOLE WASN'T GIVING UP either and vowed "to fight every step of the way." As she told a group of WCTU troops in Brooklyn, "I have been going around the country and find our women more determined than ever to hold up total abstinence as the best means of living and to support prohibition as the best means of dealing with the liquor question." Ella said as much in a letter to President Roosevelt himself in which she also insisted that Repeal would not aid America's economic recovery but instead lead to more drinking and hurt women, children, and families. She adamantly opposed the return of liquor production even though it would also mean the return of the liquor tax. "We do not believe the government should derive revenue from the vices of people," she told Roosevelt.

At the end of May, Pauline directed each of her state chairwomen to organize committees to publicize the upcoming delegate elections to the ratification conventions. This involved telephoning every WONPR member and asking them, in turn, to call those who weren't members to give them the dates of the elections and offer transportation to and from the polls. As it turned out, the Twenty-First Amendment to end Prohibition was ratified more swiftly than Pauline had dreamed. By August 31, twenty states had voted for Repeal, including the Dry strongholds of Alabama, Arkansas, Indiana, and Tennessee. A key to success in these states was the large turnout among African Americans, which the nation's Black newspapers noted Wet Whites had encouraged for their own self-serving purposes. There had been an urgent get-out-the-vote effort, including the distribution of sample ballots by the Democratic League in southern states. In Virginia, the vote ended up solidly for Repeal. As the *Afro-American* noted, "White Virginia, which uses most of its efforts to keep all colored voters away from the polls, has had a change of heart. Reason: All available votes are wanted for repeal of prohibition laws."

The disenfranchisement of Black Americans had been built into many state laws in the South. Poll taxes, discriminatory grandfather clauses, and literacy tests prevented many Black people from voting. For those who were courageous and determined enough to show up at the polls, White officials found ways to discourage them, including posting robed and hooded Ku Klux Klansmen outside polling places.

It seems that anti-liquor Whites were not as aggressive as the Wets in courting Black voters. They relied on Black churches to enforce a Dry message and did nothing to address persistent fears among Black people about the dangers to them of any tampering with the US Constitution. As Kelly Miller noted in the *New York Amsterdam News*, "Negro Americans, especially, can find no cause for rejoicing at the rescindment of the Eighteenth Amendment: Do you think that the Fifteenth Amendment is any more sacrosanct than the Eighteenth?" In Indiana, where opposition to Repeal was particularly strong among African Americans, WONPR worked hard to lobby the Black community and counter their fears. Though Indiana registered a large Dry vote on June 6, the day of its referendum, the state still came out in favor of Repeal with a 64 percent majority. In mid-July, Alabama and Arkansas registered 59 percent majorities for Repeal. In the Tennessee referendum that followed, Black people voted in larger numbers than they ever had before, making possible the state's slim 51 percent Repeal victory. "Negroes experienced no difficulty in voting," the *Pittsburgh Courier* noted. "White leaders on both sides seemed most anxious to have them register an opinion on the issue."

The South, however, was hardly unified on Repeal. North and South Carolina rejected it outright, while Louisiana, Mississippi, and Georgia didn't even bother to hold referenda on the national law. Support for the Eighteenth Amendment remained rock-solid among many Black ministers in Georgia, who, as Jonathan Eig wrote in his biography of Martin Luther King Jr., "regretted that their 'white friends' were only interested in seeing Black people vote when it suited white people's interests." A statement later signed by Reverend Martin Luther King Sr. read, "If our white ministers are really interested in our voting, let them courageously join us to fight for our elemental rights."

PAULINE WAS RELAXED ENOUGH now about the future of Repeal to take a trip with her husband, Charlie. Recently his high blood pressure had flared up, and on doctor's orders he took a break from work at the Guaranty Trust Company. Pauline had stayed with him at Bayberry Land, traveling to Manhattan several days a week for WONPR business. When Charlie was well enough, she went with him by steamer to Europe, but the trip turned out "not very beneficial to Charlie and the doctors advised our coming home," Pauline told Alice du Pont.

By the fall, Charlie seemed recovered enough for Pauline to go back on the road. On the morning of October 10, 1933, she boarded a train for Pennsylvania, which would be one of the last three of the required thirty-six states to ratify repeal. At 8 p.m. she was in the middle of giving a speech in Philadelphia, when Charlie sat down to eat in the large dining room at Bayberry Land overlooking the vast lawn stretching to the bay. The butler left the room to fetch something, and when he returned, he found Charlie slumped in his chair, his head on the table, dead of a cerebral hemorrhage. He was sixty-five. Male reporters who largely still believed a woman's place was in the home attacked Pauline for not being at her husband's side. When she'd left the house that morning, though, she had no reason to think Charlie's life was at risk. He'd played a vigorous round of golf the day before and had not seemed ill. Pauline was devastated. Aside from the tragedy of losing their baby daughter, she told the DNC chair John Raskob, they had been "completely happy. Life without him seems very futile and utterly meaningless."

James Wadsworth, who was now a lobbyist for the Association Against the Prohibition Amendment, waited a few months to allow Pauline time to grieve before offering to divorce his wife if Pauline would have him. Pauline was shocked; she never realized that Wadsworth was in love with her. "I was so dumb," she confessed after turning him down. A few weeks later Wadsworth gave Pauline a gold charm in the shape of a heart with a ruby in the center and, on the back, two engraved letters commemorating her comment, "S.D."

PROHIBITION FINALLY CRASHED on December 5, 1933, when Utah became the thirty-sixth state to ratify the Twenty-First Amendment. Fireworks exploded from rooftops across the nation. Bars everywhere reopened. Hawkers on street corners peddled leftover bathtub gin, and congressmen on Capitol Hill fired their official bootleggers. At the Department of Justice, all that remained of the Prohibition Bureau were the painted gilt letters on the door of the entrance to a suite of abandoned rooms. In New York, cheering crowds thronged Times Square. The revelers were orderly, and the two hundred extra policemen assigned to the district had little to do. By 3 a.m. they'd gone home. Among the few people still out were a group of flappers in silk dresses and cloche hats. Carrying large bolt cutters, and with their boyfriends in tow, they prowled the streets of New York from Harlem to the Bowery, severing the padlocks from speakeasy doors.

Pauline celebrated with six hundred of her Sabines at a grand
dinner in the lustrous ballroom of the Mayflower Hotel in Washington on December 7. The evening's speakers were advised by the
event's organizers to keep their tone light and humorous in deference
to the grieving Pauline's delicate feelings. "If the emotional note is
introduced," the organizers feared, "it would be very difficult for her."
"She just adored [Charlie], and I know she missed him so much, and
yet she would never say 'I miss him,'" Mrs. Willis said. "She didn't
bear her emotions to anybody."

At the Mayflower, the women dined on roast turkey with chestnut
dressing, mashed sweet potatoes, and hearts of lettuce, followed by
coffee ice cream smothered in chocolate sauce. No liquor was served,
though a few women had stashed small flasks in their garters and
could be seen at the end of the evening, laughing and tippling as they
strolled out of the hotel into the dark, boisterous night.

TWENTY-THREE

THE END OF SOMETHING

MABEL WALKER WILLEBRANDT made no public comment on Repeal. In the final days of Prohibition, she was seen hurrying through the corridors of the Treasury Department and, one columnist reported, "fluttering round" the desk of Prohibition Commissioner James M. Doran, a former chemist who was in charge with issuing permits, "breathlessly trying to get importation permits for the liquor interests she had once opposed." The press didn't specify what those interests were, though perhaps they referred to the products of California Fruit Industries, which Mabel still represented. Doran himself would switch sides the very day Repeal passed, becoming the head of the liquor manufacturers' trade association, seeming proof of Pauline Sabin's observation that Prohibition had turned even many of the most righteous Americans into hypocrites.

Texas Guinan wasn't around to join the Repeal celebration. She died a month before Prohibition passed. At the end of October, Tex had arrived in Vancouver for a run at the Beacon Theater. She'd been suffering for several days with severe stomach pains from amoebic dysentery that she'd apparently contracted in Chicago. She managed to get through several shows, but the pain became so severe that she asked to go to the hospital. She underwent surgery on November 4, but never regained consciousness and died the next morning.

Tex had requested that her funeral be held in the Actors' Chapel at St. Malachy's Catholic Church on West Forty-Ninth Street in the heart of Broadway, where she had worshipped every Sunday for years with hundreds of her fellow entertainers. But because of Tex's nightclub notoriety, church officials refused to allow it, so her funeral was held at the Frank E. Campbell Chapel between West Sixty-Sixth and Sixty-Seventh Streets, which had also been the scene of funerals for Fatty Arbuckle and Rudolph Valentino. Thousands of people filed by Tex's silver coffin, where she lay in the same sequined white chiffon gown that she'd worn in *Broadway Thru a Keyhole*, then playing at a theater nearby, under a coverlet of purple pansies and orchids that some reporters thought were artificial. She held a rosary in her left hand. Before her coffin was closed, a male relative removed the diamond rings from her fingers and a diamond necklace that encircled her lifeless neck and dropped them in his pocket.

The mourners moved on to the Gate of Heaven Cemetery in White Plains, New York, for the burial. After the graveside service, the funeral cortege departed, a black snake slinking away, and a mob of Tex's fans grabbed the wreaths and bouquets that had been left behind. Later, after dark, a group of Tex's show business and underworld friends returned to the cemetery and formed a circle around the mausoleum where she lay. No one had thought to bring candles, so Helen Morgan pulled a matchbook from her purse. Lighting match after match, she created small flickers of light until no matches were left and finally the darkness closed in.

"THE NATION IS MAD! Such decadence!" Elizabeth Tilton—a leading Cambridge, Massachusetts, temperance activist—lamented the day Repeal passed, no doubt reflecting the sentiments of her sisters in the WCTU. Earlier, in anticipating the day, she moaned that it was the "destruction of Moral Welfare Legislation with blessings for women and children painstakingly built up through long years." She refused, though, to abandon all hope. "Prohibition *will* return someday," she said, "though I might not be here to see it."

Nor did Ella Boole give up in despair. Though she kept her public comments at a lower pitch than Tilton's, Ella made clear her continued commitment to the temperance cause. "We've lost the battle, but not the war," she declared. "The nature and effect of alcohol has not been changed by Repeal. It still is a narcotic not a stimulant, and it still is habit forming. A drunken man can be reformed only by the grace of the Lord Jesus Christ." Ella retired as national WCTU president on November 1, 1933, a little more than a month before the Twenty-First Amendment went into effect. The move was considered by some reporters and citizens a harbinger of the organization's weakening and eventual demise. As the new head of the World WCTU, Ella focused now on global temperance, but she insisted the national organization was still "very much alive." Its emphasis in the coming years would be on educating the next generation of Americans on the risks of imbibing intoxicating drink. This included producing films showing the dangers of even small quantities of alcohol and circulating pamphlets cataloging the disastrous effects of liquor, wine, and beer on the body and mind. "Our ultimate goal, however," Ella said, "will be to bring back Prohibition."

It was a goal the bootleggers no doubt shared. The great irony of Repeal was that in many places of the nation it became harder to buy liquor after December 5, 1933, than during Prohibition, because the Twenty-First Amendment ceded control over alcohol laws to the states, which enforced strict rules on who could sell, buy, and consume beer, wine, and liquor. In the first three decades after Repeal, 38 percent of Americans lived in areas that had voted through local option laws to keep Prohibition. Seven states banned liquor outright. Only twenty-nine states allowed the sale of liquor by glass in restaurants and bars; twelve states approved only package sales of liquor to be consumed at home. Questions about how to control the post-Repeal liquor trade were legion: What was to be permitted—wine, beer, and spirits—and under what conditions? What hours and days should the sale of liquor be allowed? Should the state liquor boards be elected or appointed?

Pauline's chief concern was keeping newly legal liquor licenses out of the hands of "the bootlegger and racketeer," so as to drive these criminals "out of business" for good. Equally important, she believed, was deglorifying alcohol consumption, to get beyond the notion that drinking was cool, an idea that had developed when it was a forbidden treat. In what the press called one of the most stirring appeals of Pauline's four-year battle to rid America of the evils of Prohibition, she urged Americans as a nation to learn "that drinking in moderation is no different from eating in moderation. Because of the Prohibition law, people began to connive at how they could get a drink. They thought it was smart to drink and talk about drinking. It became a fixation with tens of thousands . . . every state legislature should have in mind when it formulates its liquor codes, the elimination of the thought of drinking from people's minds."

As soon as Repeal was ratified, Pauline suggested disbanding WONPR. She thought it would be a great mistake to just let it "peter out" now that it's work was finished. She didn't want WONPR to be like the old "group of fighting suffragists who, after they got the vote, didn't want to go out of the limelight into the twilight and join their respective parties," she wrote in her diary. She complained to Alice du Pont that instead, they "insisted on forming themselves into the League of Women Voters, whose activities I believe hurt the reputation of the old suffrage organization." Pauline didn't specify what those activities were, though she might have meant that by emphasizing education over organizing, the League relegated the old suffrage leaders to diminished political power. "I should hate to see us do anything of this kind," Pauline told Alice du Pont. "I dread seeing our organization disintegrate, which I believe it is bound to do unless we go out of existence with a bang." The $40,000 that was left in WONPR's coffers would be spent to honor the lease on its headquarters through April 1934 and to pay the salaries of a few employees in the national office until "Ratification is a fact," she told Mrs. du Pont. It's unknown what happened to the balance, though Pauline suggested in her letter to Alice du Pont that it be turned over "to a charity which is national in scope."

On January 22, 1934, eight of WONPR's top officers feted Pauline at a luncheon at Ione Nicoll's home. As dessert was served, Ione handed Pauline a carefully wrapped package. Inside was a small landscape by Renoir, which the women had chosen as a symbol expressing "the admiration and appreciation" the entire organization "felt for Mrs. Sabin and her great work." Pauline had a passion for French painting, and Renoir in particular. The small landscape "is a gem and has a vividness that is in a way suggestive of Mrs. Sabin herself," Alice du Pont noted in a draft of a letter intended to go to those who had contributed to the generous gift.

THE LAST TIME ELLA BOOLE and Pauline Sabin were in a room together was at the Roosevelt Hotel in Manhattan on the evening of November 19, 1934. The occasion was a banquet sponsored by the American Woman's Association (AWA), a consortium of professional women's groups, who every year gave out a medal to one woman of "eminent attainment," who in her personal and professional life exemplified "intellectual honesty, integrity, magnanimity, progressive vision, emotional stability, physical fitness, social adaptability and a sense of humor." Previous winners included Amelia Earhart, Margaret Sanger, and Frances Perkins, FDR's labor secretary and the first woman to serve in a presidential cabinet. The name of the 1934 winner had been a closely guarded secret, except to the winner herself, who had promised to attend the banquet and give a talk. The evening dragged on through five speakers and a six-course French meal that featured fruit au kirsch, striped bass, potatoes rissoles, and hearts of endive. Finally, over a dessert of bombe glacée and mignardises, Jeanie Rumsey Sheppard, of the New York State WONPR chapter, stepped to the podium to announce the winner, "a woman who has always been a crusader for good government and who was the able, courageous and victorious leader of the campaign for repeal . . . Mrs. Charles H. Sabin." Only later was it revealed that Pauline won the award over First Lady Eleanor Roosevelt, Anne Morrow Lindbergh, and Edith Wharton. In her remarks, Pauline urged the hundreds of women in attendance to get more involved in public life. "I know what women can do," she said. "I have such confidence in their fearless persuasion. I have known their loyalty to a Cause. I have seen them put principle before personalities. I have seen them brave in political battles when men were cowards."

Ella sat stone-faced in the audience, her hands in her lap as applause for Pauline rang through the ballroom. She was not the only woman "who had worked against" Pauline who had come to dinner "not knowing who they were about to honor," noted the *New York Times*. Perhaps if she had known, she would have stayed home.

EPILOGUE

MABEL WALKER WILLEBRANDT STARTED her private practice in Washington, DC, in an office in the Shoreham Building on the same floor as a John Sirica, a young attorney who decades later would become famous as the judge in the Watergate case that brought down President Richard Nixon. She got to know Sirica when she invited him to use her extensive law library, and it didn't take long for them to become close friends despite the difference in their ages. There was much to draw them together—a shared hard-driving intelligence, a fierce ambition, and a great loathing of wiretapping. Mabel so vehemently opposed it, Sirica told Dorothy Brown, that she wrote a large section of a brief against it for one of his most important cases. Their working-class backgrounds also reinforced the bond. Mabel admired Sirica's scrappiness—he was an amateur boxer—and up-from-the-bootstraps immigrant roots. She always distrusted and felt reserved around people who'd grown up in wealth and privilege, especially those from elite East Coast families, like FDR and his wife, Eleanor. Still, Mabel invited the First Lady to teas she regularly hosted at the Sulgrave Club and praised Eleanor publicly for her integrity and her example "to us all" of how to live a courageous, sincere life.

Mabel remained a bedrock Republican but found much to admire in FDR's New Deal, though she disliked several members of Roosevelt's so-called Brain Trust, his group of advisers, including Columbia University economics professor Rexford Guy Tugwell and liberal lawyers Benjamin Cohen and Thomas Gardiner Corcoran, whom she saw regularly at Washington political and social gatherings. She told Laura and Carl Lomen she thought some of those in Roosevelt's inner circle were out "to wreck the country. I never liked any of them, although all—including the ubiquitous Eleanor—were outwardly nice to me and never discarded and used me as did the 'new' Republicans," presumably a reference to Hoover and the men around him.

Nevertheless, Mabel cultivated Roosevelt, applauding him in congratulatory letters after his 1935 State of the Union message, his 1938 Labor Day speech, and his remarks opening the New York World's Fair in April 1939. In each of these speeches, Roosevelt expressed his reverence for the Constitution and the profound need for national unity, ideas Mabel also wholeheartedly supported. At the back of her mind, of course, was the hope that Roosevelt would offer her a judgeship. Despite Hoover's rebuffs, Mabel had never given up on this dream, and her letters to the president, which Dorothy Brown drew on in her book, have a tone of barely disguised obsequiousness. In 1938, she wrote Roosevelt to thank him for his "courageous stand for liberalism," and praising him for using the presidency to put forth policies to improve the lives of ordinary Americans. She also sent a letter praising Roosevelt for appointing Hugo Black to the Supreme Court, citing Black's "incorruptible courage, studiousness, resourcefulness and fairness." No doubt, she hoped Roosevelt would see that she herself possessed these qualities. Two years later, when another vacancy came up in the Supreme Court, she urged Roosevelt to appoint a woman. "Mr. President, it will be years and years, if ever, before we have a chief Executive like you with enough courage and independence to do it," she wrote FDR. She believed the other justices would accept a woman in their ranks, except, of course, Justice James Clarke McReynolds, the racist, sexist, anti-Semitic bigot who turned his back on her when she argued cases before him during Prohibition. He "feels so strongly on the subject, he might resign," Mabel noted. "But that wouldn't be an insurmountable loss!" Mabel told the president she couldn't "bear to see this opportunity" to appoint a woman "go by." But go by it did. Roosevelt ended up appointing William O. Douglas to the court.

AFTER LEAVING GOVERNMENT, Mabel bought an elegant, historic home at 3013 Dumbarton Street in the heart of Georgetown. Built in 1850, the black-shuttered red brick house had four bedrooms and fireplaces in most rooms. Mabel sent Dorothy to a series of exclusive private schools, ending with Madeira, which sat on a sprawling campus in Northern, Virginia, and where the heiresses Brooke Astor and Cornelia Vanderbilt were also students. Though Mabel had a visceral distrust of people with wealth and privilege, those were exactly the circumstances in which she was raising her own daughter. When Dorothy showed a talent for music, Mabel bought her a gleaming Steinway grand piano and hired Rose D'Amore, a popular society pianist, as her teacher. Mabel was avid for Dorothy to meet top people, including the film stars she represented, and one year arranged a birthday party for her daughter in Hollywood attended by Joan Crawford and Clark Gable, who posed with the awkward, pigtailed twelve-year-old in a photo that captured the girl's extreme unease.

Dorothy was happiest with her grandparents on the ranch in Escondido that Mabel owned with Fred Horowitz. In 1932, before Mabel sent Dorothy to the ranch to spend the summer with Myrtle and David Walker, she urged her parents to be strict with their granddaughter. "I am convinced that the only chance of [her] development is stern, constant observation so that she can get away with nothing—coupled, of course, with love and affection," Mabel wrote her mother. Wearing cowboy boots and spurs, Dorothy rode her pony through the eucalyptus groves surrounding the ranch and chased wild horses. Her grandparents gave her a pet hen and taught her how to raise and care for chickens. At the end of the summer, Myrtle convinced Mabel to let Dorothy stay the year, where she thrived in the local public school, playing the lead and singing a solo in the school play, while earning top grades. Encouraged by Myrtle, who herself wrote poetry, Dorothy tried her hand at composing verse. The girl's poems were so accomplished that her proud teacher sent them to the superintendent of schools of San Diego County.

Dorothy's country idyll didn't last, however. The following fall, Mabel brought her child back to Washington and enrolled her in the Sacred Heart School, where she chafed at the nuns' iron rule and was an indifferent student. Life perked up for Dorothy whenever her grandparents arrived for a visit. During these sojourns, David spent time at Mabel's office helping with her correspondence, while Myrtle took charge of Dorothy when the girl wasn't at school. Mabel agreed with Myrtle that Dorothy needed fresh air and nature, so in 1935 she bought a farm in Pennsylvania in the foothills of the Blue Ridge Mountains, which she called Walker Fields, where Dorothy spent many weekends hiking, riding, and helping her grandmother care for a coop full of chickens.

One afternoon while driving her parents from Walker Fields to Dumbarton Street, Mabel became frustrated by the snail's pace of a car ascending the hill in front of them, swerved around it, and crashed head-on into an oncoming vehicle. Dorothy wasn't with them at the time. David had only minor bruises, but Myrtle suffered a concussion and scalp lacerations. Despite her Christian Science beliefs, Myrtle consented to be treated by a medical doctor, who kept her in the hospital for several days. Mabel broke her arm in the crash, and a local constable charged her with passing illegally. Worse, the driver of the car she hit and his three passengers sued her for $62,000 in damages. It's unknown how the case was resolved or what became of the traffic violation. Mabel continued to drive recklessly, much to the concern and chagrin of her family. Mabel's penchant for speeding could not have been good for her mother's blood pressure, which, always high, soared during times of stress. On January 9, 1938, Myrtle died suddenly a few minutes after returning to Dumbarton Street following a drive with Mabel. The older woman had turned on the radio and settled herself on the living room couch, when she keeled over, probably from a heart attack or stroke. She was seventy-six.

With Myrtle's death, Dorothy lost her chief protection against Mabel's social ambitions. After graduating from Madeira and turning eighteen, Dorothy dutifully endured a debutante dance at the fashionable Sulgrave Club, wearing the requisite strapless gown and above-the-elbow white gloves. Mabel wanted Dorothy to "marry some high-priced lawyer or famous doctor, and she was going to do the most she could to make that happen," said Dorothy's son, Jan Van Dyke. But Dorothy had a rebellious streak and her own ideas of what she wanted her life to be. After briefly attending Bucknell University, she enrolled at Wheaton College, an evangelical Christian institution in Illinois. She began calling herself by her middle name "Rae" and fell in love with an aspiring minister, Hendrick Van Dyke, a man nine years her senior who'd returned to school after a stint in the army. When Rae wanted to leave college to marry Van Dyke, Mabel consented grudgingly, writing to Hendrick that she "detected" in his character a "a detached dependence, perhaps I should say dreaminess, that gives me concern for your future." She also worried about the difference in the couple's ages. "You took a talented girl, very young, to mold to *your* plans and purposes," Mabel scolded, "and thereby took *from* her, freedom of mind and choice and social contacts, during three or four formative years when we all learn lots by making lots of mistakes—that are our own mistakes that no one has the right to make for us. Forgoing that freedom for love of you may bring her 'sweet bondage' with deep compensations—I can . . . only hope . . . that in after years she will still feel that what she has missed is nothing, and what she has gained in love and understanding and a home, from you, is fulfillment."

Mabel seemed unable or unwilling to see that Dorothy might have a different idea than she did of what constituted a successful life. Inevitably, Dorothy resented her mother for trying to force her to be someone she wasn't. Through Dorothy remained loyal and affectionate to Mabel throughout their lives, there seemed to be "no deep love," at least on Dorothy's part, said Jan Van Dyke. Mabel sensed this, and it caused her mournful regret. The Van Dykes had three sons and moved frequently, starting out in New Jersey, where Hendrick graduated from the Princeton Theological Seminary. Once he became ordained, the Presbyterian Church moved him and his family to postings in Michigan, Delaware, Maryland, Oregon, and Alaska. As time went on, Jan Van Dyke recalled, Mabel "realized that my mom was happy with my dad," and she regretted that she had questioned Dorothy's choice of partner.

It was just one of the ways Mabel came to believe she had failed Dorothy. Throughout the girl's childhood, Mabel had been overwhelmed by work and didn't have much time for her daughter. Frequent trips to LA often kept her away from home for long periods. Her Hollywood clients, in addition to MGM chief Louis B. Mayer and his top stars, came to include the directors Frank Capra, Leo McCarey, and W. S. Van Dyke (no relation to her son-in-law). Mabel handled their tax problems and whatever other legal issues came up in their lives. She introduced them to her wide circle of Washington contacts, and entertained them when they were in town at parties attended by ambassadors, politicians, judges, and generals. At a fete director Van Dyke hosted at the Mayflower Hotel with Mable as the guest of honor, the orchestra played themes from his movies, while Mabel received guests, as the *Washington Post* noted, in a white lace, off-the-shoulder gown with a plunging back marked at the base of her spine with a cluster of white orchids. For a woman who had no interest in "girlie-girlie stuff" and had once abhorred references to her appearance in the press, she'd nevertheless learned to dress to impress.

IT WAS THE KIND OF PARTY Pauline Sabin regularly attended as a new fixture of the Washington social scene. The Repeal leader was living in the nation's capital now with her third husband, Dwight F. Davis, a widower and a former secretary of war under Coolidge. Davis also was an amateur tennis champion and the founder of the international tennis tournament, the Davis Cup. The couple had been married on May 8, 1936, in the chapel in Riverside Church in New York City with only their family members present, including Pauline's mother and sister, her two sons, Morton's wife, and Davis's two daughters from his first marriage.

The couple moved into a grand red brick house at 2145 Decatur Place NW, just a few miles from Mabel's home on Dumbarton Street in Georgetown. "It was the most enormous house I'd ever seen," recalled Pauline's granddaughter Pauline Willis, with endless rooms and a formal ballroom placed on the west side of the house to take advantage of the evening light. Pauline became one of the most popular hostesses in town, her parties as celebrated as they had been at Bayberry Land for the elegant food, drink, and entertainment, and the exciting mix of movers and shakers from Supreme Court justices and senators to industrialists, cabinet ministers, and presidents.

Pauline's Washington salon rivaled that of Alice Roosevelt Longworth, her girlhood pal and adult frenemy. The two women attended each other's dinners and parties, and it vexed Pauline to no end that Teddy Roosevelt's famous daughter got more press than she did. After one columnist quoted Alice saying "a soufflé doesn't rise twice," Pauline grumbled in her diary, "she's been credited with so many witticisms which she has not uttered, I will now wait to find out whether or not this one is original." Pauline also complained that Alice favored cocktail parties over luncheons, and Pauline loathed cocktail parties, "the invention of the Devil" in her words, which had been growing in popularity since Repeal. The idea of standing around and drinking for two hours before dinner seemed ludicrous to Pauline. She never had more than one cocktail herself, and she always felt bored sipping her drink, waiting around for the meal to begin. Drinking, she believed, dulled people's sensibilities and impeded interesting conversation—to her, the most important element of any social gathering. Pauline hosted only one cocktail party a year, in spring when her garden bloomed, and she cut the cocktail hour before her dinners to a brisk forty-five minutes.

Meanwhile, Pauline's passion for activism never diminished.

Soon after Repeal, she'd gone to work for the American Liberty League, a group of mostly wealthy conservatives who had been on her side during Prohibition and now opposed FDR's New Deal. They included Pauline's old friends James Wadsworth and Pierre du Pont, but also ranged to the Democrats Al Smith and the former DNC chair John Raskob. The president's programs to combat the Depression seemed to them to be centralizing too much power in the federal government, which had also been one of their chief objections to the Eighteenth Amendment. Pauline had hoped to drum up support for the League among the Sabines, but this never happened, and soon she turned her attention to co-chairing Fiorello La Guardia's campaign for mayor of New York. La Guardia, a popular former US congressman, was running on a Fusion Party platform supported by reform-minded Republicans, Democrats, and Independents. "No one in her social set cared a hoot about La Guardia," the short, pudgy son of Italian immigrants, said Pauline Willis, "but my grandmother did because she thought he was going to help the poor and the middle class. She thought he would get good things done." The flamboyant Tammany Mayor Jimmy Walker had been forced out of office by scandal, and Pauline was determined that La Guardia would take his place. She had joined his campaign as an independent, neither as a Republican nor as a Democrat, telling a reporter, "You can see that my politics are a little complicated."

As vice president of the Fusion Campaign Committee, Pauline had opened her headquarters in the Paramount Building in Midtown Manhattan with an appeal to all New York City women who are "alarmed and distressed by present conditions" to join the Fusion organization and get in touch with her, "in order that they may be put to work." She said she was never one who thought "all Tammany" politicians "had horns," and that her opposition was to the present Tammany Machine left behind by Walker. Mostly, though, she was for La Guardia, "who knows the city from A to Z. . . . He is honest and he would make an excellent Mayor, particularly as he is not controlled by anybody," she said.

Pauline credited LaGuardia with influencing then-Governor Franklin Roosevelt to appoint Judge Samuel Seabury to conduct the investigation into Tammany corruption that had led to Walker's ouster. "I believe that the days of bosses are over," as moribund as Prohibition itself, she declared. In the general election, La Guardia faced Tammany's Democratic incumbent John P. O'Brien and Joseph V. McKee, a lawyer and a high school teacher from the Bronx running on the new Recovery Party ticket. Pauline's approach to the Fusion campaign was the same as it had been for WONPR, a fierce drive to register members and a commitment to "carry the fight right down into the trenches," with Ione Nicoll at her side once again as her chief deputy. She organized leaders in every borough of the city and created a bureau for women speakers. When La Guardia won the election in November, Pauline rejoiced, though as Mrs. Dwight Davis of Washington, DC, she would no longer be part of the new mayor's constituency.

She still prided herself, however, on having the pulse of women in New York and throughout the nation. As a member of the District of Columbia Advisory Committee to the 1939–40 New York World's Fair, Pauline led a protest of a planned round-up of female opinion by the fair's organizers on the theme of "Peace and Freedom." The plan was to have women across America write hundred-word letters suggesting how the United States could maintain peace and freedom at a time of war. But Pauline feared that women fomenting "pacifist, Nazi, and communist propaganda" would infiltrate and taint the survey and adversely affect US foreign policy. She wrote the head of the advisory committee that she thought the round-up would be "meaningless, harmful to the Fair, and contrary to the best interests of the country. . . . While it might increase the gate receipts, [it] would in no way express the real opinion of the women of the country. Organized groups which profess various theories, and particularly subversive organizations which prate about 'Peace and Freedom' sometimes while waiting to destroy them, would all welcome the opportunity to air their views under the auspices of the World's Fair while millions of unorganized women occupied in their daily tasks, in business, on the farms, or in their homes, would not take part in such a meaningless advertising scheme." It's unknown if the survey was canceled, but it didn't receive any publicity after Pauline's protest.

Throughout World War II, Pauline directed volunteer services for the American Red Cross, overseeing a million volunteers in canteens, motor corps, and other services to the military abroad. Every day, she went to the Red Cross Auditorium, winding her way to her desk through a forest of workers sewing items for soldiers at clattering machines, dressed in the navy serge Red Cross uniform. She topped her graying blonde hair with a kepi cap like the one worn by General Charles de Gaulle himself, who was exiled in London while the Nazis occupied Paris. Though London was under siege by German bombs, the city's elites carried on an elaborate social life that required formal attire. Women, however, had no access to the new fashions, so to help Lady Nancy Astor, the first woman member of the British parliament, keep up a stylish appearance, Pauline sent her a cache of ball gowns from her own supply.

The war also saw Pauline once again on the political battlefield opposite Ella Boole and the WCTU, who had not given up on seeing Prohibition restored. With no facts to back up her claims, Mrs. D. Leigh Colvin, New York's WCTU president, argued at the group's 1944 annual convention that the return of legal liquor to America had been "primarily responsible for the increase in drunken mothers, unfaithful wives and neglected children." At the same meeting, Ella, still president of the World WCTU, declared that "the rise in venereal disease and the general lowering of moral standards" had been caused largely by alcohol. That year, the WCTU pushed Congress to pass a law to bring back Prohibition under emergency conditions, arguing that it was necessary during wartime to conserve all resources, including liquor.

Pauline reacted to Ella's efforts with fury, vowing to reignite WONPR, though none of the Sabines still around were "as young" or "so strong" as they once were. "However, I am convinced that not one of us is willing to sit complacently by and do nothing while there is any danger of a Prohibition law or anything even slightly resembling it being slipped in again," she wrote in a letter to the editor of the *New York Times* that was printed in the paper on January 12, 1944. Bowing to pressure from the WCTU and other Dry groups, a House Judiciary Committee held hearings on the matter in early January. Nothing came of them, however, and likewise with the new Prohibition bill introduced in the House by the South Carolina Democrat Joseph R. Bryson.

Never "given to being low spirited," Ella refused to be depressed and complain about the failure of the bill. "It is important to endure what we have to without grumbling," she told Margaret Munns, the national WCTU treasurer and her frequent correspondent in her later years. "There is no use being unhappy over the things we can't help." At the same time, she insisted Prohibition would not only one day be restored in the United States, but would also be imposed throughout the world. Since her election as president of the World WCTU in 1931, Ella had directed a force of anti-liquor crusaders in dozens of countries, from South Africa, France, and Italy to Germany and Scandinavia. The battle reached even tiny Pitcairn Island, a British territory in the South Pacific, where WCTU workers lectured the descendants of rum-drinking bounty mutineers on the necessity of total abstinence. On this point, Ella remained firm. At a dinner in Paris at the home of her nephew who'd married a Frenchwoman, she was dismayed to see guests flavoring their water glasses with red wine. "To convince such people there was a danger in this small amount of alcohol is difficult, especially in a Catholic country," she told Margaret Munns.

Finland—the only non-Muslim nation besides the United States that still had Prohibition during the Roaring Twenties—had ended its noble experiment in 1932, after twelve years. No other nation seemed interested in a mandatory liquor ban, a fact Ella attributed to a failure of leadership. Consequently, she spent much of her time searching out and recruiting women with forceful personalities in foreign countries to proselytize for the WCTU. "I feel that the great need of the WCTU is to develop women as we used to in the old days," she said. In Chile and Brazil, that meant enlisting Catholics, though Ella hoped local chapters in those nations would be organized with Protestant leadership whenever possible. As she told Munns, "We must be broadminded enough to invite all to join us, but in general the Catholic priests are not sympathetic with the temperance work and their women are not trained for leadership." She also approved of welcoming Jews into the WCTU, and like Catholics, placing them "at the heads of certain departments." But she felt strongly that top brass at the WCTU should forever be Protestant. She made no comment on whether Black women should have national leadership roles in the organization—perhaps the possibility had never occurred to her.

With a modest quarterly travel stipend and a salary of around $3,500 a year, Ella worked tirelessly traveling the world. "If the WCTU did not function there would be no activity against the liquor traffic," she told Munns. "I am delighted that the WCTU is holding fast to its principles in so many countries and at least the world recognizes that we are setting the right kind of example." At home in Brooklyn, she kept long hours at her desk, with only a part-time stenographer and Florence, her ever-loyal daughter, to help her with her correspondence.

After Ella developed "a cardiac condition," in the late 1930s, she remodeled the home she shared with Florence to create a bedroom/bath/office suite for herself on the ground floor, so she no longer had to walk up and down stairs. Her doctor ordered her to stop taking the subway because it involved climbing so many stairs and to cut back on work. "It is strange for me to be adopting moderation, but it is moderation in activities, not drinking," she noted sardonically. Ella cut out stair climbing but failed to ease up on work. Her largest, most complex tasks included organizing and presiding over international conferences and conventions. In June 1937, close to three thousand WCTU members from fifty-two countries met in Washington, DC. At the last minute, just in time to catch a boat sailing for the

United States, the German temperance president Frau Anna Klara Fischer got permission from Hitler to attend. The Führer "recognizes the WCTU's value," one of Ella's lieutenants told a reporter. "When the Olympics were held [in Berlin in 1936] he placed all women athletes in Frau Fischer's charge. He didn't want any training rules broken, especially the one about drinking."

Only the war slowed Ella down.

She and Florence had planned to sail for Europe in the spring of 1940 and tour the English countryside ahead of the World WCTU meeting scheduled for London in May. The trip and the convention had to be canceled when hostilities broke out. Five months later, in October, more than a year before America would enter the conflict, Ella listened on the radio to the draft lottery in Washington, DC, as a blindfolded Secretary of War Henry Stimson, with President Roosevelt looking on, reached into a giant fishbowl containing 7,836 numbers encased in small celluloid capsules and pulled out the first one. A woman in the audience at the Interdepartmental Auditorium on Constitution Avenue shrieked when 158, her son's number, was read. Ella would never forget how the mother's anguished cries pierced the airwaves.

Exacerbating the tragedy of war for Ella was the difficulty it posed for promoting temperance. "There never was a time when our work seemed to be in a more discouraging condition than just now," she reported to Munns. "The Army and the Navy [are] against us," and the military authorities are "promoting the sale of beer." She also felt outraged that the Roosevelts served champagne bought with taxpayer money at the White House. She thought temperance people had a right to demand that the First Couple pay for the champagne themselves. Similarly, she was "very sick at heart" that liquor was consumed at the summit meeting in Cairo in 1943 attended by Churchill, Roosevelt, and Chiang Kai-shek. "That the three men who have the greatest authority of anybody in the world should becloud their brains by the use of alcohol" distressed her greatly. She also didn't approve of Churchill dancing and Roosevelt composing a song at the event, though Ella insisted that she and her sisters in the WCTU were not "killjoys."

At home, she found more to vex her. She noticed that newspaper obituaries failed to reference the temperance activities of prominent people who'd once supported her cause, and she suspected "a conspiracy" on the part of editors to omit any reference to the Dry sympathies of notable people who died. On the East Coast, she had trouble finding a restaurant that didn't serve liquor. The Hotel Dennis in Atlantic City, her favorite dining spot when she and Florence vacationed in Ocean Grove, had gone Wet in 1942, "the last of the big Dry hotels" in the resort city "to surrender," she told Munns. "They will have a cocktail lounge and a bar. I am so sorry."

Ella kept up her manic traveling and lecturing until June 1947, when she retired as world chief of the WCTU. From then on, she lived quietly in Brooklyn with Florence, who continued to cook and take care of her mother. Her siblings and stepchildren through William Boole were all dead, and she felt regretful that she had not stayed in better touch with them when they were alive. "I gave up all my family interest during the years I was [WCTU] president," she confessed, and now she and Florence were "almost without relatives." Like Mabel, she regretted that she'd always put work over family. "I see now that it was a mistake, but it is too late to remedy that mistake now."

Ella lived five more years, dying at home on March 13, 1952, after suffering a stroke. She was ninety-three.

LIKE ELLA'S FINAL YEARS, the last decade of Pauline Sabin's life was marred by family sorrow. She had been married to Dwight Davis for nine years when he fell ill and died of a heart attack at home on November 28, 1945, widowing Pauline for the second time. She sold the couple's Decatur Place home and moved first to an estate on Foxhill Road, then to a more modest house on S Street in Georgetown, where she enjoyed a view of the Washington Monument from her bedroom window.

The loss of her third husband might have sharpened Pauline's sense of the brevity and precarity of life and the preciousness of family, and softened her feelings toward her firstborn, Morton Smith. But this did not happen. Mother and son remained estranged. Pauline's hopes that Morton's second marriage to Alice Rand would lead to stability and an end to his drinking were never fulfilled. His union with Alice produced three children, a son and two daughters, but his drinking never abated. Morton's marriage collapsed, he lost his job at an investment firm, and Pauline cut him off financially. He ended up living in Florida, though his children don't know how he supported himself.

Pauline stayed close to her younger son, who, in sharp contrast to his brother, led a life of great purpose and high achievement. After graduating from Harvard and Columbia Law School, Jimmie Smith served as a navy pilot during World War II and went on to become assistant secretary of the navy under President Dwight Eisenhower.

Though Pauline considered Morton's ex-wife Alice immature and unprepared for motherhood—after all, Alice had been just nineteen years old when she married—Pauline continued to support her in an apartment in Manhattan, where Alice was raising her children. Alice's daughters, however, acknowledge that, like Pauline, their mother wasn't very maternal. When the girls and their brother were four, five, and six, Alice left them alone with a cook and governess while she went out around town and traveled. Several years later, when Alice was remarried to a travel and sportswriter, Pauline stepped in and took the children to live with her.

They never knew their grandfather, their father's father and Pauline's first husband, J. Hopkins Smith. Pauline Willis and her brother met him only once a few days before Pauline died. They knew he existed, however, because they'd see his name on the pad by the telephone in the pantry whenever the butler James Coker took messages from him for Pauline and J.'s son Jimmie. Pauline rarely spoke to her ex-husband. Usually, if she had something to communicate to him about their children and grandchildren, she'd have her secretary call his secretary.

Pauline didn't want to have anything to do with her ex-husband.

"Granny would never waver on anything. If she was through with someone, she was through with them," Mrs. Willis said. "One of her favorite expressions was 'fish or cut bait.' I used to hear that a lot in childhood." Pauline was the queen, and she would hurl aside people she became furious with or who didn't come up to her standards. No one in the family could compete with her iron will; no one dared challenge her decisions. Sometimes, when Pauline "was too harsh with us, the English nanny would step in and say, 'Now, Madam, they're only children,'" recalled Mrs. Willis. Ironically, Mrs. Willis notes, "Some of the choices Granny made with us came from the same strengths that led her to accomplish so much politically." Once as a young child, when Mrs. Willis was at Southampton Hospital with strep throat during the national polio scare, Pauline entered her room "and everyone just dropped out of the way. It was a total takeover," Mrs. Willis recalled. Pauline saw to it that the family doctor, who was known to be one of the hospital's top physicians. cared for the little girl, who it turned out had escaped polio. "Her word was go. You never said 'no' to her," said Mrs. Willis. "I had no choice about anything, even my own wedding."

A second granddaughter, Sheila Cochran, wasn't a good test taker, so her grades suffered. "I think I was the only person at St. Timothy's boarding school who failed current events, which is pretty hard to do, though I don't think Granny ever knew," she said. Still, Pauline decided Sheila shouldn't go to college. Instead, she treated Sheila to a several months-long tour of Europe. On their return, Pauline helped her granddaughter get a job as a secretary at the CIA, where Sheila worked until her marriage.

And yet, Pauline loved her grandchildren fiercely—a love they returned equally fiercely—and she wanted them to enjoy their young lives. The girls and their brother thrived during summers at Bayberry Land, when "there was a lot of laughter," Mrs. Willis recalled. Appearances also were important. To help her maid's brother who struggled as a cobbler in Boston, Pauline sent the children's shoes to him at the end of the school year to be repaired and shined. One spring, saleswomen from Henri Bendel and Bergdorf Goodman in New York arrived by train to Washington with trunks of clothes for the girls to try on. "Granny had a huge dressing room and we'd try on all these dresses. She bought five dresses for each of us," said Mrs. Willis. Once, during the height of the Cold War, Pauline took the girls with her to the White House where she was advising on art for the presidential walls. While Pauline discussed paintings with the head of the National Gallery, David Finley, the girls were left alone to wander the mansion, ending up in the basement exploring the vast bomb shelter.

In 1949, Pauline sold Bayberry Land, but kept on the staff, including her longtime butler. She dressed in formal attire every night for dinner whether she dined with fifty guests or just one. After Dwight Davis's death, she often entertained James Forrestal, President Harry Truman's brilliant but troubled secretary of defense. "Forrestal dined here" and "Forrestal came in" for cocktails, she often noted in her diary.

Forrestal was attracted to Pauline "not only by her beauty and style but also by her conspicuous intelligence and competence," wrote his biographers Townsend Hoopes and Douglas Brinkley. "She had a frank and gracious way of meeting and dealing with people of every background and persuasion. She was warm and feminine, yet seriously interested and informed about major political issues." Pauline told a friend she wanted to make Forrestal her fourth husband. Still, her granddaughters don't think they were lovers, as it would have been difficult for Pauline to have an affair without involving her staff in an awkward way. "Her maid always dressed and undressed her, and it would have taken the maid ten minutes just to undo the complicated buckles on my grandmother's T-strap shoes," said Mrs. Willis. What's more, Forrestal could never bring himself to divorce his alcoholic wife. Then, in May 1949, he committed suicide by jumping out of a window at Bethesda Naval Hospital, where he was being treated for depression. Pauline was shattered.

Ione Nicoll had died the same way nine years earlier, in August

1940, in a sixteen-story fall from a room at New York Hospital, where she was being treated for an undisclosed ailment, possibly a depression sparked by the death of her husband in 1938. Though the police called Ione's death accidental, her family believes she committed suicide. She plunged to her death soon after a visit from a doctor she'd been dating, who, according to family lore, told her he planned to marry another woman.

After Forrestal's death, Pauline found herself without romantic prospects for the first time since adolescence. By then, however, her health was failing. She would not have had the energy for a love affair, even if an interesting man had been available. Nor did she have the strength for another political fight. Still, the McCarthy Red Scare of the early 1950s inspired Pauline's desire to organize again—this time a watchdog body to protect the civil liberties of Americans. But Pauline was suffering from amyotrophic lateral sclerosis (ALS), or Lou Gehrig's disease, and she was too sick to do it. One of her last political acts, performed as she lay dying in her home on S Street, was to write a letter to the *Washington Post*, condemning "the sickness of fear, of mutual suspicion, of unhealthy credulity" provoked by the McCarthy witch-hunts. "An energetic organization is needed to take the part of victims who have nowhere to turn when agents of their own government unjustly decide to destroy them," she wrote, thinking back to her glory days leading the fight for Repeal. She vowed to stand in spirit as she had throughout her life "with other right-thinking citizens, if such an organization is formed."

Her last years had been eased by her close relationship with her younger son, Jimmie, and with her seven grandchildren. At the time of her death at sixty-eight on December 27, 1955, she had not seen her elder son, Morton, for fourteen years. Jimmie had Pauline's gravestone etched with her dates, 1887–1955, and her legal name, Pauline Sabin Davis. Charlie, though, was the great love of her life, and so Pauline chose to be buried next to him in Southampton Cemetery on Long Island, and not with Davis, who was laid to rest at Arlington Cemetery. She wanted to spend eternity with the husband who stood beside her in her finest hour, when she led America's fight to repeal Prohibition.

AT THE TIME OF PAULINE'S DEATH, Mabel was no longer her neighbor. She had sold her Dumbarton house and Pennsylvania farm and moved to California full-time, sharing a home with her father at 5718 N. Loma Street in Temple City. She also bought a date farm in Indio, California, that she named Walkersands and where she entertained friends on the weekends and holidays.

By now, Mabel had given up all hope of becoming a judge, though she had held on to this dream until after World War II. In November 1948, she wrote Hoover, then America's only living ex-president, asking him to put in a good word for her with President Harry Truman. "Could you have it in your heart to recommend me for an appointment to the Circuit Court of Appeals for the 9th Circuit (California) to President Truman?" she wrote him. "I'm 59, my daughter has her own family; my father's 88. I have enough to live on, but I am alone. There are twelve to fifteen years ahead of me that I'd like to devote to something worthwhile in my profession. I'd try to be a good judge and make you proud of me." Though Truman was a Democrat, Mabel believed he might be open to appointing her, unlike Roosevelt, who before his death in 1945, "only appointed New Dealers and personal friends" to the bench. Mabel thought Truman "might *like* to demonstrate that he now represents *all* the people," and he "might take pride in appointing a woman and a Republican if you put it up to him." Hoover, who had failed to make her the nation's first female attorney general twenty years earlier, disappointed her once again. "My dear, I would do anything for you," he scrawled disingenuously across the top of Mabel's letter, perhaps to be typed up later by his secretary as a reply. "But my relations with the man you mention would do you more harm than good. I will inquire for a better proposer." He never did.

Mabel felt at home in Los Angeles with Hollywood's self-made moguls who'd come from nothing and risen to the top of American life, and they relied on her unfailingly shrewd advice. She was "our guiding light, our glue, our coherence," the director Al Rogell told Dorothy Brown. In 1938, Mabel represented Hollywood's directors in the new Screen Directors Guild in their dispute with film producers and won for them a limited work week of sixty hours and six days, the right to approve the first cut of a film and to have some say in casting. "Mabel helped us to survive," the guild's National Executive Secretary Joseph Youngerman told Brown.

She also shared with these men a fierce anti-communism. Mabel confided to the Lomens that "the Commies" had tried to infiltrate the Directors Guild, "but fortunately, they didn't get elected, so we are to have a good, conservative American group to work with next year." In the early 1950s, Mabel represented two fathers who sought custody of their children on the grounds that the youngsters' mothers were unfit because they associated with communists. She also supported Wisconsin Senator Joseph McCarthy's campaign to purge the government of communists in the early 1950s, another example of the kind of spectacular misstep she made during the Smith/Hoover campaign of 1928. "Good old Senator McCarthy! He certainly does not mind sticking his neck out," she wrote the Lomens.

Mabel's fear of communists had less to do with a simplistic view of patriotism, however, than a commitment to a worldview that valued, above all, her own sense of morality, personal integrity, and spiritual values. Loyalty to old friends mattered, too. She kept an office in LA in the Title Insurance Building, on the same floor as her old mentor, Frank Doherty. When Doherty worked (unsuccessfully, as it turned out) to secure the Republican presidential nomination for Senator Robert A. Taft, the fiercely anti-communist and anti–big government candidate, in 1940 and 1948, Mabel helped him get Taft endorsements from some of Hollywood's top figures, including Clark Gable, Sam Wood, Hedda Hopper, Clarence Brown, and Leo McCarey.

As always, Mabel was generous with money. One day in 1951, when Louis B. Mayer in a fit of rage threatened to fire his longtime assistant, her friend Ida Koverman, Mabel waived her retainer fee for the year to cover Koverman's salary so Mayer would keep her on. (Koverman was ill at the time and died four years later.)

One friend she did not stay close to was her foster sister, Maud Hubbard Brown, whom Mabel had helped financially over the years. In 1940, Maud sued Mabel and David Walker to regain title of a house in Temple City, California, where Maud had lived intermittently, though Mabel paid the mortgage. When Maud moved to China with her husband and sons, she deeded the house to David Walker, who arranged to have it rented out. Now Maud was divorced and back on the West Coast and claiming full ownership of the house. There was a trial, and a judge ruled that the home belonged to Mabel. Embarrassingly, the case had played out in splashy coverage in the Los Angeles papers, and Mabel was particularly chagrined that her beloved father had been dragged into such an ugly public fight.

Mabel was in Europe on business in August 1954 when David Walker died at ninety-three after suffering a series of debilitating strokes. She rushed home to arrange the funeral and burial next to Myrtle in Powersville, Missouri. Dorothy flew in from Alaska, her husband's most recent church posting. Mabel's grandson Jan Van Dyke recalls occasional trips to California to visit Mabel, who "was thin and frail and smoked a lot," and the elegant possessions she handed down to the family that didn't fit into their simple, nomadic life: a rolltop desk that was the replica of the desks used by legislators in Washington, a hand-carved chest from China, a large oriental rug, and a historic 1828 colonial dresser.

After her father's death, Mabel sold the home they shared in Temple City and bought a one-story house in the West Hollywood Hills, close to her new office at 9110 Sunset Blvd. She treasured the sporadic visits from Dorothy and her family, and as the years went on, she regretted more and more deeply that she had not been a better parent. One Mother's Day, she wrote her daughter, "I want you to know that every memory you have given me throughout all your life is precious—rewarding and cherished as the golden threads

throughout the years too wasted on law and other things that tar-
nish. I realized so many times how grievously I failed you." Mabel
felt an aching remorse that she'd been so demanding and unyielding
as a mother, trying to mold Dorothy into her own image of driven
ambition and achievement, when all Dorothy wanted was a simple
life of home and family. It no longer mattered, Mabel assured her
daughter, that Dorothy had not become an academic star or married
a hard-charging professional. She felt "full of pride" at the "useful-
ness" of Dorothy's quiet life. Dorothy returned this pride and respect.
She understood the importance of her mother's career, that she was,
in Frank Capra's words "an unforgettable example of courage among
the timid, integrity among the hypocrites, morality among the point-
shavers—a lifelong one-woman lib movement with brains."

In the late 1950s, Mabel's friend Grace Knoeller, the Prohibition Bureau lawyer who'd helped her through the crisis of the 1928
election, introduced her to a young priest, Father Robert McCor-
mack, with whom Mabel developed a close friendship. Faith in God
had been a cornerstone of her childhood and a strength throughout
her life. She'd been searching for a spiritual home since her days in
Washington, first flirting with Christian Science at her mother's urging. As she aged, she felt an intense desire "to pour out" her heart in
prayer, and she discovered that the Catholic Church was "very rich
in books of prayer." Father McCormick's discussions with her about
Catholicism and about the church's social activism and firm anti-
communist stand, appealed greatly to her. She liked that the church
"stood for something."

With John Sirica as her sponsor, Mabel became a Catholic in
1954. Perhaps her religious conversion played a part in her attraction to her fellow Catholic, the 1960 Democratic presidential candidate John F. Kennedy. Despite her lifelong Republicanism, Mabel
admitted to Knoeller that she found herself "more and more secretly
rooting in my heart for Kennedy." Also, she hated his Republican
rival, Richard Nixon. "I just do *not* like Nixon; I do *not* trust him,"
she told Knoeller.

Mabel's hearing loss was exacerbated by two operations that only briefly improved her hearing, with the second operation causing her severe balance problems. Sometimes, as she staggered from a party or a restaurant, Mabel was horrified to overhear strangers whispering "that she was drunk," according to Dorothy Brown. Even more alarming, her smoking habit had ruined her health. She suffered from angina and had trouble breathing. When she was diagnosed with lung cancer, she moved into a small house in Riverside, and she died there on April 6, 1963, at seventy-four.

Among the many letters of condolence Dorothy received was one from Judy Odlum, who with her husband, the Hollywood producer Bruce Odlum, owned a home near Mabel's country retreat in Indio. "I know she must have been a very difficult person to have as a mother," Odlum wrote. "On the other hand, I always admired her for her ability to analyze and admit her mistakes."

AT THE TIME OF MABEL'S "HOMEGOING," as Ella would have called her old ally's death, Mississippi was the only state in the nation that still had Prohibition, which it wouldn't rescind until 1966. Much to Ella's horror, alcohol consumption had been steadily rising in the United States since Repeal, as membership in the WCTU sharply declined. Today, the organization barely exists, with fewer than a thousand members.

The WCTU is mostly remembered as an intimidating political lobby of humorless, self-righteous women determined to create a liquor-less America at all costs. Part of the group's legacy, however, is the same as WONPR's: It offers an example of how to build a successful grassroots coalition to effect change. The seeds of contemporary activism are discernible in the high-minded striving of Ella and Pauline. In leading their crusades from opposite sides of the ideological divide, they lifted women's voices across the land. Those voices are lifted still.

ACKNOWLEDGMENTS

T HIS IS THE SECOND BOOK I've set in the Jazz Age, an era in which I feel very comfortable, and which is as real to me as my own fraught time, filled as it is now and was then with craven politicians, fake news, and a Congress in the grip of a fanatical minority. The late historian David McCullough once said, "There is no such thing as the past, only other people's presents," apt words for a biographer to write by. Letters, diaries, newspaper and magazine articles brought me close to my characters' "presents." I touched Pauline Sabin's life even more directly through her granddaughters Sheila Morton Smith Cochran and Pauline Sabin Smith Willis, who provided a living link to the documents I was studying. Mrs. Cochran and Mrs. Willis invited me into their homes and shared their reminiscences of the woman they called "Granny" who raised them from the time they were small children. Mrs. Cochran gave me access to Pauline Sabin's scrapbooks and photo albums, and Mrs. Willis, who bears an uncanny resemblance to her luminous grandmother, graciously answered my many email and phone queries. Wendell Willis Livingston, Mrs. Willis's daughter and the family genealogist, generously shared her knowledge and the many photographs she's collected over the years of her great-grandmother's political activities. My conversations with these women were highlights of my research.

I'm also indebted to Mabel Walker Willebrandt's grandson Jan Christopher Van Dyke, who shared photographs and letters that he had inherited from his mother, Mabel Willebrandt's daughter, Dorothy Rae Willebrandt Van Dyke, and which provided a valuable insight into Mabel Willebrandt's character.

Eileen Nicoll and Katrina Wagner, granddaughters of Ione Nicoll, lent me Ione's large scrapbook filled with newspaper clippings cataloging WONPR activities. Katrina also provided the beautiful portrait of Ione in this book.

Firebrands has benefited immensely, too, from the generosity of Dorothy Brown, Mabel Walker Willebrandt's biographer, and Louise Berliner, Texas Guinan's biographer, who patiently answered my queries.

Librarians and archivists are the great unsung heroes of biography, and at the top of the list of those I'm indebted to is Janet Olson, archivist at the Frances Willard House Museum and WCTU Archives in Evanston, Illinois. Janet guided me through the collection, directed me to sources I never would have discovered on my own, tracked down quotes and stories in the *Union Signal*, researched information I was unsure about, and answered my endless questions about Ella Boole.

Satu Haase-Webb helped me with research at the Library of Congress, while Lori Azim was a shrewd and exacting fact-checker who made what's usually a tedious process surprisingly enjoyable with her smart, humorous comments in the margins of my book. I would also like to thank the librarians and archivists at Northwestern University Library, the Schlesinger Library, the Billy Rose Division of the New York Public Library for the Performing Arts, the Hagley Museum and Library, and the Manuscript Division of the Library of Congress.

Thanks, also, to my editor Tim Mennel for seeing the value of this book and his insightful suggestions for improving it; to his assistant, Andrea Blatz, for her patience and attention to detail; to Erin DeWitt for expert copyediting; and to everyone at the University of Chicago Press who helped shepherd the manuscript through to publication.

I'm grateful to my agent Flip Brophy for her belief in me and my writing and her unfailingly astute guidance. Thanks also to her lieutenant, Jessica Friedman, for her spot-on judgment on all things book related.

My posse of indispensable friends cheered me on throughout the research and writing of this book. Thank you once again to Jonathan Black, Maureen Dowd, Ted Fishman, Brenda Fowler, Brooke Kroeger, Victoria Lautman, Trish Lear, Kaarina Salovaara, Julie Shelton, Rachel Shteir, Dinitia Smith, Christine Sneed, Sara Stern, Monica Vachher, and Joyce Wadler.

Finally, eternal thanks to my husband, Richard Babcock, for his all-enabling love and devotion over the course of four decades. He and our son, Joe, are the reason I live and write.

A NOTE ON SOURCES

THE CHIEF SOURCES FOR THIS BOOK were documents in the WCTU Archives in Evanston, Illinois; the Mabel Walker Willebrandt Papers at the Library of Congress; the Pauline Sabin Davis Papers at the Schlesinger Library at the Radcliffe Institute for Advanced Study at Harvard University in Cambridge, Massachusetts, and Pauline's scrapbooks in a private collection; material related to the Women's Organization for National Prohibition Reform at the Hagley Museum and Library in Wilmington, Delaware; and the Texas Guinan material at the Billy Rose Theatre Division of the New York Public Library.

Though my characters were born in the nineteenth century and died long ago, a few of their close relatives are still living, including Pauline Sabin's granddaughters and Mabel Walker Willebrandt's grandsons, and they provided a link to the past by sharing their reminiscences and insights of the women profiled here.

I've also drawn on the work of the historians, scholars, biographers, and journalists who've come before me. The bibliography contains a list of these sources. In quoting from published material, I've sometimes corrected spelling errors for clarity.

ABBREVIATIONS

FWMLA   Frances Willard Memorial Library and Archives
HHP   Herbert Hoover Papers
HJP   Hiram Johnson Papers
JSGH   John S. Stein and Grace Hayward, "Hello, Sucker! The Life of Texas Guinan" (unpublished ms., 1941)
MWW   Mabel Walker Willebrandt
MWWP   Mabel Walker Willebrandt Papers
PS   Pauline Sabin
PSDP   Pauline Sabin Davis Papers
RWONPR   Records of the Women's Organization for National Prohibition Reform

Mabel Walker Willebrandt's diary and all of her correspondence unless otherwise cited are from the collection of her papers at the Library of Congress (MWWP).

Ella Boole's letters are from the Boole Correspondence Files in the WCTU Archives in Evanston, Illinois.

NOTES

PROLOGUE

x "WOMEN WHO DOOMED": *New York World-Telegram*, June 30, 1932.

xi "THE MANUFACTURE, SALE": Constitution of the United States, Amendment 18 (1919).

xiii "HAVE YOU IMPRESSED": Publicity—General 1930–1932, reel 14, RWONPR.

CHAPTER ONE

2 "THE VERY PERMANENCY": *Star Gazette* (Elmira, NY), September 2, 1920.

3 "HALLMARK OF GENIUS": Stanley Walker, "With Ella in the Desert," *Outlook and Independent*, April 9, 1930.

3 "STUFFY WITH CAUSES": *New Yorker*, October 22, 1932.

3 "WHIMPER": *Outlook*, April 9, 1930, 565.

4 "PROHIBITION HAS MADE" ... "YOUNG PEOPLE": *Outlook*, April 9, 1930, 567.

4 "SCALP": *New York Evening World*, January 27, 1920.

5 "WILL NO LONGER" ... "A SPADE": Goodier, *No Votes for Women* (ebook edition), loc. 2683.

5 "SEND A MOTHER": *Star Gazette* (Elmira, NY), September 11, 1920.

6 "ATTRACTIVE TO THE EYE": *New York Daily News*, September 20, 1929.

6 "THE UNBOSSED CANDIDATE": *New York Times*, September 14, 1920.

6   "CENTER OF DEGENERACY": *Brooklyn Daily Eagle*, April 19, 1926.

7   "EVERY MAN AND WOMAN" . . . "THE CONTRIBUTION": *Star Gazette* (Elmira, NY), August 30, 1920.

8   "SHUT OUT" . . . "THERE WAS NO CREED": Ward, *The White Ribbon Story*, 10.

8   "MODERATE" . . . "TOTAL ABSTINENCE": Ward, 10.

9   "ANGELS IN THE HOUSE": Coventry Patmore, *The Angel in the House*, Parts I & II (London: Macmillan, 1863).

9   "ALMOST OVERNIGHT": Jed Dannebaum, "The Origins of Temperance Activism and Militancy among American Women," *Journal of Social History* 15, no. 2 (Winter 1981): 235–52.

9   "THE VERY MOMENT": Schrad, *Smashing the Liquor Machine*, 344.

11   "I FIRST DISCOVERED": *Outlook*, April 9, 1930.

12   "THE ARCH ENEMY": *New York Daily News*, July 29, 1931.

12   "THE MARRIAGE OF A CAUSE": *New York Daily News*, July 26, 1931.

12   "THE NEIGHBORHOOD SIMPLY": *Outlook*, April 9, 1930.

13   "IS A PROPER SUBJECT": *Brooklyn Daily Eagle*, December 10, 1913.

14   "THE HOUSE AND SENATE SPONSORS": Okrent, *Last Call*, 57.

15   "SMALL, SLENDER": *New York Daily News*, July 31, 1931.

16   "NOTIFY MRS. ELLA A. BOOLE" . . . "MENTALLY SICK": *Brooklyn Daily Eagle*, July 8, 1918.

17   "THE VOICE OF MRS. BOOLE": *Outlook*, April 9, 1930, 565.

17   "THE MODERATE DRINKER": *Union Signal*, September 12, 1918.

18   "*IF YOU BELIEVE*": *Democrat and Chronicle* (Rochester, NY), October 26, 1920.

CHAPTER TWO

19   "I THINK THOSE": *New York Times*, May 11, 1927.

21   "AN EDUCATION" . . . "WELL, YOU GET": Cordery, *Alice*, 429.

21   "I'VE ALWAYS THOUGHT": Isabel Leighton, *Smart Set*, March 1930.

21   "IT'S A POWERFUL": *Washington Evening Star*, November 15, 1914.

22   "HE DIDN'T WANT": Author interview with Wendy Livingston, April 4, 2018.

22   "SHE FLOURISHED" . . . "HE DIDN'T FEEL THREATENED": Author interview with Sheila Cochran, April 18, 2018.

23   "MY GRANDMOTHER DIDN'T SUFFER": Author interview with Pauline Willis, April 4, 2018; Burns and Novick, *Prohibition*.

23   "HER FACE WAS CONSTANTLY": Pauline Willis to the author in an email, January 14, 2022.

23   "FELL ALL OVER" . . . "THEY WERE ALL": Author interview with Pauline Willis, April 4, 2018.

23   "SHE LOVED": Author interview with Pauline Willis, April 4, 2018.

23   "I WAS NEVER": *Washington Post*, December 12, 1939.

24   "WOMEN TEND TO VOTE": Esther A. Coster, *Brooklyn Daily Eagle*, January 18, 1925.

24   "I GOT MY FIRST": Coster, *Brooklyn Daily Eagle*, January 18, 1925.

24   "POLITICS IS WOOING": *Asbury Park (NJ) Evening Press*, October 30, 1924.

26   "THE MEN THOUGHT": *New York Herald Tribune*, July 24, 1920.

26   "SEX WAR" . . . "WOMEN WHAT TO DO": Gustafson, Miller, and Perry, *We Have Come to Stay*, 102.

28   "MRS. BOOLE IS AND SHE WOULD BE" . . . "TOO SMALL A MAN": *Times Herald* (Olean, NY), October 25, 1920.

28   "TO STICK IT OUT": *New York Tribune*, September 12, 1920.

29   "SUPREME" . . . "THE ENTIRE EXTINCTION": WCTU Press Release, Willard House, September 2, 1920, FWMLA.

29   "WE WANT" . . . "WADSWORTH'S PLACE": *Brooklyn Daily Eagle*, October 26, 1920.

29   "HAD TO SAY AGAINST": *Brooklyn Daily Eagle*, October 26, 1920.

29   "A REMARKABLY STRONG": *New York Times*, November 14, 1920.

30   "TO MAKE A REAL FIGHT": *Crainsville (MO) News*, September 27, 1928.

30   "A WEAK AND COLORLESS": Dean, *Warren G. Harding*, 67.

30   "IMMORALITIES" . . . "OFTEN PROVED A RIDE": *New York Times*, December 28, 1922.

31   "HEAVY WITH TOBACCO": Cordery, *Alice*, 300.

31   "THE TRUTH IS": *Baltimore Sun*, October 30, 1932.

CHAPTER THREE

33   "STOP IT!" . . . "TO LIVE UP TO": *Good Housekeeping*, May 1928.

33   "WAS ALWAYS INTERESTED": *Kansas City Star*, June 15, 1928.

34   "BECAUSE SHE COULDN'T GO": *Kansas City Star*, June 15, 1928.

35   "MOST CHERISHED HOPE": *Good Housekeeping*, May 1928.

36   "TO WALK THE TIGHT-ROPE": *Smart Set*, February 1930.

37   "THE ONLY MAN": Brown, *Mabel Walker Willebrandt*, 40.

38   "HE IS SO THOUGHTFUL": Myrtle Walker to MWW, n.d., MWWP.

38   "THAT IS THE KIND" . . . "THAT ALL GOOD JEWS": Myrtle Walker to MWW, December 22, 1921, MWWP.

39   "SHE IS ONE": Brown, *Mabel Walker Willebrandt*, 46.

39   "SO HARD" . . . "THOSE EVENING CONFIDENCES": MWW to parents, Christmas 1922, MWWP.

39   "INCONSEQUENTIAL GROOVE": MWW to parents, Christmas 1922, MWWP.

40   "YOU ARE SPLENDID" ... "IN THAT CASE": *Union Signal*, February 25, 1928; *New Yorker*, May 8, 1920.

CHAPTER FOUR

43   "AS DEVOID OF HONESTY": MWW, *The Inside of Prohibition*, excerpt in the *New York Times*, August 8, 1929.

44   "IF THE FACTS" ... "WHAT IS ENCOURAGING": *Dayton Herald*, September 15, 1921.

44   "WORN WHITE RIBBONS": *Union Signal*, December 7, 1922.

44   "WHERE SHE HAD THE WHITE RIBBON": *Record of Los Angeles*, October 2, 1928.

45   "PROTECTION OF PROHIBITION": *Union Signal*, September 8, 1921.

46   "I'M GETTING SO SPOILED": MWW to parents, May 19, 1923, MWWP.

46   "IT WAS A STAG PARTY": MWW diary, March 20, 1923, MWWP.

46   "SHE MUST ALWAYS BE": *Union Signal*, February 25, 1928.

46   "RATHER MASCULINE": Margaret Smith to the Walkers, October 11, 1922, MWWP.

46   "EXPECTED A LARGE, LOUD WAIL": *San Francisco Chronicle*, October 9, 1921.

47   "MRS. WILLEBRANDT PRESENTED": *Washington Post*, October 2, 1921.

47   "GIRLIE-GIRLIE": MWW to parents, March 22, 1922, MWWP.

47   "OTHER ASST. A.G.'S": MWW to parents, August 11, 1923, MWWP.

47   "I AM SO VERY PROUD": Margaret Smith to Myrtle Walker, October 11, 1922, MWWP.

48   "HE HAD TO HOLD" ... "WAS APPARENT": MWW, *The Inside of Prohibition*, excerpted in the *New York Times*, August 15, 1929.

48   "BEGAN WITH A WHOOP": Fitzgerald, *My Lost City*, 132.

49   "EACH MONTH SEEMS": MWW to parents, Christmas 1922, MWWP.

49   "THE INWARD TERROR": MWW to parents, Christmas 1922, MWWP.

49   "POLISH, BEAUTY OF DICTION": MWW to parents, March 9, 1926, MWWP.

49   "THE DREAD SHADOW": MWW to parents, Christmas 1922, MWWP.

49   "DAMN, YOU THINK": MWW to parents, Christmas 1922, MWWP.

50   "THE FINEST, BIGGEST" ... "HUNDREDS TURNED AWAY": MWW diary, November 3, 1922, MWWP.

50   "AS SMOOTHLY": MWW diary, November 3, 1922, MWWP.

51   "THE CHILDREN OF MY MIND": Myrtle Walker to MWW, 1921, MWWP.

51   "DOTTED WITH ESTABLISHMENTS": Lerner, *Dry Manhattan*, 138; *Variety*, October 14, 1921.

52   "JUST SUPPOSE": "Impossible Interviews," *Vanity Fair*, January 1933.

CHAPTER FIVE

53   "BUTTER AND EGG MAN": Berliner, *Texas Guinan*, 101.

54   "ADVICE" ... "LAUGH PROVOKING": JSGH, 340.

54   "IF THEY PADLOCK": *Brooklyn Daily Eagle*, April 9, 1929.

54   "A WHOLE CABOODLE": JSGH, 14.

54   "THAT MEAN, MEASLY REFORMER": JSGH, 20.

55   "WAS ALWAYS HUNGRY": JSGH, 23.

55   "IF YOU BECAME A MODEL WIFE": JSGH, 32.

56   "ACTRESS QUACK": *Chicago Tribune*, December 17, 1913.

56   "NEVER JILT": *The Gun Woman*, (Triangle Film Corp., 1918).

57   "TO TEXAS GUINAN": Louis Sobol, "The Voice of Broadway," *New York Evening Journal*, November 7, 1933.

57   "TIRED OF KISSING HORSES": Berliner, *Texas Guinan*, 89.

57   "YOU COULDN'T PUT": Winchell, *Winchell Exclusive*, 49.

58   "I WOULD RATHER HAVE": Leo Trachtenberg, "Texas Guinan: Queen of the Night," *City Journal*, Spring 1998, https:/www.city-journal.org /article/texas-guinan-queen-of-the-night.

59   "KLEPTOMANIA": JSGH, 290.

60   "ANOTHER WAS WITH A GANGSTER": Granlund, *Blondes, Brunettes and Bullets*, 139.

61   "HELLO, SUCKER": Berliner, *Texas Guinan*, 102.

61   "YOU MAY BE ALL": *New York Daily News*, April 10, 1932.

61   "GIVE HER A GREAT BIG HAND!": JSGH, 154.

62   "PROSTIPRETTIES": Winchell, *Winchell Exclusive*, 116–17.

62   "THE PRISONER'S SONG": Berliner, *Texas Guinan*, 119.

62   "I LIKE YOUR CUTE LITTLE JAIL": Trachtenberg, "Texas Guinan," *City Journal*, Spring 1998.

CHAPTER SIX

63   "PUERILE": Brown, *Mabel Walker Willebrandt*, 56.

64   "EVERYBODY IN WASHINGTON": MWW to parents, January 2, 1923, MWWP.

64   "SOME OF THE HIGHEST PRAISE": MWW to parents, January 2, 1923, MWWP.

65   "WHOM I LOVE" ... "IT IS REGARDED": MWW to parents, January 2, 1923, MWWP.

65   "TO A TRUE HANDMAIDEN": *Union Signal*, February 25, 1928.

65   "THIS STORY OF THE BIG BATTLE": *Union Signal*, September 11, 1924.

65   "GOOD PUBLICITY WORK": *Union Signal*, September 11, 1924.

65   "TO USE AS HE SAW FIT": Ella Boole to MWW, February 1, 1927, MWWP.

66   "IF YOU COULD SEE": MWW to parents, Christmas 1923, MWWP.

66   "THEIR CONSECRATION": MWW, *The Inside of Prohibition*, excerpted in the *New York Times*, August 14, 1929.

66   "REPELLED": *New Yorker*, February 16, 1929.

66   "TRUE WOMANHOOD": Bernard O'Reilly, *The Mirror of True Womanhood* (Classic Reprint Series, Forgotten Books, 2018).

67   "WOMEN ALL OVER": *New York Times*, July 29, 1923.

67   "EVERY STATE THAT THREATENS": *New York Times*, July 29, 1923.

67   "WAS RATIFIED" . . . "PROBABLY PERMANENTLY EMBEDDED": MWW, *The Inside of Prohibition*, excerpted in the *St. Louis Post-Dispatch*, August 24, 1929.

68   "UNCANNY FEELING" . . . "IT SEEMS THAT IT MAY": MWW to parents, Christmas 1923, MWWP.

68   "JUDICIAL": MWW to David Walker, September 2, 1923, MWWP.

69   "A CONSPIRACY WORTHY OF LENIN": Gage, *G-Man*, 97.

69   "I BELIEVE": MWW diary, December 14, 1922, MWWP.

69   "VERY LOVELY TO ME": MWW diary, December 14, 1922, MWWP.

69   "SEEMED TO IGNORE": Giglio, *H. M. Daugherty and the Politics of Expediency*, 137–38.

69   "SECRETARY, GREETER": Gage, *G-Man*, 91.

69   "WERE THE MOST INTIMATE FRIENDS": Masters, *Crooked*, ebook, loc. 223.

70   "DON'T PAY ANY ATTENTION": Abbott, *Ghosts of Eden Park*, ebook, loc. 677.

70   "LOOKING BETTER": MWW diary, June 18, 1923, MWWP.

70   "FEARFUL PAIN": MWW diary, June 18, 1923, MWWP.

70   "HE IS WITH HER": MWW diary, June 18, 1923, MWWP.

70   "CAP THE CLIMAX": MWW diary, June 18, 1923, MWWP.

70   "UNLESS I COMPLETELY COLLAPSE" : MWW diary, June 18, 1923, MWWP.

71   "YOU'VE DONE SO WONDERFULLY" . . . "THE *BEST* APPOINTMENT": MWW diary, June 18, 1923, MWWP.

71   "THO OUTWARDLY" . . . "IF THIS HAD COME": MWW to parents, January 29, 1925, MWWP.

72   "MABELMEN": *Akron Beacon Journal*, June 12, 1929; *New Yorker*, May 4, 1929.

72   "STEALING BALLOTS" . . . "SLUGGING": MWW, *The Inside of Prohibition*, excerpt in the *Chicago Daily News*, August 17, 1929.

72   "WHISPERING WIRES": MWW, *The Inside of Prohibition*, excerpt in the *New York Times*, August 19, 1929.

72   "CODE SIGNALS" ... "WHEN THE COAST": MWW, *The Inside of Prohibition*, excerpt in the *New York Times*, August 19, 1929.

73   "THOROUGHLY DISAPPROVED": MWW, *The Inside of Prohibition*, excerpt in the *New York Times*, August 19, 1929.

73   "RIGHT TO BE LET ALONE": Okrent, *Last Call*, 286.

73   "FROZEN": "Jill Lepore on Why It's so Hard to Amend the Constitution—and Why That Matters," *The New Yorker Radio Hour*, podcast, June 30, 2023.

73   "ALWAYS THE WIELDERS": *Louisville Courier Journal*, April 25, 1924.

74   "THE DRYS WILL SAY": MWW to parents, February 19, 1924, MWWP.

74   "I MIGHT AS WELL" ... "DO LITTLE REAL GOOD": MWW to parents, January 6, 1924, MWWP.

74   "I HAVE TO APPEAR": MWW to parents, April 4, 1924, MWWP.

75   "THE FOREMOST WOMAN": MWW to parents, June 30, 1924, MWWP.

75   "LACK OF VIRILITY": MWW to mother, October 13, 1926, MWWP.

75   "SOME BOOTLEGGERS" ... "IT MAKES ME FEEL": MWW to parents, February 15, 1924, MWWP.

75   "PHYSICAL EXERTION": MWW diary, August 11, 1922, MWWP.

76   "A COLD EASTERN": Myrtle Walker to MWW, October 11, 1924, MWWP.

76   "I WOULD REJOICE": Myrtle Walker to MWW, October 11, 1924, MWWP.

76   "A MAGNIFICENT LOOKING MAN" ... "'MAMA IS SURE DIPPY'": Myrtle Walker to MWW, August 30, 1923, MWWP.

77   "SHE COULDN'T DECIDE": MWW diary, August 1922, MWWP.

77   "MY NATURE": MWW to parents, Christmas 1922, MWWP.

77   "ALWAYS KNEW" ... "LOTS OF MONEY": MWW to Myrtle Walker, May 13, 1923, MWWP.

77   "DEAREST MABEL": MWW diary, December 16, 1922, MWWP.

77   "I WONDER": MWW diary, December 16, 1922, MWWP.

77   "TO HIS STENOGRAPHER" ... "WAS TOO GOOD": Myrtle Walker to MWW, May 2, 1924, MWWP.

77   "SOMEONE ELSE WOULD MARRY HER": Myrtle Walker to MWW, May 2, 1924, MWWP.

78   "OH, I'VE JUST FINISHED": MWW, fragment, October 1924, MWWP.

78   "ABSTRACT IN HIS THOUGHTS": MWW to parents, September 21, 1927, MWWP.

78   "TO BE VERY GRACIOUS" ... "A LITTLE TENSE AND STRAINED": MWW to parents, January 6, 1924, MWWP.

78   "HE GAVE A LIMP HAND": MWW to parents, January 6, 1924, MWWP.

79   "HARD": MWW to parents, May 11, 1924, MWWP.

79   "SUCH A ROTTER": MWW to parents, January 2, 1923, MWWP.

79   "THE LOVE THAT UNLOCKS" . . . "THE JUSTICES JUST HELPED": MWW diary, December 8, 1922, MWWP.

80   "WHY SHOULD SOCIETY": MWW diary, April 13, 1923, MWWP.

80   "PUT ME INTO A PERFECT": MWW to parents, October 28, 1925, MWWP.

80   "STUTTER AND WANT": MWW to parents, October 28, 1925, MWWP.

80   "PETTED DARLINGS": Brown, *Mabel Walker Willebrandt*, 128.

80   "AN IMMENSE INFLUENCE": *Oakland (CA) Tribune*, June 15, 1924.

80   "LEADER OF WOMEN": unidentified clipping, PS Scrapbooks.

81   "ALL THE IMPORTANT CONFERENCES": unidentified clipping, PS Scrapbooks.

81   "SAY SO": unidentified clipping, PS Scrapbooks.

81   "A GREAT COMING OUT PARTY": unidentified clipping, PS Scrapbooks.

81   "HELD SOME NEGATIVE CONNOTATIONS": unidentified clipping, PS Scrapbooks.

81   "DOESN'T [PAULINE]": unidentified clipping, PS Scrapbooks.

81   "MRS. SABIN IS SO PRETTY": *Grand Island (NE) Independent*, June 12, 1924.

82   "THE GOP DIP": unmarked clipping, PS Scrapbooks.

82   "POLITICAL ACTIVITY IS EXPECTED": Wolbrecht and Corder, *A Century of Votes for Women*, 78.

82   "WAS QUITE HIGH": Wolbrecht and Corder, 61.

82   "STATES . . . WITH THE MOST STRINGENT": Wolbrecht and Corder, 73.

83   "I THINK IT IS FAIRLY OBVIOUS": Eleanor Roosevelt, "Women in Politics," *Good Housekeeping*, March 1940.

83   "FLAPPER": Zeitz, *Flapper*, 5.

84   "FAT DANCES" . . . "LOVELY NEGRO SINGING": MWW to parents, March 22, 1922, MWWP.

85   "I'M SO HAPPY FLYING": MWW to father, July 30, 1928, MWWP.

85   "WHITE AS A SHEET": MWW to father, July 30, 1928, MWWP.

86   "CAUTION ARTIST": MWW to parents, n.d., MWWP.

86   "A LOVELY MOONLIGHT RIDE": MWW diary, April 6, 1923, MWWP.

CHAPTER SEVEN

87   "GUIDING PROPHET": *Outlook & Independent*, April 9, 1930.

87   "A SCORNED": Mark Lawrence Schrad, "Why Do We Blame Women for Prohibition?," *Politico*, January 13, 2019.

88   "IT IS IMPOSSIBLE": Fiorello La Guardia, Senate Subcommittee of the Committee on the Judiciary, *The National Prohibition Law: Hearings to Amend the National Prohibition Act*, 69th Cong., 1st sess. (1926), vol. 1, 42.

88   "THE JAZZ MAYOR": *Fort Worth Star Telegram*, February 21, 1928.

88   "AND SLEPT HALF THE DAY": MacKaye, *Tin Box Parade*, 3–4.

88   "DRANK TOO MUCH": MacKaye, 3–4.

88   "DO EVERYTHING": Evans, *Do Everything*, 1.

88   "WOMEN ARE RELIEVED": Emma Boole, radio address, in Burns and Novick, *Prohibition*.

88   "AN APPLIER OF PRESSURE": Walker, *Outlook and Independent*, April 9, 1930.

89   "JUST VERBAL PRESSURE": Boole, "The Reminiscences of Ella Boole, 1950," part IV, no. 24, p. 18.

89   "FIRSTHAND KNOWLEDGE": Mark Lawrence Schrad, "Why Do We Blame Women for Prohibition?," *Politico*, January 13, 2019.

89   "RACE TRAITORS": Lerner, *Dry Manhattan*, 203.

90   "ANY NEGRO WOMAN": *Amsterdam News*, December 21, 1927.

90   "TALK OF GIVING": Schrad, *Smashing the Liquor Machine*, 360.

90   "BUILD A CHRISTIAN COMMUNITY": Gilmore, *Gender and Jim Crow*, 49.

90   "HIGH OFFICIAL" ... "SERVE ME": MWW to parents, March 14, 1927, MWWP.

91   "THE DRAWING OF A COLOUR LINE" ... "HOW LONG WILL": "The WCTU and the Coloured Question," *Anti-Caste*, March 1895.

92   "I WILL BE SEPARATED": Gilmore, *Gender and Jim Crow*, 185.

92   "FREE, WHITE": *Afro-American* (Baltimore, MD), January 26, 1929.

92   "I'M FREE": *Strangers May Kiss*, dir. George Fitzmaurice (Metro Goldwyn Mayer, 1931).

92   "REPULSIVE": *Chicago Defender*, March 2, 1935.

93   "THE PROBLEM IS": Illinois WCTU 1924 Annual Report.

94   "WIDE-AWAKE CITY ORGANIZER": "Report of the Work among the Colored People," National WCTU Meeting Minutes, Atlanta Georgia, 1914, FWMLA.

94   "A NATIONAL CHARACTER": *Independence (KS) Daily Reporter*, June 29, 1922.

95   "NATIONAL DEPARTMENT" ... "EASY FLOW": *Union Signal*, October 19, 1922, 12.

95   "SHE HAS JUST FINISHED": *Saline (KS) Evening Journal*, July 7, 1922.

95   "WAS ESPECIALLY NOTEWORTHY": *Union Signal*, October 19, 1922, 12.

95   "SHE AROUSED": *Union Signal*, October 19, 1922, 12.

95   "WHO ARE SERIOUSLY DEVOTED": *Afro-American*, May 30, 1931.

96   "THE FIFTEEN MILLION" ... "WE DO NOT WANT" ... "WE MUST
      LIVE": *Hearings Before the Subcommittee of the Committee of the Judi-
      ciary*, US Senate, 69th Cong., 1st sess., April 5–24, 1926, on Bills to
      Amend the Prohibition Act., Vol. 1, 689.

97   "TOY": *Baltimore Sun*, April 8, 1926.

97   "WERE REPETITIONS": *New Yorker*, May 1, 1926.

97   "WHAT COMMUNITY": *New York Times*, April 20, 1926.

98   "TOTAL ABSTINENCE": *Handbook of the National Woman's Chris-
      tian Temperance Union* (Evanston, IL: National WCTU Publishing
      House, 1926), 80.

98   "HAS RESULTED IN BETTER": *Brooklyn Daily Eagle*, April 19, 1926.

98   "WE BELIEVE THE VOLSTEAD": *Brooklyn Daily Eagle*, April 19,
      1926.

98   "DO YOU THINK" ... "NOW THAT APPLAUSE": *Brooklyn Daily
      Eagle*, April 19, 1926.

99   "THE MODIFICATIONISTS" ... "DELIGHTED HER HEARERS":
      Union Signal, May 1, 1926.

CHAPTER EIGHT

100   "I MISS YOU": MWW to Annabel Matthews, June 26, 1926, Papers of
      Annabel Matthews, Schlesinger Library, Radcliffe Institute, Harvard
      University.

101   "ONLY *DESIRED*" ... "I *WISH*": MWW to Myrtle Walker, July 21, 1925,
      MWWP.

101   "YOU WILL BE": Mrytle Walker to MWW, July 2, 1925, MWWP.

102   "AN UNUSUAL FIND": MWW to parents, August 15, 1925, MWWP.

102   "I'D LOVE HER": MWW to Myrtle Walker, August 25 & 26, 1925,
      MWWP.

102   "YOU SHOULD SEE HER" : MWW to Myrtle Walker, August 25 & 26,
      1925, MWWP.

102   "THE DEAREST": MWW to Myrtle Walker, August 25 & 26, 1925,
      MWWP.

102   "A ROMP": MWW to parents, August 15, 1925, MWWP.

103   "COULD EASILY" ... "DR. STANLEY": MWW to parents, April 2, 1926,
      MWWP.

104   "TO BREAK OFF": MWW to Fred Horowitz, December 2, 1925, MWWP.

104   "YES, THE YOUNG UNKNOWN" ... "ALL MY SELF-REPRESSIONS":
      MWW to Fred Horowitz, December 2, 1925, MWWP.

104   "THE CRUEL WORLD" ... "SHOULD EXACT": MWW, *Smart Set*, Feb-
      ruary 1930.

104 "THAT'S MORE THAN POSSESSION": MWW to Dearest, December 2, 1925, MWWP.

104 "TOOK ALL" . . . "THE SAME THING": Fred Horowitz to MWW, December 1, 1928, MWWP.

105 "A GREAT INNER PEACE": MWW to parents, February 15, 1925, MWWP.

105 "MARRY THAT CAPITAL": MWW to parents, February 15, 1925, MWWP.

105 "TO THE POINT": MWW to parents, February 15, 1925, MWWP.

105 "A BUSINESS ARRANGEMENT": Author interview with Jan Christopher Van Dyke, June 4, 2020.

105 "YOU'VE DONE SO MUCH": MWW to parents, Christmas Day, 1926, MWWP.

105 "STROLLING WITH": MWW to parents, July 26, 1926, MWWP.

106 "SOMEHOW I FELT WORSE": MWW to parents, Christmas 1926, MWWP.

107 "TEN JUDGESHIPS": MWW to parents, February 11, 1924, MWWP.

107 "SHE WOULD SELL": Hiram Johnson to Frank Doherty, July 31, 1926, HJP.

107 "THOUGH SHE HAS PERFORMED" . . . "A DEVOTEE": Hiram Johnson to Harold Ickes, May 22, 1926, HJP.

108 "FUTILE AND PERNICIOUS": unidentified clipping, September 14, 1926, PS Scrapbooks.

108 "CERTAIN ORGANIZATIONS" . . . "IT SEEMS STRANGE": *New York Times*, October 24, 1926.

108 "SOMETHING WHICH WAS HANDED": *Brooklyn Daily Eagle*, October 4, 1926.

108 "SEE TO IT": *Brooklyn Daily Eagle*, October 26, 1926.

109 "COURAGE": *New York Times*, April 14, 1926.

110 "CONSIDERED IT JUST AS IMPORTANT": Cook, *Eleanor Roosevelt*, 374.

110 "BEEN DRINKING" . . . "I'M WONDERING": ER to Elinor Morgenthau, April 29, 1927, FDR Archives.

110 "SUMPTUARY POLICE STATUTE": *New York Times*, October 16, 1926.

110 "MR. WADSWORTH IS A LEADING": *New York Times*, October 16, 1926.

111 "COUNTRY SQUIRE" . . . "AS I UNDERSTAND IT": *New York Times*, October 19, 1926.

111 "SINGULARLY UNCOMMUNICATIVE": *New York Times*, October 19, 1926.

111 "EVERYONE KNOWS" . . . "TAMMANY HALL": *New York Times*, October 5, 1926.

112   "A WOMAN WHO" . . . "ABOUT ALL [THE MEN]": *New York Times*, November 6, 1926.

112   "FOR BEING TOTALLY UNFAIR": *New York Times*, November 6, 1926.

112   "WHILE POLLS": Lerner, *Dry Manhattan*, 230.

                          CHAPTER NINE

114   "HAD ACCEPTED BRIBES": Masters, *Crooked*, 246–47.

114   "I HATE TO CAUSE": Giglio, *H. M. Daugherty and the Politics of Expediency*, 190.

115   "ANY HARM CAN COME": MWW to parents, February 13, 1927, MWWP.

115   "YOU ARE REALLY ONE" . . . "I HAVE NOTHING": *New York Times*, February 18, 1927; *Chicago Daily Tribune*, February 18, 1927; *Evening Star* (Washington, DC), February 18, 1927.

115   "A PECULIAR CHARACTERISTIC": *Chicago Daily Tribune*, February 18, 1927.

115   "THE BEST WAY": *Chicago Daily Tribune*, February 18, 1927; *Evening Star* (Washington, DC), February 18, 1927.

115   "THE DEPARTMENT OF EASY VIRTUE": Masters, *Crooked*, 247.

116   "A LITTLE FORTIFYING": James Wadsworth to Charles Sabin, January 16, 1927, folder: Pauline Sabin Correspondence, James Wadsworth Family Papers.

116   "RED LETTER DAY": *Union Signal*, January 15, 1927, 10.

116   "THE TURNING OF THE TIDE": quoted in *New York Times*, November 5, 1926.

117   "A HUMMING BIRD": *Washington Post*, September 25, 1930.

118   "ON BEHALF OF THE NATIONAL": Ella Boole to MWW, February 1, 1927, MWWP.

118   "THE APPREHENSIONS": *New York Daily News*, August 2, 1931.

119   "VAUDEVILLE": *Collier's*, February 6, 1926.

119   "WAS FULL OF WHISKY": *Chicago Tribune*, April 5, 1924; *New York Times*, May 9, 1924.

120   "A MISREPRESENTATION": *Long Islander*, May 2, 1924.

120   "THE POWER AND THE GLORY": Coolidge, *Autobiography*, 139.

121   "HIS OWN VIGOR": MWW to parents, February 19, 1924, MWWP.

121   "A SPECTACULAR MAN" . . . "HE IS BY ALL ODDS": MWW to parents, January 15, 1928, MWWP.

121   "OUGHT TO BE" . . . "DECENT WHITE FOLK": MWW to parents, February 14, 1924, MWWP.

121   "I SAY UNHESITATINGLY": *Washington Post*, April 12, 1928.

122 "she is the fountainhead" ... "she is a very forceful person": *Washington Post*, April 13, 1928.

122 "i promised all": Oral History of Bradley Nash, July 31, 1968, 45, HHP.

122 "peculiarly fitted": *Outlook*, April 9, 1930.

122 "the pause between": Burner, *Herbert Hoover*, 218–19.

123 "a clear-cut": Boole, "The Reminiscences of Ella Boole, 1950," 25.

123 "one plank minds": *Chicago Tribune*, March 9, 1930.

123 "the worst hated": Okrent, *Last Call*, 246.

123 "politics like a man": *Daily Notes* (Canonsburg, PA), October 9, 1929.

124 "i was one" ... "gets tremendous publicity": *Outlook*, June 13, 1928.

124 "is greatly diminishing": *Outlook*, June 13, 1928.

124 "it is true": *Outlook*, June 13, 1928.

124 "only to find": *Outlook*, June 13, 1928.

125 "republican principles": *Suffolk County News*, August 31, 1928.

CHAPTER TEN

126 "undoubtedly would continue": *Kansas City Star*, June 10, 1928.

126 "try and think": *Kansas City Star*, June 10, 1928.

127 "beneath the veneer" ... "are refused serious": *Redbook*, April 1928, 79.

127 "when meetings": *Redbook*, April 1928, 79.

127 "infinitely more examples": *Redbook*, April 1928, 79.

128 "they must learn": *Redbook*, April 1928, 79.

129 "the widow mccormick": quoted in *Time*, June 25, 1928, 13.

129 "to feminine maneuvers": *Kansas City Star*, June 5, 1928.

129 "in the eyes": *New York Times*, June 12, 1928.

129 "the most conspicuous": *Time*, June 25, 1928.

130 "only as women": *Kansas City Times*, June 6, 1928.

130 "nobody looking": *New York Times*, June 12, 1928.

131 "into a rousing": *New York Times*, June 12, 1928.

131 "calmly, undisturbed": *Washington Evening Star*, June 13, 1928.

131 "we don't want hoover": Associated Press, June 13, 1928.

131 "her appearance on the stand": Associated Press, June 13, 1928.

131 "as fresh as a daisy": Associated Press, June 13, 1928.

132 "she got tangled up": *Time*, June 25, 1928.

132   "ATTA BOY": *Tulsa (OK) Tribune*, June 13, 1928.
132   "EASY TO TRACE": *Kansas City Star*, June 15, 1928.
132   "MARVEL FOR CLEARNESS": "My Trip," David Walker journal, June 13, 1928, MWWP.
132   "JUBILATED": *Time*, June 25, 1928.
132   "INITIATED A GREAT BUSINESS" . . . "EVEN THE LARGE": *Washington Evening Star*, June 15, 1928.

CHAPTER ELEVEN

134   "AT HIGH SPEED": Boole, *Give Prohibition Its Chance*, 135.
134   "ORDERING OUR WOMEN": Boole, "The Reminiscences of Ella Boole, 1950."
134   "BURNED AND BLAZED": Boole, *Give Prohibition Its Chance*, 136.
135   "THE PRESIDENTIAL HIGHWAY": *Union Signal*, September 8, 1928.
135   "THE SINISTER LOBBYING": *New York Times*, March 9, 1923.
135   "IF THAT WOULD GET US": *Union Signal*, July 31, 1928.
135   "WHICH IS AND OUGHT TO BE": *Brooklyn Daily Eagle*, May 9, 1924.
136   "FAILURE TO SUPPRESS": *Baltimore Sun*, September 22, 1928.
136   "PLAYED A TRICK" . . . "AS SOON AS": Boole, *Give Prohibition Its Chance*, 137.
136   "IT WAS SEIZED UPON": Boole, 137.
137   "IF YOU ONCE REPEAL": *Philadelphia Tribune*, October 9, 1930.
138   "IS THERE A DEFINITE": National League of Republican Colored Women to MWW, August 4, 1928, Nannie Helen Burroughs Papers, Library of Congress.
139   "BLACK VOTERS WANT TO BE": Report by Miss Nannie Helen Burroughs, Burroughs Papers, Library of Congress.
139   "PERCEIVED HIM": Samuel O'Dell, "A Mild Rejoinder," *Phylon* 48, no. 1.
140   "NOW THE RACE": *Chicago Defender*, March 20, 1926.
140   "WE HAVE RESOLVED": *Chicago Defender*, March 20, 1926.
140   "THE NEGRO IS": *Afro-American News*, November 8, 1930.
140   "THE CRIMINAL STATISTICS" . . . "THE POOR, UNDERPRIVILEGED": *Afro-American News*, November 8, 1930.

CHAPTER TWELVE

143   "GET GUINAN": JSGH, 209.
143   "HELLO, DENVER": *Brooklyn Daily Eagle*, April 9, 1929.
143   "WELL, EVERYBODY KNOWS": *New York Daily News*, April 9, 1929.

143   "FOLKS, WE ARE ENFORCEMENT": *New York Herald Tribune*, June 30, 1928.

144   "MABEL'S MOPPERS": *New York Daily News*, November 16, 1928.

144   "SOMETHING WAS UP": *Washington Post*, June 30, 1928.

145   "SHE'S A GREAT WOMAN": *Times* (Shreveport, LA), August 6, 1928.

145   "WHOLE CONTINENT DANGLES": *New Yorker*, August 25, 1928.

145   "THE OLD SCHOOL MARM": JSGH, 200.

145   "IF WILLEBRANDT CAN MAKE": JSGH, 204.

145   "TO DEMOLISH GUINAN": JSGH, 204.

145   "AN EIGHTH-GRADE SCHOOL CHILD": *Evening Star* (Newark, NJ), August 31, 1928.

146   "DRAGNET": *New York Herald Tribune*, August 22, 1928; *New York Daily News*, August 24, 1928.

146   "GAUDY ROMAN HOLIDAY": *Washington Post*, August 21, 1928.

146   "TWO COLORED WOMEN": *Washington Post*, August 21, 1928.

146   "A FISHING EXPEDITION": *Washington Post*, August 21, 1928.

146   "CHEAP NEWSPAPER": MWW to John G. Sargent, quoted in Brown, *Mabel Walker Willebrandt*, 67.

146   "UNTOLD DAMAGE": MWW to John G. Sargent, quoted in Brown, 67.

147   "PITILESS PUBLICITY": *New York Times*, August 28, 1928.

147   "I AM TRYING": *Minneapolis Star Tribune*, August 27, 1928.

147   "MRS. MABEL WALKER WILLEBRANDT": *Richmond Planet*, July 28, 1928.

148   "IN A POLITICAL ORDER": Neil R. McMillen, "Perry W. Howard, Boss of Black-and-Tan Republicanism in Mississippi, 1924–1960," *Journal of Southern History* 48, no. 2 (May 1982): 209.

148   "INVITED CORRUPTION": McMillen, 210.

148   "DURING THE PRESIDENTIAL": McMillen, 209–10.

149   "A STAYING-IN": Bunche, *The Political Status of the Negro in the Age of FDR*, 81.

149   "A BETTER LILY-WHITE": Bunche, 434.

149   "MODERN DAY PORTIA" ... "A WHITE WOMAN": *New York Amsterdam News*, June 5, 1929.

150   "HONORED JIM CROW": McMillen, *Dark Journey*, 68.

150   "IF SOMEONE IN AUTHORITY": *Richmond Planet*, August 25, 1928.

151   "NOT TO WORRY": Ruth Fessler Lipman, Oral History, 44, box 26, HHP.

151   "CLASH WITH THE SPIRIT": *Union Signal*, August 18, 1928.

151   "I OWE NOTHING": MWW to parents, March 28, 1933, MWWP.

152   "30,000 PEOPLE": MWW to parents, August 21, 1928, MWWP.

152   "DISCOURAGEMENT WHICH I MUST NOT": MWW to parents, August 21, 1928, MWWP.

152   "I SEEM TO BE A SORT": MWW to Herbert Work, file 44-42-1, Mail and Files Division, DOJ.

152   "IT IS TOO HARD WORK": MWW to Hubert Work, file 44-42-1, Mail and Files Division, DOJ.

153   "HAD REARED HIM" . . . "THERE ARE 2,000 PASTORS": *New York Times*, September 8, 1928.

153   "THE NATURE OF THE AUDIENCE ": Okrent, *Last Call*, 307.

153   "BARBARIC": Ruth Fessler Lipman, Oral History, 46, box 26, HHP.

154   "NO ONE IN AUTHORITY": *New York Daily News*, September 27, 1928.

154   "ATTORNEY GENERAL SARGENT'S OFFICE": Brown, *Mabel Walker Willebrandt*, 166.

154   "A DISGRACE": *New York Times*, September 26, 1928.

154   "NEVER ASKED A MAN'S": *Washington Post*, September 24, 1928.

155   "FREE-LANCE": *Time*, October 8, 1928.

155   "LACK OF BACKING": MWW to Hubert Work, September 27, 1928, MWWP.

155   "NOT MADE A SINGLE SPEECH": MWW to Hubert Work, September 27, 1928, MWWP.

155   "SURELY YOU AND SARAH": Willebrandt, *Inside Prohibition*, excerpted in *Chicago Daily News*, August 5, 1929.

155   "I DO ENJOY": Willebrandt, *Inside Prohibition*, excerpted in *Chicago Daily News*, August 5, 1929.

155   "SHE HAS PERFORMED": Hiram Johnson to Harold Ickes, May 22, 1926, HJP.

155   "NEVER SYMPATHIZED" . . . "CULTIVATES A CERTAIN PRIDE": *New Yorker*, February 16, 1929.

156   "THE SOLEMNITY": *Independent Record* (Helena, MT), October 3, 1928.

156   "TO REMAIN AS DIVORCED": *Chicago Daily Tribune*, September 27, 1928.

156   "IS A VERY FINE MAN": *Los Angeles Record*, October 2, 1928.

156   "TO JUDGE FROM THE STORY": Eugene Suter to MWW, October 1, 1928, file 44-4, 2–3, Mail and Files Division, DOJ.

156   "JUST TOO MUCH": Brown, *Mabel Walker Willebrandt*, 168.

157   "SHE SHOWED THE TEXTS": Brown, 168.

157   "A VERY GRAVE MISTAKE": *New York Times*, July 25, 1928.

157   "FLYING SQUADRON": *New York Times*, September 5, 1928.

158   "WE WOMEN ARE BEGINNING": Associated Press, *Indianapolis Star*, September 3, 1928.

158 "THIS YEAR THE PRESIDENT": *New York Times Magazine*, October 21, 1928.

158 "WHICH HE ALONE": Boole, *Give Prohibition Its Chance*, 140.

158 "CONTRARY TO EXPECTATIONS": Corder and Wolbrecht, *Counting Ballots*, 197.

159 "NOBLE EXPERIMENT": Inaugural Address of Herbert Hoover, March 4, 1929. (Hoover's actual words were "Our country has deliberately undertaken a great social and economic experiment, noble in motive and far reaching in purpose.")

CHAPTER THIRTEEN

161 "I CAN'T STAND": Root, *Women and Repeal*, 11.

161 "IT'S A GREAT SATISFACTION": *New York Times*, August 24, 1965.

162 "THE WORST EVIL": Hoover Inaugural Speech, the 36th Presidential Inauguration, March 4, 1929.

162 "IN LESS THAN TEN MINUTES": Boole, *Give Prohibition Its Chance*, 140.

163 "I HAD THOUGHT": Root, *Women and Repeal*, 10.

164 "CATHOLICS FLOCKED": Okrent, *Last Call*, 309.

165 "IT CONFLICTS WITH MY VIEWS": *New York Times*, April 4, 1929.

165 "THERE WAS A LARGE GROUP": Root, *Women and Repeal*, 11.

165 "TALKED THINGS OVER": *New York Sun*, June 14, 1932.

165 "SHE GOT THEM EXCITED": Author interview with Pauline Willis, April 4, 2018.

166 "BECAUSE AS YOU KNOW": Eleanor Roosevelt to Anne Hinkley, July 17, 1932, Gilder Lehrman Collection, Gilder Lehrman Institute of American History, New York, NY.

166 "EASY FOR ALL" . . . "the STATES SHOULD BE GIVEN": Eleanor Roosevelt to Anne Hinkley, July 17, 1932, Gilder Lehrman Institute of American History.

166 "BECAUSE I BELIEVE": *Brooklyn Times Union*, June 21, 1929.

167 "THE COMMON PEOPLE": Heckman, "Prohibition Passes," 215.

167 "DAMNED MILLIONAIRES": *New York Times*, April 22, 1930.

167 "THEY WERE AGAINST PROHIBITION": *Baltimore Sun*, October 30, 1932.

168 "THE GREATEST PIECE": Rose, *American Women and the Repeal of Prohibition*, 96.

168 "WAS NOT A SNOB": Author interview with Pauline Willis, April 4, 2018.

168 "I AM AMAZED": *New York Times*, June 10, 1930.

169 "ONE OF THE MOST BEAUTIFUL": *New York Times*, April 14, 1907.

169   "PRETTIEST SPELLBINDERS": *New York Daily News*, September 4, 1932.

169   "THE MOST INTERESTING THING": unmarked clipping, Ione Nicoll Scrapbook.

169   "ONE'S KNOWLEDGE OF PEOPLE": unmarked clipping, Ione Nicoll Scrapbook.

169   "A CONCISE QUALITY": Root, *Women and Repeal*, 92.

170   "IT WAS HER WAY" . . . "THERE WAS NEVER A PROBLEM": Root, 92, 158.

171   "THE OLD SUFFRAGE DAYS": *Vogue*, September 1930.

171   "CIDER, SIR?": Post, *Etiquette in Society, in Business, in Politics and at Home*, 205.

172   "COCOANUT CONGRESSMEN": *Toledo Blade*, June 12, 1945.

172   "THE STORY SHOWS": *Current Biography Yearbook* (H. W. Wilson Co., 1946), 336.

173   "WHO WERE LIKE DANGEROUS ANIMALS" . . . "ONE GIVING US": Ida Tarbell, *Is Prohibition Forcing Civil War?*, 26.

173   "THE BETTER CLASS": Organization Committee for Delaware, May 6, 1933, RWONPR Papers.

174   "I HAD THREE MOTHERS" . . . "RACE CONSCIOUS AND MILITANT": Oral History, Pauline A. Young Papers, Atlanta University Center, Robert W. Woodruff Library.

175   "I WAS RUNNING": Oral History, Pauline A. Young Papers.

175   "THE WOMEN I REPRESENT" . . . "OUR POLITICAL AFFILIATIONS": "Anti-Prohibitionist Sentiment Expressed," June 13, 1932 (Movietone Story, MVTN 14-860).

176   "LIKE A FLASH": Root, *Women and Repeal*, 158.

176   "I AM HUMAN ENOUGH": Pauline Sabin diary, May 3, 1924, PSDP.

176   "HONESTLY, DIDN'T YOU ENJOY": Root, *Women and Repeal*, 157.

177   "NEVER FORGET": Pauline Sabin diary, May 23, 1947.

177   "OUR WOMEN WERE MORE AMIABLE": Root, *Women and Repeal*, 24.

177   "NEARLY 600,000": *Union Signal*, October 5, 1929.

178   "WHOLE ECONOMIC MESS" . . . "THAT PROHIBITION IS THE SECRET": *Vanity Fair*, August 1931.

179   "I KNOW THERE ARE NOT ENOUGH": *Union Signal*, September 14, 1919.

180   "THAT YOUNG AMERICA": *New York Times*, July 2, 1929.

180   "IT'S NONE OF YOUR BUSINESS": Heckman, "Prohibition Passes," 379.

CHAPTER FOURTEEN

181 "THESE VEHEMENT WORDS": *Chicago Tribune*, September 9, 1930.

182 "YOUNG, PRETTY AND INTELLIGENT": *Vanity Fair*, August 1931.

182 "VIGOROUS MOVEMENT": Root, *Women and Repeal*, 7–8.

182 "WOMEN WILL NOT DESERT": Boole, *Give Prohibition Its Chance*, 141.

183 "PERMANENT MASCULINE HEGEMONY": Murdock, *Domesticating Drink*, 180.

184 "SHE WILL DO OUR CAUSE" . . . "MENTION ANYTHING": M. Louise Gross to Mrs. David Holmes Morton, April 7, 1929, M. Louise Gross Papers, Manuscripts and Archives Division, New York Public Library.

185 "THAT THE POWER": Rose, *American Women and the Repeal of Prohibition*, 142–43.

185 "FANATIC" . . . "BEEN BEHIND": *New York Times*, April 4, 1929.

185 "WHETHER MY BOYS DRANK": S. J. Woolf, "A Woman Crusader for the Wet Cause," *New York Times Magazine*, May 8, 1932.

185 "NOT SINCE THE CIVIL WAR": Ione Nicoll Scrapbook.

185 "I KNOW OF NOTHING": *New York Times*, December 2, 1931.

186 "BLINDLY SWAYED": William O. Finish to Mrs. Alice Berlin du Pont, April 28, 1932, RWONPR.

186 "PROBABLY THE MOST INTERESTING": *Baltimore Sun*, December 26, 1928.

186 "THE LOVELIEST TRIBUTES": MWW to parents, February 12, 1929, MWWP.

186 "GET BACK NOT ONLY": MWW to parents, February 12, 1929, MWWP.

186 "AS I AM WITH HER": MWW to parents, February 12, 1929, MWWP.

186 "WON'T YOU TRY": MWW to parents, February 12, 1929, MWWP.

187 "FRAYIM" . . . "IT'S TAKEN EVERY OUNCE": MWW to parents, July 28, 1929, MWWP.

187 "DO YOU REALIZE" . . . "IN THE PRESS OF BUSINESS": David Walker to MWW, March 30, 1929, MWWP.

188 "WOULD BE UNWISE" . . . "MABEL, IF YOU COULD SEE": Myrtle Walker to MWW, April 1929, MWWP.

188 "THE MOST NOTORIOUS": *New York Times*, November 22, 1928.

188 "PAPA DEAR": MWW to parents, July 28, 1929, MWWP.

189 "DOER WHO COULD INSPIRE" . . . "LESSER LEGAL LIGHT": MWW to Herbert Hoover, February 8, 1929, Presidential Appointments, Men Considered, HHP.

190 "ANYONE ON THE LINE?" . . . "I JUST WANTED": MWW to parents, February 22, 1929, MWWP.

190   "A DEMOCRAT" ... "DEAN ROSCOE POUND": Brown, *Mabel Walker Willebrandt*, 175.

190   "AT LEAST FOR A WHILE" ... "STAY A WHILE": MWW to parents, February 22, 1929, MWWP.

190   "IT GOES TO PROVE": MWW to parents, February 22, 1929, MWWP.

190   "IN SUCH A FUROR": MWW to parents, February 22, 1929, MWWP.

191   "ANY PLAN WHICH DRAWS": *Chicago Daily Tribune*, March 17, 1929.

CHAPTER FIFTEEN

192   "A SOMEWHAT ENTERTAINING THRILLER": *New York Times*, March 18, 1929.

192   "FROM THE SERENITY": JSGH, 210.

192   "A TEMPORARY ECLIPSE": *Standard Union* (Brooklyn, NY), April 1, 1929.

192   "ALL RISE!" *Brooklyn Daily Eagle*, April 10, 1929.

193   "THE WORLD KNEW": Berliner, *Texas Guinan*, 133.

193   "PRETTY MUCH AS SHE PLEASED": Berliner, 134.

193   "HAD TO" ... "WANTED TO": *Brooklyn Daily Eagle*, April 10, 1929.

193   "VERY, VERY DRUNK" ... "OUT THE WINDOW": JSGH, 218.

193   "HE IS FROM CHICAGO": *Brooklyn Daily Eagle*, April 10, 1929.

193   "VERY, VERY MUCH": JSGH, 217.

193   "TO PAINT THE TOWN RED": *New York Daily News*, April 10, 1029.

194   "I'M AFRAID YOU THINK" ... "OH NO": JSGH, 219.

195   "THOSE PEOPLE" ... "THIS IS NOT A SHOW": *New York Daily News*, April 10, 1929; *Brooklyn Daily Times*, April 11, 1929.

195   "I CAN'T HELP": *Brooklyn Times Union*, April 11, 1929.

195   "ME A NUISANCE?" ... "MABEL WALKER WILLEBRANDT IS MY IDEA": *New York Daily News*, April 9, 1929.

195   "THE CASE BECAME" ... "HOW ANY JURY": JSGH, 242.

196   "THE PRISONER'S SONG": JSGH, 250.

196   "IF MISS GUINAN": *Brooklyn Daily Eagle*, April 12, 1929.

196   "CONGRATULATIONS" ... "WE ALL GIVE": JSGH, 251.

197   "DISGUSTING PIECES": *Chicago Tribune*, April 13, 1929, 6.

197   "YOU AND I": "Jealous, Replies Tex," *New York Daily News*, April 14, 1929.

197   "PERSECUTION": JSGH, 268.

198   "HAD SCHEMED": *New York Daily News*, April 18, 1929.

198   "WE HAD TO HAVE": *New York Daily News*, April 18, 1929.

CHAPTER SIXTEEN

199   "THE WCTU AND THE CHURCH CROWD": Myrtle Walker to MWW, May 27, 1929, MWWP.

199   "HELPED": Bartlett C. Jones, "A Prohibition Problem: Liquor as Medicine 1920–1933," *Journal of the History of Medicine and Allied Sciences* 18, no. 4 (October 1963): 360–61.

200   "WOULD BE CRUCIFIED" . . . "DAMN NEAR RAN": Braitman, *She Damn Near Ran the Studio*, 102, xii; *Los Angeles Times*, June 12, 1929.

201   "INDEBTEDNESS": Herbert Hoover to MWW, May 28, 1929, box 21, Executive Department, Justice, Presidential Papers, HHP.

201   "IT IS NOT PROPOSED": Herbert Hoover to Laurence Richey, June 3, 1929, box 1, Executive Department, Justice, Presidential Papers, HHP.

201   "INDISPENSABLE" . . . "HEART OF THE CAUSE": *Union Signal*, June 15, 1929.

201   "IT IS NOT SURPRISING": *Union Signal*, June 15, 1929.

203   "WILLEBRANDT WINE": *Times Herald* (Port Huron, MI), September 2, 1931.

203   "ONCE THE JOAN OF ARC": *New York Daily News*, August 2, 1931.

203   "MABEL'S GRAPE BRICKS": United Press International, *Daily Northwestern* (Oshkosh, WI), November 9, 1931.

204   "VERY DISAPPOINTED" . . . "WHAT A PITY": Elise Giles to MWW, September 10, 1931, MWWP.

204   "IGNORANT CRITICISM" . . . "MRS. WILLEBRANDT HAS NOT": David Walker to Elise Giles, October 10, 1931, MWWP.

204   "LIKE ALL OTHER HONEST": David Walker to Elise Giles, October 10, 1931, MWWP.

205   "I'VE NEVER SEEN": Maud Hubbard Brown to MWW, December 10, 1932, MWWP.

CHAPTER SEVENTEEN

207   "BABY BLONDE ALIBI": *Philadelphia Inquirer*, April 21, 1929.

208   "MURDER, INC.": Sifakis, *The Mafia Encyclopedia*, 2005.

208   "I HEARD OF A FELLOW": "Texas Guinan Says," *Milwaukee Leader*, May 10, 1931.

208   "LITTLE CHILDREN": *Cincinnati Enquirer*, April 12, 1929.

208   "TROUBLE": *New York Daily News*, March 25, 1930.

209   "FEETS": JSGH, 331.

209   "FOR KEEPING YOUR MOUTH SHUT": *New York Daily News*, March 31, 1930.

209   "YOU ARE EITHER NOTORIOUS": JSGH, 323.

210 "MEN DO NOT WANT": *Nebraska State Journal,* May 21, 1930; *Journal Star* (Lincoln, NE), May 20, 1930.

211 "WHO DO YOU THINK" . . . "YES, AND THE POLICE": JSGH, 289.

213 "AN ARROGANT EGOMANIAC": Applegate, *Madam,* 268.

CHAPTER EIGHTEEN

214 "TWENTY-FIVE MILLION CHILDREN": *Democrat and Chronicle* (Rochester, NY), January 17, 1930.

215 "THIS YEAR FINDS CONGRESS" . . . "POVERTY IS": *Chicago Tribune,* January 17, 1930.

215 "IT'S IN THE CONSTITUTION": *New York Daily News,* July 20, 1931.

216 "I REPRESENT" . . . "I SAID TO MYSELF": *Kansas City Star,* July 24, 1932.

217 "RID THIS COUNTRY": *New York Times,* February 11, 1931.

217 "TEN YEARS IS NOT" . . . "I AGREE": *New York World-Telegram,* February 11, 1931.

217 "KNOW JUST WHAT FINGER": *Union Signal,* May 10, 1930.

217 "TORCHES OF FREEDOM": *Record* (Hackensack, NJ), April 11, 1929; *Boston Globe,* July 19, 1998.

218 "WE HOPE THAT WE": *Record* (Hackensack, NJ), April 11, 1929; *Boston Globe,* July 19, 1998.

218 "DRUNKEN AND IMMORAL": Root, *Women and Repeal,* 110–11.

218 "DEPRIVING THE POOR" . . . "BACCHANALIAN MAIDENS": Lerner, "Dry Manhattan," 415.

218 "EVERY EVENING": Kyvig, *Repealing National Prohibition,* 126.

219 "INSTEAD OF A BONA FIDE" . . . "CHARGED WITH BEING AFRAID": *Pittsburgh Press,* February 28, 1930.

219 "IT WOULD BE DIFFICULT": unidentified clipping, PS Scrapbook.

219 "HAVE BEEN TESTED": *Philadelphia Enquirer,* February 13, 1930.

220 "TO REFUTE THE CONTENTION" . . . "NO IMPROVEMENT": *Prohibition Amendment Hearings on H. J., Res. 11,* 38, 99, 114, 219 & 246; 71st Cong., 2nd sess., 1930, 41–44.

220 "WE JUST CAME TO SEE": Root, *Women and Repeal,* 53–54.

220 "THE RICH" . . . "EVERY DRUNKARD": *Prohibition Amendment Hearings,* 41–44.

221 "DIVINE GUIDANCE": *New York Daily News,* July 20, 1931.

221 "THE DISAPPEARANCE OF THE SALOON": *New York Times,* April 9, 1930.

221 "THE RESIDENTS OF GREENWICH": *New York Times,* April 9, 1930.

221 "WE ARE GLAD" . . . "WINEBIBBER": *New York Times,* April 9, 1930.

222 "ARE THESE THE IDLE RICH" . . . "I'M USED TO IT": *New York Times,* April 9, 1930.

CHAPTER NINETEEN

223 "IN A VERITABLE FLOOD": Root, *Women and Repeal*, 27.

224 "*DANGEROUS* EXPERIMENT": *New York Herald Tribune*, April 15, 1931.

225 "SUDDENLY REALIZED" . . . "HE HAS TO AT LEAST": *New York Evening Post*, April 15, 1931.

225 "THE PROTEST AGAINST" . . . "I AM VERY GLAD": *New York Evening News*, April 15, 1931.

226 "COOPERATION WITH LABOR": Matthew Woll to Pierre S. du Pont, April 24, 1932, RWONPR.

227 "OUR SITUATION WILL REMAIN": *Indianapolis Star*, November 24, 1931.

227 "IF ELECTED, WILL YOU SUPPORT": Essential Part of Instructions from the National Office of WONPR to State Chairmen Regarding the Poll of Candidates for Congress, fall 1932, General Correspondence 1932, reel 14, RWONPR.

227 "IS IT REALLY POSSIBLE" . . . "I AM WRITING": Root, *Women and Repeal*, 53.

228 "THE GREAT NEED": Root, 50.

228 "WORSE. BASED ON": *New York Daily News*, August 4, 1931.

228 "WAS A WOODEN HORSE": *Louisville Courier Journal*, July 12, 1931.

229 "IT SEEMS A BIT STRANGE": *Atlanta Daily World*, September 2, 1934.

229 "FINE INTELLIGENCE": *Atlanta Constitution*, March 3, 1932.

230 "STAGE THE LARGEST": *Charleston News and Courier*, February 12, 1932.

230 "IS NOT A QUESTION" . . . "SPEAK OUT": *Charleston News and Courier*, March 2, 1932.

231 "BEAUTY" . . . "PLATFORM PERSONALITY": *Atlanta Constitution*, March 3, 1932.

231 "SOCIALLY PROMINENT": *Union Signal*, April 23, 1932.

231 "THE PROHIBITION AMENDMENT": *Baltimore Sun*, April 15, 1932.

231 "TEMPERANCE ORGANIZATIONS" . . . "THE CHIEF ALLIES": *Baltimore Sun*, April 15, 1932.

231 "OF AN INTOLERANT, FANATICAL": *Syracuse (NY) Herald*, April 13, 1932.

232 "ABSOLUTELY NOT!": *Evening Star* (Washington, DC), April 13, 1932.

232 "WEAR THE WET LABEL": *Rochester (NY) Democrat and Chronicle*, May 16, 1932.

CHAPTER TWENTY

236   "ONE NEED NOT": *New York Evening Post*, April 14, 1931; *Daily News* (New York), August 8, 1931.

236   "WE ARE ALL DELIGHTED": *New York Telegram*, June 4, 1932.

237   "WE ARE IN THE WORST": *New Haven (CT) Citizen*, February 1931.

237   "THE REAL TRAGEDY": *Detroit Evening News*, May 30, 1932.

237   "HER EXPRESSIVE EYES" . . . "TO HERSELF WHAT SHE WANTS": United Press International, *New York World-Telegram*, June 14, 1932.

238   "DRY LOYALTY" . . . "WET PROPAGANDA": *Baltimore Sun*, June 12, 1932.

238   "FOR OUR SAKE": *Chicago Tribune*, June 15, 1932.

239   "THE IRON CHANCELLOR": *New York Daily News*, July 18, 1931.

239   "PERT AND CONFIDENT": unidentified clipping, PS Scrapbooks.

239   "THE OPPONENTS": *Union Signal*, June 25, 1932.

239   "THE WOMEN WHO": *Union Signal*, June 29, 1932.

240   "SHOW ME A WOMAN": Murdock, *Domesticating Drink*, 147.

240   "GIGANTIC STRADDLE": *Albion (NE) News*, June 16, 1932.

240   "TO ISSUES RATHER THAN CANDIDATES": *New York Times*, August 16, 1933.

240   "TO SEEM DRY": *Chicago Tribune*, June 16, 1932.

241   "WENT AS WET": *New York Times*, June 30, 1932.

241   "DESERTED THE AMENDMENT": . . . "DEMOCRACY, LIKE SATURN": *New York Times*, June 30, 1932.

241   "SILK STOCKING BEAUTIES": *Lawrence (MA) Telegram*, June 27, 1932.

241   "WELL, *YOU* OUGHT": *Wilmington (DE) Journal*, June 30, 1932.

241   "PERFECTLY SWELL!" . . . "I AM SIMPLY GIBBERING": *New York Times*, July 3, 1932.

241   "TO THE MEN AND WOMEN" . . . "RESTORE AMERICA": The American Presidency Project, Franklin D. Roosevelt, Address Accepting the Presidential Nomination at the Democratic National Convention in Chicago, July 2, 1932.

242   "THE SOLE TEST": *Boston Globe*, July 11, 1932.

242   "I AM VERY SORRY": *Chicago Tribune*, July 12, 1932.

242   "DON'T BRING ME": *New York Times*, July 12, 1932.

242   "THAT POLITICS IS THICKER": *Christian Science Monitor*, July 15, 1932.

242   "IS WEAKER THAN TISSUE": Elizabeth Tilton diary, Papers of Elizabeth Tilton, 1914–1949, Schlesinger Library, Radcliffe Institute, Harvard University.

243   "WE HAVE JUST BEGUN": United Press International, *San Mateo (CA) Times*, June 30, 1932.
243   "THE POPULOUS CLASS": *Time*, July 18, 1932.

CHAPTER TWENTY-ONE

244   "THE GREATEST HANDICAP": *Time*, August 26, 1929.
244   "WET OR EVEN DAMP": *New York Times*, October 30, 1932.
244   "THE EIGHTEENTH AMENDMENT CAN BE": *New York Times*, October 30, 1932.
245   "NO MORAL SPEED LIMITS": JSGH, 194.
245   "SORT OF QUEEN": Berliner, *Texas Guinan*, 170.
246   "LOCAL BANDITTI": Gabler, *Winchell*, 155.
249   "LAID HANDS": Epstein, *Sister Aimee*, 210.
249   "WHITE SLAVERY": Gilbert King, "The Incredible Disappearing Evangelist," *Smithsonian*, June 17, 2013.
251   "I HAVE GIVEN MY LIFE": JSGH, 385.
251   "I HAVE ALWAYS": JSGH, 385, 386.

CHAPTER TWENTY-TWO

252   "DREW A HEAVY" ... "ALTHOUGH IT'S ONLY IN RECENT YEARS": *Tampa Bay Times*, November 9, 1932.
253   "LITTLE ORGANIZATION": Lerner, "Dry Manhattan" (diss.).
253   "I AM GLAD": *New York Times*, February 17, 1933.
253   "A WALK-OVER": *Des Moines Iowa Tribune*, May 9, 1933.
254   "WE REPEALISTS" ... "WE HAVE SHOWN": *Des Moines (IA) Tribune*, May 9, 1933.
254   "SAFELY WET" ... "GOOD PROSPECTS": WONPR Press Release, WONPR Records, Pennsylvania Division 1930–1934.
254   "WE HAVE DECIDED": WONPR Press Release, WONPR Records, Pennsylvania Division, 1930–1934.
254   "TO FIGHT" ... "I HAVE BEEN GOING": *New York Times*, February 17, 1933.
254   "WE DO NOT BELIEVE": Roosevelt Library, Record Group of 75, Folders, Prohibition: In Favor of, 1933–1937, A–I.
255   "WHITE VIRGINIA": *Afro-American*, October 7, 1933.
255   "NEGRO AMERICANS": *New York Amsterdam News*, July 26, 1933.
256   "NEGROES EXPERIENCED": *Pittsburgh Courier*, July 29, 1933.
256   "REGRETTED THAT" ... "IF OUR WHITE MINISTERS": Eig, *King*, 38.
256   "NOT VERY BENEFICIAL": Pauline Sabin to Alice du Pont, August 16, 1933, RWONPR.

257   "COMPLETELY HAPPY": Pauline Sabin to John Raskob, October 6,
      1932, file 2017, John J. Raskob Papers, Hagley Museum and Library,
      Wilmington, Delaware.

257   "I WAS SO DUMB": Author interview with Pauline Willis, April 4,
      2018.

258   "IF THE EMOTIONAL": Committee on Arrangements for Final
      WONPR dinner to Mrs. Pierre (Alice) Paul du Pont, November 30,
      1933, RWONPR.

258   "SHE JUST ADORED HIM": Author interview with Pauline Willis,
      April 4, 2018.

                      CHAPTER TWENTY-THREE

259   "FLUTTERING ROUND" ... "BREATHLESSLY TRYING": *Capital
      Times* (Madison, WI), December 9, 1933.

260   "THE NATION IS MAD": Elizabeth Tilton diary, December 5, 1933,
      Papers of Elizabeth Tilton, 1914–1949, Schlesinger Library, Radcliffe
      Institute, Harvard University.

260   "DESTRUCTION OF MORAL WELFARE" ... "PROHIBITION *WILL*
      RETURN": Elizabeth Tilton diary, March 28, 1933.

261   "WE'VE LOST THE BATTLE": *Brooklyn Daily Eagle*, March 14, 1952.

261   "VERY MUCH ALIVE": Boole, "The Reminiscences of Ella Boole,
      1950," 26.

261   "OUR ULTIMATE GOAL": *Camden (NJ) Courier Post*, November 1,
      1933.

262   "THE BOOTLEGGER AND RACKETEER": *Indianapolis Times*,
      November 24, 1933; *Knoxville News-Sentinel*, November 26, 1933.

262   "THAT DRINKING IN MODERATION": *Indianapolis Times*, November 24, 1933; *Knoxville News-Sentinel*, November 26, 1933.

262   "PETER OUT": Pauline Sabin to Mrs. Pierre (Alice) du Pont, August
      29, 1933, RWONPR.

262   "GROUP OF FIGHTING SUFFRAGISTS": Pauline Sabin diary, 1942,
      2, PSDP.

262   "INSISTED ON FORMING" ... "I SHOULD HATE TO SEE": Pauline
      Sabin to Alice du Pont, August 29, 1933, RWONPR.

262   "RATIFICATION IS A FACT" ... "TO A CHARITY": Pauline Sabin to
      Alice du Pont, August 29, 1933, RWONPR.

263   "THE ADMIRATION" ... "IS A GEM": Alice du Pont to "My dear," January 22, 1934, RWONPR.

263   "EMINENT ATTAINMENT" ... "INTELLECTUAL HONESTY": *New
      York Times*, November 20, 1934.

263   "A WOMAN WHO HAS ALWAYS": *New York Times*, November 20,
      1934.

263   "I KNOW WHAT WOMEN": Pauline Sabin speech, November 20, 1934, American Woman's Association Press Release, PS Scrapbooks.

263   "WHO HAD WORKED AGAINST": *New York Times*, November 21, 1936.

EPILOGUE

265   "TO US ALL": MWW, Women in Government Speech, given at the Ebell Club, Los Angeles, November 1952, MWWP; Brown, *Mabel Walker Willebrandt*, 215.

266   "TO WRECK THE COUNTRY": MWW to Laura and Carl Lomen, n.d., Carl Lomen Papers; Brown, *Mabel Walker Willebrandt*, 216.

266   "COURAGEOUS STAND": MWW to FDR, September 3, 1938, PPF, box 1986, FDR Papers.

266   "INCORRUPTIBLE COURAGE": MWW to FDR, August 17, 1937, OF 41, box 51, FDR Papers; Brown, *Mabel Walker Willebrandt*, 216.

266   "MR. PRESIDENT": MWW to FDR, February 16, 1939, PPEF, box 1986, FDR Papers; Brown, 218.

267   "FEELS SO STRONGLY" ... "BEAR TO SEE": MWW to FDR, February 16, 1939, MWWP.

267   "I AM CONVINCED": MWW to Myrtle Walker, May 14, 1932, MWWP.

269   "MARRY SOME HIGH-PRICED": Author interview with Jan Van Dyke, June 4, 2020.

269   "A DETACHED DEPENDENCE" ... "YOU TOOK A TALENTED": MWW to Hendrick Van Dyke, November 3, 1943, private collection.

270   "NO DEEP LOVE": Author interview with Jan Van Dyke, June 4, 2020.

270   "REALIZED THAT MY MOM": Author interview with Jan Van Dyke, June 4, 2020.

271   "IT WAS THE MOST": Author interview with Pauline Willis, April 4, 2018.

271   "A SOUFFLÉ DOESN'T": Pauline Sabin diary, 1948, 62, PSDP.

271   "THE INVENTION": Pauline Sabin diary, 1948, 22, PSDP.

272   "NO ONE IN HER SOCIAL SET": Author interview with Pauline Willis, May 26, 2022.

272   "YOU CAN SEE": *New York Times*, October 4, 1933.

272   "ALARMED AND DISTRESSED": *New York Times*, October 4, 1933.

272   "ALL TAMMANY" ... "WHO KNOWS THE CITY": *New York Times*, October 4, 1933.

273   "I BELIEVE": *New York Times*, October 4, 1933.

273   "CARRY THE FIGHT": *New York Times*, October 4, 1933.

273   "PEACE AND FREEDOM" ... "PACIFIST, NAZI": *The New York Times*, May 4, 1940.

274   "MEANINGLESS, HARMFUL": *New York Times*, May 4, 1940.

274   "PRIMARILY RESPONSIBLE" . . . "THE RISE IN VENEREAL": *Brooklyn Daily Eagle*, January 22, 1944.

274   "AS YOUNG" . . . "HOWEVER, I AM CONVINCED": Pauline Sabin, letter to the editor, *New York Times*, January 12, 1944.

275   "GIVEN TO BEING LOW" . . . "IT IS IMPORTANT": EB to Margaret Munns, October 9, 1940, FWMLA.

275   "TO CONVINCE SUCH PEOPLE": EB to Margaret Munns, March 18, 1939, FWMLA.

276   "I FEEL THAT": EB to Margaret Munns, December 20, 1940, FWMLA.

276   "WE MUST BE BROADMINDED" . . . "AT THE HEADS": EB to Margaret Munns, November 8, 1943, FWMLA.

276   "IF THE WCTU": EB to Margaret Munns, July 20, 1942, FWMLA.

276   "A CARDIAC CONDITION" . . . "IT IS STRANGE": EB to Margaret Munns, March 28, 1939, FWMLA.

277   "RECOGNIZES THE WCTU'S VALUE": *State* (Columbia, SC), May 30, 1937.

277   "THERE NEVER WAS": EB to Margaret Munns, July 30, 1942, FWMLA.

277   "VERY SICK" . . . "THAT THE THREE MEN": EB to Margaret Munns, December 8, 1943, FWMLA.

278   "KILLJOYS": *Brooklyn Daily Eagle*, July 14, 1938.

278   "A CONSPIRACY": EB to Margaret Munns, December 12, 1940, FWMLA.

278   "THE LAST OF THE BIG": EB to Margaret Munns, June 26, 1942, FWMLA.

278   "I GAVE UP" . . . "I SEE NOW": EB to Margaret Munns, June 23, 1947, FWMLA.

280   "GRANNY WOULD NEVER WAVER": Author interview with Pauline Willis, April 4, 2018.

280   "WAS TOO HARSH": Author interview with Pauline Willis, April 4, 2018.

280   "AND EVERYONE JUST DROPPED" . . . "HER WORD WAS GO": Author interview with Pauline Willis, April 4, 2018.

280   "I THINK I WAS": Author interview with Sheila Cochran, April 18, 2018.

280   "THERE WAS A LOT": Author interview with Pauline Willis, April 4, 2018.

281   "GRANNY HAD A HUGE": Author interview with Pauline Willis, April 4, 2018.

281   "FORRESTAL DINED HERE": Pauline Sabin diary, 1947–1949, PSDP.

281   "NOT ONLY BY HER BEAUTY": Hoopes and Brinkley, *Driven Patriot*, loc. 4866.

281 "HER MAID": Author interview with Pauline Willis, April 4, 2018.

282 "THE SICKNESS OF FEAR" ... "WITH OTHER RIGHT-THINKING": *Washington Post*, May 29, 1953.

283 "COULD YOU HAVE IT": MWW to Herbert Hoover, November 11, 1948, Post Presidential File, box 558, HHP.

283 "ONLY APPOINTED" ... "MIGHT *LIKE* TO DEMONSTRATE": MWW to Herbert Hoover, November 11, 1948, MWWP.

283 "MY DEAR" ... "BUT MY RELATIONS": MWW to Herbert Hoover, November 11, 1948, MWWP.

284 "OUR GUIDING LIGHT": Brown, *Mabel Walker Willebrandt*, 236.

284 "MABEL HELPED US": Brown, 241.

284 "THE COMMIES" ... "BUT FORTUNATELY": Brown, 243–44.

284 "GOOD OLD SENATOR": Brown, 243.

285 "WAS THIN": Author interview with Jan Van Dyke, June 4, 2020.

285 "I WANT YOU TO KNOW": MWW to Dorothy Van Dyke, n.d., MWWP.

286 "FULL OF PRIDE": MWW to Dorothy Van Dyke, n.d., MWWP.

286 "AN UNFORGETTABLE EXAMPLE": Capra, *The Name Above the Title*, 428.

286 "TO POUR OUT" ... "STOOD FOR SOMETHING": Brown, *Mabel Walker Willebrandt*, 253.

286 "MORE AND MORE SECRETLY": Brown, 251.

287 "THAT SHE WAS DRUNK": Brown, 261.

287 "I KNOW SHE MUST": Judy Odlum to Dorothy Van Dyke, April 4, 1963, MWWP.

SELECTED BIBLIOGRAPHY

ARCHIVES AND MANUSCRIPT COLLECTIONS

Boole, Emma. "The Reminiscences of Ella Boole, 1950." Individual Interviews Oral History Collection, Columbia Center for Oral History, Columbia University.

Davis, Pauline Sabin. Papers, Schlesinger Library, Radcliffe Institute for Advanced Study, Harvard University, Cambridge, MA.

Du Pont, Alice (Mrs. Pierre S. du Pont), Papers. Hagley Museum and Library, Wilmington, DE.

Gilder Lehrman Collection. Gilder Lehrman Institute of American History, New York, NY.

Hoover, Herbert. Papers. Herbert Hoover Presidential Library and Museum, West Branch, IA.

Ickes, Harold. Papers. Library of Congress, Washington, DC.

Johnson, Hiram. Papers. Bancroft Library, University of California, Berkeley.

Lomen, Carl. Papers. University of Alaska, Fairbanks.

Matthews, Annabel. Papers. Schlesinger Library, Radcliffe Institute of Advanced Study, Harvard University, Cambridge, MA.

National League of Women Voters. Papers. Library of Congress, Washington, DC.

Roosevelt, Eleanor. Papers. Franklin D. Roosevelt Presidential Library, Hyde Park, NY.

Roosevelt, Franklin D. Papers. Franklin D. Roosevelt Presidential Library and Museum, Hyde Park, NY.

Tilton, Elizabeth. Papers. Schlesinger Library, Radcliffe Institute of Advanced Study, Harvard University, Cambridge, MA.

Wadsworth, James. Family Papers. Library of Congress, Washington, DC.
Willebrandt, Mabel Walker. Papers. Library of Congress, Washington, DC.
Woman's Christian Temperance Union Archives and Collections. Frances Wil-
    lard Memorial Library and Archives, Evanston, IL.
Women's Organization for National Prohibition Reform. Pennsylvania Divi-
    sion Records. Hagley Museum and Library, Wilmington, DE.
Work, Hubert. Papers. Hoover Institution, Stanford University, Stanford, CA.

DOCUMENTARY

Burns, Ken, and Lynn Novick, dirs. *Prohibition*. PBS documentary, 2011.

IN PRIVATE COLLECTIONS

Pauline Sabin Scrapbooks
Ione Nicoll Scrapbook

THESES AND DISSERTATIONS

Fulton, Crystal. "The Women's Organization for National Prohibition Reform,
    1929–1933." MA thesis, Western Ontario University, 1990.
Heckman, Dayton E. "Prohibition Passes: The Story of the Association Against
    the Prohibition Amendment." PhD diss., Ohio State University, 1939.
Krinitsky, Nora. "The Politics of Crime Control: Race, Policing, and Reform
    in Twentieth-Century Chicago." PhD diss., University of Michigan,
    2017.
Lerner, Michael A. "Dry Manhattan: Class, Culture, and Politics in Prohibition-
    Era New York City, 1919–1933." PhD diss., New York University, 1999.
Morrison, Glenda E. "Women's Participation in the 1928 Presidential Cam-
    paign." PhD diss., University of Kansas, 1928.

UNPUBLISHED MANUSCRIPT

Stein, John S., and Grace Hayward. "Hello, Sucker! The Life of Texas Guinan."
    1941. Billy Rose Theatre Division, New York Public Library for the Per-
    forming Arts, New York City.

WORKS BY MABEL WALKER WILLEBRANDT

"First Impressions." *Good Housekeeping*, May 1928, 38–39, 219–29.
"Give Women a Fighting Chance!" *Smart Set*, February 1930, 24–26, 106–7.
The Inside of Prohibition. Indianapolis: Bobbs-Merrill, 1929.

"The Republican Platform as Viewed by Mrs. Mabel Walker Willebrandt." *McCall's Magazine*, November 1928, 18, 119.

"Will You Help Keep the Law?" *Good Housekeeping*, April 1924, 72–73, 235–40.

BOOKS

Abbott, Karen. *The Ghosts of Eden Park: The Bootleg King, the Women Who Pursued Him, and the Murder That Shocked Jazz Age America*. New York: Crown, 2019.

Allen, Frederick Lewis. *The Big Change: America Transforms Itself, 1900–1950*. New York: Harper & Brothers, 1952.

Allen, Frederick Lewis. *Only Yesterday: An Informal History of the Nineteen Twenties*. New York: Harper & Brothers, 1931.

Allen, Frederick Lewis. *Since Yesterday: The 1930s in America, September 3, 1929–September 3, 1939*. New York: Harper & Row, 1939.

Ambrose, Hugh, and John Schuttler. *Liberated Spirits: Two Women Who Battled over Prohibition*. New York: Berkley, 2018.

Anderson, Lisa M. F. *The Politics of Prohibition: American Governance and the Prohibition Party, 1869–1933*. Cambridge: Cambridge University Press, 2013.

Applegate, Debby. *Madam: The Biography of Polly Adler, Icon of the Jazz Age*. New York: Doubleday, 2021.

Baker, Jean. *Sisters: The Lives of America's Suffragists*. New York: Hill and Wang, 2005.

Berliner, Louise. *Texas Guinan: Queen of the Nightclubs*. Austin: University of Texas Press, 1993.

Boole, Ella A. *Give Prohibition Its Chance*. Evanston, IL: National Woman's Christian Temperance Union Publishing House, 1929.

Braitman, Jacqueline R. *She Damn Near Ran the Studio: The Extraordinary Lives of Ida R. Koverman*. Jackson: University Press of Mississippi, 2020.

Brown, Dorothy M. *Mabel Walker Willebrandt: A Study of Power, Loyalty, and Law*. Knoxville: University of Tennessee Press, 1984.

Brown, Dorothy M. *Setting a Course: American Women in the 1920s*. Boston: G. K. Hall, 1987.

Bunche, Ralph. *The Political Status of the Negro in the Age of FDR*. Chicago: University of Chicago Press, 1973.

Burner, David. *Herbert Hoover: A Public Life*. New York: Knopf, 1979.

Cook, Blanche Wiesen. *Eleanor Roosevelt*. Volume 1: *1884–1933*. New York: Viking, 1992.

Coolidge, Calvin. *The Autobiography of Calvin Coolidge*. Wilmington, DE: Intercollegiate Studies Institute, 1921.

Corder, J. Kevin, and Christina Wolbrecht. *Counting Women's Ballots: Female Voters from Suffrage Through the New Deal.* Cambridge: Cambridge University Press, 2016.

Cordery, Stacy A. *Alice: Alice Roosevelt Longworth, from White House Princess to Washington Power Broker.* New York: Viking, 2007.

Dean, John W. *Warren G. Harding.* New York: Henry Holt, 2004.

Dober, Lawrence. *Westerleigh: The Town That Temperance Built.* New York: Westerleigh Improvement Society, 2000.

Dobyns, Fletcher. *The Amazing Story of Repeal.* Evanston, IL: Signal Press, 1974.

Eig, Jonathan. *King: A Life.* New York: Farrar, Straus and Giroux, 2023.

Epstein, Daniel Mark. *Sister Aimee: The Life of Aimee Semple McPherson.* New York: Harcourt, 1993.

Evans, Christopher H. *Do Everything: The Biography of Frances Willard.* New York: Oxford University Press, 2022.

Fitzgerald, F. Scott. *My Lost City: Personal Essays, 1920–1940.* Cambridge: Cambridge University Press, 2005.

Gabler, Neal. *Winchell: Gossip, Power, and the Culture of Celebrity.* New York: Vintage, 1995.

Gage, Beverly. *G-Man: J. Edgar Hoover and the Making of the American Century.* New York: Viking, 2022.

Giglio, James N. *H. M. Daugherty and the Politics of Expediency.* Kent, OH: Kent State University Press, 1978.

Gilmore, Glenda Elizabeth. *Gender and Jim Crow: Women and the Politics of White Supremacy in North Carolina, 1896–1920.* 2nd ed. Chapel Hill: University of North Carolina Press, 2019.

Goodier, Susan. *No Votes for Women: The New York State Anti-Suffrage Movement.* Champaign: University of Illinois Press, 2013.

Graham, Frances W. *Sixty Years of Action, 1874–1934: A History of Sixty Years' Work of the Woman's Christian Temperance Union of the State of New York.* Lockport, NY, 1934.

Granlund, Nils T. *Blondes, Brunettes, and Bullets.* Philadelphia: McKay, 1957.

Griffin, Elisabeth. *Formidable: American Women and the Fight for Equality, 1920–2020.* New York: Pegasus Books, 2022.

Gustafson, Melanie S., Kristie Miller, and Elisabeth Israels Perry. *We Have Come to Stay: American Women and Political Parties (1880–1960).* Albuquerque: University of New Mexico Press, 1999.

Hallett, Hilary A. *Inventing the It Girl: How Elinor Glyn Created the Modern Romance Novel and Conquered Early Hollywood.* New York: Norton, 2022.

Hoopes, Townsend, and Douglas Brinkley. *Driven Patriot: The Life and Times of James Forrestal.* Annapolis, MD: Naval Institute Press, 1992.

Kyvig, David E. *Repealing National Prohibition*. Chicago: University of Chicago Press, 1979.

Lerner, Michael A. *Dry Manhattan: Prohibition in New York City*. Cambridge, MA: Harvard University Press, 2007.

Levy, Shawn. *The Castle on Sunset: Life, Death, Love, Art, and Scandal at Hollywood's Chateau Marmont*. New York: Doubleday, 2019.

Lichtman, Allan J. *Prejudice and the Old Politics: The Presidential Election of 1928*. Chapel Hill: University of North Carolina Press, 1979.

MacKaye, Milton. *Tin Box Parade: A Handbook for Larceny*. New York: R. M. McBride, 1934.

Masters, Nathan. *Crooked: The Roaring Twenties Tale of a Corrupt Attorney General, a Crusading Senator, and the Birth of the American Political Scandal*. New York: Hachette, 2023.

Maxwell, Gilbert. *Helen Morgan: Her Life and Legend*. New York: Hawthorn, 1965.

Mayer, Martin. *Emory Buckner: A Biography*. New York: Harper & Row, 1968.

McGirr, Lisa. *The War on Alcohol: Prohibition and the Rise of the American State*. New York: Norton, 2015.

McMillen, Neil R. *Dark Journey: Black Mississippians in the Age of Jim Crow*. Champaign: University of Illinois Press, 1990.

Mencken, H. L. *Heathen Days: 1890–1936*. New York: Knopf, 1943.

Miller, Kristie. *Ruth Hanna McCormick: A Life in Politics, 1880–1944*. Albuquerque: University of New Mexico Press, 1992.

Murdock, Catherine Gilbert. *Domesticating Drink: Women, Men, and Alcohol in America, 1870–1940*. Baltimore: Johns Hopkins University Press, 1998.

Okrent, Daniel. *Last Call: The Rise and Fall of Prohibition*. New York: Scribner, 2010.

Perry, Elisabeth Israels. *After the Vote: Feminist Politics in La Guardia's New York*. Oxford: Oxford University Press, 2019.

Root, Grace Cogswell. *Women and Repeal: The Story of the Women's Organization for National Prohibition Reform*, authorized by Mrs. Charles H. Sabin. New York: Harper & Brothers, 1934 (digitized version).

Rose, Kenneth D. *American Women and the Repeal of Prohibition*. New York: New York University Press, 1996.

Rymph, Catherine. *Republican Women: Feminism and Conservatism from Suffrage through the Rise of the New Right*. Chapel Hill: University of North Carolina Press, 2006.

Sarlot, Raymond, and Fred E. Basten. *Life at the Marmont: The Inside Story of Hollywood's Legendary Hotel of the Stars—Chateau Marmont*. New York: Penguin, 2013.

Schrad, Mark Lawrence. *Smashing the Liquor Machine: A Global History of Prohibition*. Oxford: Oxford University Press, 2021.

Sellers, James Benson. *The Prohibition Movement in Alabama, 1702–1943*. Chapel Hill: University of North Carolina Press, 1943.

Shirley, Glenn. *Hello Sucker! The Story of "Texas" Guinan*. Austin: Eakin Press, 1989.

Sifakis, Carl. *The Mafia Encyclopedia*. New York: Facts on File, 2005.

Sirica, John J. *To Set the Record Straight*. New York: Norton, 1979.

Walker, Stanley. *The Nightclub Era*. New York: Blue Ribbon Books, 1933.

Ward, Sarah F. *The White Ribbon Story: 125 Years of Service to Humanity*. Evanston, IL: Signal Press, 1999.

Weiss, Elaine. *The Woman's Hour: The Great Fight to Win the Vote*. New York: Penguin Books, 2019.

Winchell, Walter. *Winchell Exclusive*. New York: Prentice-Hall, 1975.

Wolbrecht, Christina, and J. Kevin Corder. *A Century of Votes for Women: American Elections since Suffrage*. Cambridge: Cambridge University Press, 2020.

Zeitz, Joshua. *Flapper: A Madcap Story of Sex, Style, Celebrity, and the Women Who Made America Modern*. New York: Crown, 2006.

INDEX